LET THEM JOURNEY

TRUE STORIES UNITING THE PAST
WITH THE FUTURE

compiled by

Jennifer Hall and **Pesah Leah Porat**

of

the Telshestone English Library

Distribution:

Urim Publications, P.O. Box 52287, Jerusalem 91521 Israel
Lambda Publishers Inc., 3709 13th Avenue,
Brooklyn, New York 11218 U.S.A.
Tel: 718-972-5449 Fax: 718-972-6307, mh@ejudaica.com
www.UrimPublications.com

Cover illustration by Tirtsa Peleg
Book Design by Alalim Ltd

Published by the Telshestone English Library
who can be contacted at
P.O. Box 456, Kiryat Telshestone
D.N. Harei Yehudah 90840, Israel

Printed in Israel

וַיֹּאמֶר ה׳ אֶל־מֹשֶׁה מַה־תִּצְעַק אֵלָי דַּבֵּר
אֶל־בְּנֵי־יִשְׂרָאֵל וְיִסָּעוּ:

שמות פרק יד פסוק טו

"Hashem said to Moshe "Why do you cry out to Me?
Speak to the Children of Israel and let them journey."

רש"י: **מה תצעק אלי** – למדנו שהיה משה עומד ומתפלל,
אמר לו הקב"ה לא עת עתה להאריך בתפלה שישראל נתונין
בצרה. דבר אחר מה תצעק אלי עלי הדבר תלוי ולא עליך, כמו
שנאמר להלן (ישעיה מה יא) על בני ועל פועל ידי תצוני:
דבר אל בני ישראל ויסעו – אין להם אלא ליסע שאין הים
עומד בפניהם, כדאי זכות אבותיהם והם והאמונה שהאמינו בי
ויצאו, לקרוע להם הים:

Why do you cry out to Me? This verse teaches us that Moshe
was standing and praying.
The Holy One Blessed is He said to him "Now is not the time to
prolong in prayer, when Israel is placed in distress. Another
interpretation: "Why do you cry out to Me?" Upon Me the matter
depends and not upon you, as it is stated in Isaiah 45:11, "Concerning
My sons and concerning the work of My hands do you command
Me?"

Speak to the Children of Israel and let them journey There is
nothing for them to do but to travel, for the sea does not stand in their
way. The merit of their fathers and their own faith in Me when they
went forth from Egypt are sufficient to split the sea for them..

עיריית ירושלים

Municipality of Jerusalem

بلدية اورشليم – القدس

ראש העיר
Mayor of Jerusalem
رئيس البلدية

Jerusalem, February 12, 2006
14 Shvat, 5766

The holiest spot on earth for the Jewish people is Jerusalem – the location of the Temple and the seat of the Royal house of David. Jerusalem has always been the focal point for the Jewish people blending the past and the future since we pray constantly for the rebuilding of the Temple in Jerusalem.

Almost five hundred years ago during the time of the Ottoman rule, Suleiman the Magnificent, standing at the helm of one of the largest Empires known to man, initiated the construction of the wall around the Holy City, which was completed fifteen years later.

At this time the Jewish population of Jerusalem was negligible, but by the middle of the nineteenth century it had grown to ten thousand residents. The severe overcrowding within those city walls was life threatening, since the primitive infrastructure was ill equipped to handle the strain placed upon it.

In 1855 Sir Moses Montefiore was the initiator behind the building of the first Jewish owned dwellings outside the city walls. This dwelling was named Mishkenot Sha'anim – the dwellings of serenity.

The second area to be built outside the walls was Nachalat Shivah – the inheritance of the seven; named after the seven men who agreed together to build houses on the site.

The success of Nachalat Shivah emboldened and inspired others within the city to make the courageous decision to move into the wilderness beyond the city walls. Over a hundred men convened a meeting and on Rosh Chodesh Kislev 1873 Meah Shearim officially came into existence. The parshah that Shabbos was Parshas Toldos in which it states, verse 26-12, 'Yitzchak sowed in that land and that year reaped a hundredfold – meah shearim - for Hashem blessed him.'

Jerusalem has always been multi cultural and today it is a hustling, bustling modern city; whose residents, like many of the storytellers in this book, have made their way from all corners of the world.

We have been waiting for you to visit us for two thousand years – come soon – a warm welcome awaits you.

With best wishes,

Uri Lupoliansky

Contents

Footsteps
Rachel Greenblatt *11*

Peddlers, egg eaters and Mr Finkelstein
Dr David Kranzler. *13*

The Mezuzah of Jerusalem
Avraham Rosenthal
Mayor of Kiryat Yearim Telshestone. *17*

Are a Whistle and a Bell still enough?
Jennifer Hall: Librarian of the Telshestone
English Library *20*

Of Ostlers and Ostrich Feathers boas
Esther Deyong born in 1864 . . . . *28*

Pickled cucumbers, wieners and Jewish foie-gras
Uri ben Shimon *32*

'Grandmother was insistent; she had to have a cow'
Margola Levin niftar in the late 1930's *38*

'Hot bricks heated the bed'
Belle Rabinowitz born in 1911 . . . . *42*

'So you would have another dresske in the closet?'
Pincus Trachtenberg born in 1879 . . . . *44*

All aboard Halley's comet
Moshe Zalman Feiglin born in 1875 . . . . *47*

'Every family had a spinning machine'
A Lady born in 1914 . . . . *51*

'They are not speaking Jewish and they are not
speaking gentile'
  Yoel Yosef Phetersen born in 1923 56
'A dressmaker wants to open a school'
  A pupil of Sarah Schenirer born in 1912............ 61
'I want one of you to go out to the East
and create light'
  Bertha Gitleman born in 1914..................... 64
'Mother slept on the stove'
  Leah Perl born in 1906 70
'Well bought is half sold'
  Isaac Gaba born in 1882.......................... 73
Guardian of the Wall
  Rabbi Menachem Porush born in 1915 79
'It never rains here so you don't need a roof'
  Yetta Bloch born in the late 1880's................. 84
'It cost five shillings to go to Yeshiva'
  Rev. Shalom Camissar born in 1918 89
'So the Rabbi tied his peyos to the ticket counter'
  A Gentleman born in 1925........................ 94
Growing up in the Netherlands East Indies
  Jacqueline Philips born in 1924..................... 98
One knife, which everyone shared
  Claire Rose born in 1923.......................... 103
'n'egg n'arf f'r apenny'
  Speranza born in 1922............................ 106
'Juden Unerwuenscht' – Prohibited to Jews
  Ruth bat Frumet born in 1925..................... 110

'We had no telephones and no loshon hora'
A Lady born in 1920 115

A diamonds true worth
Solomon Joseph Cohen born in 1893 121

'Aleh leben, schtizeh neitik' All are alive,
support needed
Rabbi Yehuda Braver born in 1891 126

'Mother, if you buy from the Jew I shall report you'
Max Oestreich born in 1909 133

'The Jewish people in my village had a wonderful
Pesach that year'
Rabbi Ya'akov Baker born in 1914 138

Paying homage to the inhabitants of Yedwabne
Aleksander Kwasniewski 143

'How can you see a girl if your cufflinks are different?'
Miriam Pollack born in 1903 146

'At what time would you like your order delivered?'
Joan Sklan born in 1928. 151

'Until the Olympia they left the Jews alone'
Zipporah Hess born in 1921 158

'In the goldene medina you had to be American'
Esther bat Leah born in 1925 163

'The Steipler would take me out of my crib
to quieten me'
Rabbi Yisroel Orlansky born in 1925 168

'Brother can you spare a dime?'
Selma Kaminetsky born in 1918. 175

'For years the Governor preserved old Jerusalem'
Oscar Mareni born in 1907. 178

Holidays, lazy days and spies
  Speranza born in 1922.......................... 186

'I still daven in the Mir minyan'
  Rabbi Yehudah Broyde born in 1918.............. 191

'My father handed over the shul to the Mir Yeshiva'
  Cissie [Simcha] Flegg born in 1924................ 198

'I have seen nothing but war in my life'
  A Lady born in 1917............................. 206

'It was the bread that saved them'
  Hanna Yeret born in 1923 210

A blood libel in America.
  Sorelle Parker born in 1923....................... 214

A broken leg for Shabbos
  Shlomo Aaron ben Ya'acov born in 1900 217

'I never wore black boots again'
  Nini Neufeld born in 1926 221

A wedding band or a piece of bread?
  Rochel Klueger born in 1937..................... 226

'Mussar teaches that simcha should not be
uncontrolled happiness'
  Tuvia Nadel born in 1923 233

'A world where you could have as much bread
as you wanted'
  Pinchas Ofner born in 1932 239

By any name – a Jew
  Mendel Yeret born in 1921 246

'We are going to hang out our washing on the
Siegfried line'
  Joan Sklan born in 1928......................... 250

'This woman has six fingers'
Simon Braun born in 1918 257

Stick telephones, hobos and crystal sets
Bernard Kraus born in 1914 260

'Father slept on the counter'
Max Todes born in 1892 266

Mandlebaum's Gate
Simcha Mandelbaum born around 1870 268

'In cattle wagons deep into Siberia'
Esther Liebes born in 1924 271

'Deutschland iber alles Juden kaput'
Tzipora Morganstren Gilbert born in 1923 277

Grey days and penny chocolate bars
Gerry Benson born in 1935 284

'Do you think we ate every day?'
Michel Nager born in 1937 289

'Jerusalem is not on the moon'
Emmanuel Boruch born in 1916 294

'The poor lived and died on the streets'
William Sopher born in 1923 301

'I am alive and I am coming home'
Matil Miryam bat Shmuel Meir born in 1911 305

'Come, sit by me'
Rabbi Michoel Boruch born in 1929 310

'Yosef, someone is trying to take a picture of me,
but nothing will come out'
Rabbi Yoel Teitelbaum born in 1887 314

'The Foreign Minister was asked to reinstate
the name of King George'
Ezra Yakhin born in 1928 316

'We were learning to live without money'
Shirley Granovetter born in 1927 324

'That was the Shalom Aleichem that saved America'
Rabbi Yehuda Davis 328

Charred mealies, pootu and Zulus
Rivka Leah Silver born in 1875................... 333

Suppers consisted of only a piece of bread
and an onion
Rabbi Dr. Joseph Kaminetsky born in 1911 337

'I believe you have to be Jewish first, everything
else is second'
Herman Greenstein born in 1949.................. 342

'There are no open miracles, but there are many
ways of hashgacha'
Simon Braun born in 1918...................... 347

'A fabulously wealthy gift – of two onions'
Katya Brajtman born in 1976 350

'The Queen, he replied, likes to keep everything'
Jack Krantz born in 1912 355

'Mille et mille fois'
Etta bat Shlomo HaLevi born in 1912 360

Fifty years is half a century
Noach Haltrecht born at the end
of the age of elegance........................... 366

Dedications 371

Rachel Greenblatt

Footsteps

Traversing the ancient pathways of my land
I wonder whose steps do I take as I walk?

Are they the weary steps of my brethren in Egypt?
Bent under their heavy load?

Are they the steps of a multitude of holy Jews?
Who wandered in the desert for forty years?
Or maybe the steps of a warring nation ready for battle?

Are they the rhythmic steps of my people
celebrating a glorious celebration in their Temple,
or the defeated and broken step of a nation on it's way to exile?

Or maybe they are the footsteps of the haughty
who dare to enter the halls of Greek learning,
or the marching steps of a Maccabean soldier,
in line for the battle of the weak against the strong.

Are they the proud steps of our people in a Golden Spanish
Age,
or the light-footed perilous steps of fear of inquisition?

Are they the quaking, fearful steps,
bristling at the sound of a pogrom,
or the light and happy steps
of a shtetl bridegroom.

Are they the tortured and terrified steps
of those demented in the hell of Germany,
or the feverish dancing steps of those who kiss the
ground of the land of Israel?

Do my footsteps take me across the bow of a creaking boat,
through muddy riverbeds,

across undulating sand dunes,
or through green fields?

Do they take me to Shanghai, New York,
to Gateshead, to Cape Town or to Antwerp,

As I walk,
do I run,
do I dance,
do I falter and fall,

Am I young,
am I old,
am I rich,
am I poor?
and to whom do these steps of mine belong?

Are they maybe, the wide and steady steps
of a successful American businessman,
or the solid plodding steps of the South African gold-digger,
the tempered, measured steps of the English land-owner,
or the Russian Professor's thoughtful steps in the halls
of Muscovite learning?

Who's steps do I take,
as I traverse your land Hashem?
As many and diverse as the stars up above,
are the wanderings of Your people Israel.

One thing is for sure,
on all our journey's,
and throughout all the ages,
all paths lead...
... to **You** Hashem.

*Dr **David Kranzler***

Peddlers, egg eaters
and Mr. Finkelstein

J ewish life in the Diaspora is marked by wandering. Since the 1880's, following a series of pogroms and with the ever-tightening restrictions imposed on a growing Jewish population throughout the Russian Empire, Jewish people sought freedom around the world. Hundreds of thousands of them crossed the borders of the Russian and Austro-Hungarian Empires, as well as Romania, to find freedom and economic opportunities across the ocean in an expanding United States, Canada and South America, particularly in Argentina. The usual route was to travel to the German port of Hamburg, where Jewish organizations temporarily supported the refugees. From Hamburg, they would proceed to England and then onwards to the western hemisphere, particularly to the United States.

In South America many Jewish people were provided with farmland by the great Jewish philanthropist, Baron Hirsch, who envisioned they would settle the land and become farmers, and thereby reduce anti-Semitism. This belief was based on a widespread misconception that anti-Semitism was caused by the many Jews too heavily involved in business and intellectual pursuits, at the expense of conforming to the gentile's world, where tillers of the soil were the majority and were highly valued. Ironically, this warped view would soon suffer a reversal with the advance of industrialization, technology and modernization, and the business and intellectual world of the Jews became the ideal focus of the non-Jewish nations, as thousands left their farms to move to the cities in pursuit of these values.

Since fewer people were required to till the soil, universal education was becoming a more widespread phenomenon in a rapidly changing world. That is why, despite his good intentions, most of the Baron Hirsch farms in South America and the United States failed to endure. Nevertheless, more than two million Jewish souls were able to escape oppressive countries before the First World War, and found economic opportunities, security and religious freedom elsewhere.

Above all, with hindsight, we know that Hashgochah Protis (Hashem's Hand) decreed that these people, subjected to the cruelty of life as refugees and forced to wander around the world, would be saved from the Holocaust. It was these Jews who were to become the major supporters of European and other Jewries through-out the world, and eventually, these refugees, seeds from the tree, who established great Torah centres wherever they landed.

At the time many Jewish refugees initially became peddlers. They travelled throughout the countryside selling all kind of products to farmers, who welcomed the opportunity to purchase things that were usually only available in the cities. Many of these Jewish peddlers, who frequently ate only hard-boiled eggs to maintain *kashrus*, even under difficult circumstances, were known to the American Indians as "egg-eaters." The more fortunate among them eventually opened stores in the growing cites of the United States and Canada, while a smaller number pioneered the idea, and eventually built, the great department stores such as Macys and Gimbels. One department store in New Haven, owned by a Mr.

Finkelstein, remained *Shomer Shabbos* well into the twentieth century.

Smaller numbers of Jews went to South Africa, almost exclusively from Lithuania, until the 1930's, when German Jewish refugees joined the Lithuanian community in building Yiddishkeit in South Africa. There, for the first time, Jews encountered the racial situation known as "Apartheid."

Still fewer migrated to Palestine, in an attempt to build up Eretz Yisroel and expand the cities. Initially, a large proportion was Orthodox, but many secular Zionists soon followed them from Germany, and they sought to build a socialist state. This was contrary to the Orthodox view of Yishuv Ha'aretz and remains a major schism in the Jewish world of Eretz Yisroel, even today.

This book illustrates the story of Jewish migration in the last hundred years, from an unusual perspective. There is no faceless narrator sweeping the characters along the tides of history; the stories are told by the people themselves, unaltered and with all the poignancy of memory intact. These people, their lives overshadowed and sometimes obliterated by catastrophic events, relate in their own voices what it was like to be a Jew in such a world and under such conditions.

It is precisely this extremely personal view, which answers the larger question of how G-d, in His great mercy, cares for His creation.

This collection of vignettes provides the human face and reflects the varied and wide-ranging Jewish experience of the migration of several million Jewish refugees during the late nineteenth and early twentieth centuries. These include stories of adventure, heroism, *mesiras nefesh* for Yiddishkeit and obvious instances of *Hashgochah Protis*. For example, there are the stories of the young Jews, among many thousands, drafted into the Czar's Army to fight the Japanese during the Russo-Japanese War of 1904-05, who managed to elude the Russian authorities to embark on a long trek to freedom.

Little did they know that it was an American, Jewish banker, Jacob Schiff (grandfather of Dorothy Schiff, for many years the publisher of the New York Post), whose several loans to a fledgling Japanese nation, was crucial to her winning the war. His loans, together with several additional ones, floated with the help of Schiff's cousin, the Jewish bankers M. Warburg in Germany and Sir Ernest Cassel of England, were offered at a time when no other nation had any confidence in Japan's ability to defeat the giant Russian Empire. Incidentally, Schiff was the first westerner to be honoured by the Emperor, a factor in the later rescue during the Shoah, of 18,000 Jewish refugees, including the entire Mirrer Yeshiva.

During the pointless war of 1914-1918, over one and a half million Jews served in the armies of both sides, and there are many tragic stories of Jews discovering, too late, that they had killed a fellow Jew. Despite the large number who volunteered, even for the Czar's army, the Jews were called "slackers," and draft dodgers. Thus, almost all countries made an official count, and proved the charges to be baseless. But truth, supported by hard facts, didn't stop the anti-Semitism.

The recollections related in this book provide an interesting, enlightening and informative panorama of the varied Jewish experiences in the twentieth century. This book should be in every Jewish library.

✦ ✦ ✦

David Kranzler Ph.D., M.A., M.L.S. is a prolific author and scholar who received his Ph.D. in Jewish history from Yeshiva University.

המועצה המקומית קרית-יערים (טלזסטון)

ת.ד. 101 ד.נ. הרי יהודה מיקוד 90840
טל: 02-5332735 פקס: 02-5332736, 5332737

Kiryat Yearim Telshestone –
The Mezuzah of Jerusalem

I was born in 1947 shortly before the State of Israel was established. When Statehood was declared in 1948, Jerusalem was under siege and a state of war was in effect. People hid in bomb shelters and supply routes were disrupted causing great hunger throughout the city. My mother's milk supply was low from malnourishment, and my father had to run under bombardment of shells and bullets, risking his life to buy milk powder from the pharmacy to feed me.

After Statehood was proclaimed, life in Jerusalem during the years I was growing up was very difficult. In the fifties basic nourishment such as bread was readily available, but fruit, vegetables, meat and fish were scarce commodities, which we did not get on a regular basis. One apple was shared between three children, sometimes even four. Relatives in America sent us second-hand clothing, which were altered as necessary to fit the children of the family.

Despite the hardships of life during this time we maintained our learning, even though, sometimes, learning took the place of food.

Jerusalem was much smaller then, because the partition between East and West Jerusalem was still in place. Everybody knew almost everybody else. Whilst economically and physically things were hard, on the other hand we grew spiritually and prospered socially. Families lived close together, and they visited each other frequently, in contrast to the present time, when the situation is far better economically, but nobody has time to visit friends and relations.

In the early sixties preceding the Six Day War, the situation in Jerusalem was very tense. Disturbances increased day by day until Monday the 26th Iyar 5727, when the war began. At the sound of the sirens we ran to the shelters. The air was full of smoke and fire and the Jordanian planes were dropping bombs above our heads. In the shelters we prayed unceasingly and said *Tehillim* fervently, pleading with the Almighty to save our lives. On the first and second nights it was impossible to sleep but on Wednesday, the 28th Iyar the Kotel was liberated.

That day is etched firmly on my memory. The fighting was very close to us and we heard thundering noises accompanied by a lot of activity. And then suddenly — it was over. The tension dissolved and we cried tears of thanksgiving. When we learned that the Old City and the Western Wall were liberated, we embraced each other crying and laughing with joy. We lived in Meah Shearim and heard the Shofar blown by Chief Rabbi Goren in front of the Kotel and the song "Jerusalem of Gold" sung by the soldiers.

Words are inadequate to describe our happiness in that moment of liberation when everyone took to the streets, dancing and singing. Later we learnt that the Golan Heights, Sinai and the whole of the West Bank, including our historic towns of Beit El and Beit Lechem were also liberated. Above all, our beloved Jerusalem was open to everyone and the streets were again safe.

We visited the Kotel on Shavuot, after the war, together with tens of thousands of fellow Jews, in order to pray in front of the giant stones of the Western Wall of the Second Temple. We prayed that Hashem would "rebuild [His] House as it was at first, and restore the service of the Kohanim, and the Levites to their song and music."

Later I married and moved out of Jerusalem, although I always yearned to return. One day in 5737 my family and I visited a new village just outside Jerusalem. The beauty of the village, which was surrounded by mountains and which had a quiet, enchanted and pastoral atmosphere, immediately entranced me. It seemed far from the noisy bustle of the city, but nevertheless was close to it. Many Yeshivas were located there to give the bochurim a quiet location to focus on their learning. It appeared to be an excellent environment to bring up children. My wife and I agreed to settle here until the day that we would return to live in Jerusalem. That was almost thirty years ago.

The holy atmoshpere that permeates the village we believe is due to the fact the Aron, containing the *luchos*, was located in Kiryat Yearim for twenty years before Dovid HaMelech took it the short distance to Jerusalem. We hope that the Geulah will come soon, and we will be collected on the way to Jerusalem...

אברהם רוזנטל
הראש המועצה
קרית יערים

Jennifer Hall
Voluntary Librarian of the Telshestone English Library
Born in the year cars were first manufactured
without running boards

Are a Whistle and a Bell still enough?

Jennifer Hall

While we were sitting in a waiting room in Israel, my son picked up a magazine that was lying on a nearby table. Unused to such reading matter, we both stared in amazement at the advertisements. We saw the most magnificent photograph of a car with an on board navigational computer.

I laughed as I reminded myself, and my son, that my parents' first car did not have automatic electric ignition.

There was a hole in the front of the car into which the driver inserted a handle, which cranked up the engine. When the driver had turned the handle a sufficient number of times the engine turned over and was ready to go. The driver then extracted the handle, ran to his seat, flung the handle onto the back seat of the car and put the car into gear before the engine died and he had to start all over again.

When my mother took the children on a picnic to Bradgate Park, near Leicester, England, it was the pinnacle of excitement. The eight horsepower engine was not strong enough to climb the hill, thereupon all the children would get out and walk.

Horsepower! With eight horsepower engines you didn't have synchromesh on the gearbox. In order to change gear the driver needed to double-declutch. The window by the driver was left open, even in the winter, in order to make hand signals to indicate the car's direction. You failed your driving test if you failed to make them. Using the car's semaphore arms was simply not enough. On the driver's side only was a windscreen wiper. The car manufacturer did not regard putting a wiper on the passenger's side as a necessity. When the driver put his foot on the accelerator the air left the wiper tank and the wiper stopped working. When it rained one could either accelerate or have a working wiper — but not both.

As I was gardening recently, I noticed a friend sitting disconsolately on a nearby bench. Did she want to use a telephone, have a message conveyed to someone, or did she simply need a glass of water?

None of these. She was sitting next to a gleaming, new, white car; the kind that still has the smell of expensive leather when you sneak a look inside.

She passed me a black plastic keypad and said, 'I can't turn the alarm off and without doing that first I can't start the car.' I suggested pushing the car to an incline, putting it in gear and away she would go. She looked at me with total incomprehension. 'The car won't start if I can't turn the alarm off.' She cradled the keypad in her warm palms and eventually she was able to turn off the alarm and start the car.

I grew up in wartime Britain, where blackout material shut off light to the street. There was no street lighting for the same reason. There were no milestones to tell you how far you were to the next village. All the milestones were removed so that the German enemy would not know where he was if he infiltrated the country.

However, it was safe to walk the streets. Also walking the streets was the local policeman. The "bobby on the beat" was armed with nothing more than a whistle to summon help and a truncheon for his protection. Help was at hand at some street corners in strategically placed police boxes that housed a telephone. The local bobby was fortunate that he had the back up of the local police car, which announced its arrival by the loud clanging of its hand-operated bell.

Life in wartime Britain was in some ways not unlike living in Israel today. Our bomb shelter was in the garden. Everyone had one, or access to a communal shelter. My husband, who lived in London at the time, remembers the day his sister had an asthma attack just as they were leaving the flat to go to Sunday morning cheder. Consequently, the family was not at the bus stop when the bombs fell there.

In Israel the radio is always on, to advise citizens of the current situation. In wartime Britain the picture was the same. The family crowded around the wireless to listen to the latest war news, or a speech by Winston Churchill or, on special occasions, a speech by the King. It was a miracle of modern science. From time to time one needed to take the accumulator to the local repair shop to be recharged or to replace burnt out wireless valves.

Remembering the wartime, I never leave food on my plate. If the grandchildren complain about some trivial matter concerning food, I tell them about Ration Books. In my childhood, if you wanted to buy some basic foodstuffs, all that was available, you had to go to the shop with your Ration Book. After the purchase of a small pat of butter or a few ounces of sugar and flour, which had to last the entire week, the grocer cut out the relevant coupons from the Ration Book. Of course the grocer served you. He was on one side of the counter with food stacked up on the shelves behind him. You bought what you needed. If you wanted cheese, the grocer cut it on a cheese board with the cheese wire.

Of course, it wasn't just food that was rationed. In my mind's eye I can still see my mother standing deep in thought when I asked her for a new dress for school. One needed coupons to buy clothes. A wedding dress took a year's supply of coupons.

My family does not understand my preoccupation with electric lights. I turn them off when I leave a room. If you have to put coins in a meter to buy electricity, you don't waste it.

The local Library was free, therefore I read books. When I wasn't reading a book from the library, I was gardening – growing food for the war effort. If you didn't have a garden, you could rent an allotment from the local council. An allotment could support a family of four in vegetables for most of the year. In wartime Britain gardeners learned how to grow vegetables cheek by jowl. In gardening parlance one grows catch crops. Radishes were grown on the hillocks of pota-  toes, onions or garlic grown as companion plants of tomatoes. The halachos of Kalayim do not apply to vegetable growing outside Israel,

where such planting is forbidden.

I can't recollect having any toys except one doll, sent from America. My toys were pegs and saucepans. Before my mother used the pegs for their proper purpose, she would scrub the clothes clean on a scrubbing board and then put the clothes through a mangle to take out the excess water, before pegging them on the clothesline to dry. In the winter the clothes would freeze and when you bought them into the house they were as stiff as a board. In the winter the smell and sight of damp clothes hanging on the clothes pulley was part of the kitchen scene.

When my children were still young we took them to a museum that showed life as it used to be. We went from the 1920's kitchen to the 1930's, and then to the 1940's. I gasped to my children, 'that's my mother's kitchen,' with its coal fired cooking range and clothes pulley, exactly like the kitchen that was still being used by my mother.

A young friend told me recently that her husband had just bought her a second washing machine, since one was simply not enough. Her girls use a towel only once before depositing it in the laundry basket. With six children living at home, if my friend doesn't do five washes one day, she does ten washes the next. How, I wondered to myself as my friend related this to me, would today's generation manage with a scrubbing board and a mangle?

Post war Britain was the era of the rag and bone man, with his horse and cart trotting along the street calling out for everyone's unwanted iron bedsteads and old tin baths. Today's generation think that they have invented recycling. The kitchen was the place where you had your bath, in a large sized tin bathtub placed strategically close to the fire for warmth. The water was boiled in the kettle placed on the coal-fired range. I can still remember my mother filling my bath in this manner.

How many of today's generation realise, as they check that their mobile phones are with them when they leave the house that, in those days, if you wanted to make a long distance telephone call, that is, any call that wasn't local, you booked an appointment with the telephone operator. A caller wrote a letter to the person they wished to call, arranging a day and time that both of them would be free to speak on the telephone. There was of course no guarantee that one could obtain a line. It was common to wait many years, sometimes ten years, to obtain a line. And then there was no guarantee that you had the sole use of it. It was not unusual to share a line, called a party line, with another subscriber, or even more than one.

How would today's throwaway society have managed in an era when you didn't throw away even one piece of paper? In my school, the children were instructed to write on both sides of every sheet of paper, when they weren't writing on slates. I carefully save every scrap of paper from any source, to write out shopping lists or notes. It grieves me to see people collecting their mail from the mailbox, and then throw the unwanted circulars on the street. I tell the young mothers to use the unwanted mail as scrap paper for the kids. They stare at me in complete bewilderment.

In my childhood, everything was made to last. When you bought a refrigerator or a perambulator, you were still using them many decades later. I perambulated my children in a baby carriage, with large wheels, which was roomy enough for baby to sleep in comfort. I had a dozen or so terry towelling nappies that I put on the babies and washed when they were dirty. The same nappies were used for all my children. I eventually threw them away, but only when I had no more babies who needed them.

Since this was the era of coal fires in every hearth, fog in the winter was a major hazard. It was not uncommon for the fog to be so thick that it was impossible to see your hand in front of your face while walking in the street. A bus that still needed to reach its destination would have a policeman walking in front of it, with a lantern in his hand, to assist it to reach the safety of the bus terminal.

My husband remembers his forays into London's Hyde Park in the wartime. Children would wait for the German planes to fly over throwing down rolls of specially treated silver paper that the Germans hoped would foil the British radar. Barrage balloons were tethered in Hyde Park above the soldiers waiting with their anti aircraft guns. When a German plane flew over it was hoped that they would become entangled in the strings attached to the barrage balloons and would then be easy targets for the waiting soldiers. The children were also waiting for the soldiers to finish firing and then they watched as the guns were being cleaned.

What will be the vignettes of my grandchildren's bygone yesterday?

For this book we interviewed many people who lived in the twentieth century. A turbulent period in our history, which saw millions of Jews forced to flee for their life, from country to country, until they reached a land that would take them in. Not only could they take no possessions, they also, often, went alone. And who said you had to eat every day? These stories are memories from the cedar chests of time, describing a period of history that has disappeared in the mists of time, but which we felt should not be forgotten.

Dear Reader, as you read these stories, please bear in mind that these are the memories of people who have lived for many decades and whose desire to tell their story often surpassed the strength needed to do so.

Even as this book is being prepared for publication, we have sadly received news of the passing of some of our storytellers. May their memories be for a blessing.

This is not the work of a 'master storyteller' and rather than 'rewrite' the stories we have chosen not to alter, add to, embroider or exaggerate the interviews with our storytellers.

The vignettes in this groundbreaking book are fascinating glimpses into their lives, and we are grateful to them for their contribution of words and photographs.

Words do not just appear on paper. We also acknowledge the help we have received from countless others who have donated their time and literary skills to enable us to bring this book to you.

We are grateful to the archive departments of the Municipality of Jerusalem and of the State of Israel for allowing the use of archive material, which we hope will add to your reading pleasure.

Esther Deyong
born in 1864
Told by her granddaughter

Of Ostlers and
Ostrich feather boas

*Esther Deyong on the beach
in Bournemouth*

M y grandmother lived with her parents in the City of London. Our family tree can be traced back to the return of the Jews to England in the seventeenth century during the Parliament of Oliver Cromwell.

As children, we would listen spellbound, while grandmother described outings she had with her mother. When she was five or six years of age, around 1870, her mother would take her to watch the arrival of the stagecoaches, mainly from Kent, at the gates of the City, Aldgate and Bishopsgate. She would re-enact her childhood excitement as she described the coaches approaching at speed, pulled by steaming horses; their manes flying. The passengers would sit inside the coach, while the baggage on the roof, swayed precariously.

Amid shouts and the sound of the post-horn, the horses were reined to a halt outside a coaching inn. Ostlers emerged from the inn as passengers left the coach and collected their luggage. The ostlers lead the horses away to be rubbed down, fed, watered, stabled and rested before the next journey.

Grandmother described her excitement when the River Thames froze over in the winter. She would watch Londoners skating on the frozen Thames, and there would be festive ox roasting on the thick ice.

One of grandmother's early memories was of challah baking. In her day, all bread was baked in the oven at home. Some domestic ovens were too small to cook the Shabbos meal for a large family as well as baking loaves of challah. There was a certain woman, with a large oven, who would make space for the challahs of several families. My grandmother would run round with the uncooked challahs and then return to collect them. This woman eventually became her mother-in-law.

Pesach matzos were not usually baked at home but bought from Levy's matzo bakery. When I was a child in the 1930's, grandmother took me with her to order her matzos and to show me how they were made.

We descended a steep staircase, built against the wall of a large circular underground room, well lit and very hot. At its centre, reaching from ceiling to floor was a huge circular oven, with arched openings at intervals around it. At each opening a baker worked, wielding what appeared to be a very long-handled garden hoe with its end like a very large fish slice. The fire inside was visible through the openings and there was a great, flat circular stone turning slowly within.

Workers collected on their trolleys the thin flat rounds of dough, which had been fed through rollers with rows of retaining pins, which produced the tiny holes in the finished matzot. With the long-handled slice a baker

Bevis Marks Shul

rapidly trans-
ferred, from the
trolley into the
central oven, the
thin, uncooked
rounds of matzot.
The trolley was
frequently re-
plenished and
brought to his
side by another
worker. The mat-
zot were turned and finally withdrawn, fully baked, within
the halachically prescribed time. I went to look for Levy's
after the Second World War, but unfortunately it no
longer existed.

At the time of the restoration of the Monarchy, after
the Cromwellian era, when Charles the Second succeeded
to the throne in 1660, there were at least two well
established and fully attended Jewish synagogues in the
City of London.

One was the small Sephardi Synagogue, in Creschurch
Lane, the other, for Ashkenazi worshippers, occupied a
house in nearby St Helen's. By 1702 a large, new Sephardi
Synagogue, had been consecrated in Bevis Marks Road.
Although its name was Sharei Shamayim, it became
known as the Bevis Marks Synagogue, because of its
location.

Queen Anne presented to the synagogue, when it was
under construction, timber from a naval man-of-war to be
used as a roof beam. This roof beam is still in place. The
Quaker builder, Joseph Aris, returned his profit on the
construction, not wishing to gain by building a house of
prayer. Some of the furnishings still in use in the Bevis

Marks Synagogue, are benches and other items transferred from Creschurch Lane, which date back well before 1650. The Ashkenazi community also outgrew its early premises in St Helens. In 1722, in Dukes Place, they built an elegant synagogue not far from Bevis Marks. It was damaged by bombs during the Second World War.

When talking to us about her childhood grandmother would recall how, on Friday mornings, the front door step and pavement to every Jewish home, in the area of Bevis Marks, was scrubbed, either by a housemaid at the more affluent houses, or by the housewife herself. Since whole streets were, in many cases, in full Jewish residency, there was an almost continuous shining, clean path to the synagogues. Grandmother said that in dry weather, the women walked to Friday night services without needing to lift the trains of their dresses.

As a girl she loved to see the women in their Shabbos finery, with jewels, ostrich feather boas and elaborate hats. These hats were also adorned with ostrich feathers, which at that time were the height of fashion. They would walk, with unhurried dignity in an elegant procession, on the arms of their top hatted spouses. With deep nostalgia, Grandmother described this Friday night atmosphere as 'Magical, like visiting a Palace.'

Uri ben Shimon

Pickled cucumbers, wieners and Jewish foie-gras

M y mother was born in what is today the Czech Republic. She appeared somewhere among the middle of nine children of a Jewish innkeeper and his farmer wife. They lived in a small Moravian village close to the Austrian border, which featured green, rolling countryside, lots of fruit trees, corn, vegetables and livestock, and a very rural atmosphere. We used to refer to this area as the "pickled cucumber country" because of the excellent sweet pickles produced in the region.

There was indeed much sweetness and simplicity about this place, and life proceeded at a much slower pace than in hectic Vienna, my hometown. The Jewish innkeeper was a well-known figure in those days in Central, and particularly Eastern Europe. The inns were usually of a simple kind, where the local peasants came in for their glass of schnapps. The innkeeper had to deal often with drunk and rowdy customers. My grandfather was well suited for that job. A stern, bearded patriarch, he presided over the goings on in the inn. He ruled his wife and their nine children with an iron hand and, in the case of the latter, sometimes with a birch.

As a special treat once in a while, the children loved wieners with sauerkraut, but kosher wieners were only available on those rare occasions when father went to town on business. At the beloved meal that featured these delicacies, each of the children showed their appreciation for the food in their own way. My mother Hedi, a high spirited, vivacious girl, wolfed down the wieners with gusto, while her younger sister, Rosie, ate them much more slowly, savouring each bite and always leaving a choice piece of sausage to the end. The look of this delicious morsel would tantalize my mother, who had long finished her portion, and she waited for the moment when Rosie's attention temporarily strayed whereupon she would quickly snatch and devour it, to the wails of poor Rosie. I am sure that my mother must have been punished for this and other escapades.

Growing up as country kids, my mother and her siblings walked barefoot every day several miles to and from school through the green landscape dotted with tempting fruit trees. As a strong wall usually protected the best orchards, in order to get at the fruits, Hedi's brothers would help her climb over the wall and then let her down. With fruits in her hand, they would hoist her back by her long black pigtails.

My grandfather's inn, which was a square two story building, had a courtyard in its center, in the middle of which stood a large and gnarled pear tree. The branches would knock gently in the wind against the windowpanes of the second floor bedroom in which I sometimes slept when I came for visits as a small boy. I remember a circular bench that surrounded the tree, on which one could sit on summer evenings to listen to stories told by an uncle or aunt, or to answer riddles with any cousins who might be present. In those days before television, and with radio in its infancy, we loved riddles.

When my grandfather became too old to manage the inn, they sold it and moved into a smaller house in a larger village nearby. That house also had a large yard, with fruit trees, chickens and even geese. I used to watch with fascination when the servant girl would force-feed the geese. Sitting on a low stool, she would take the goose between her legs, hold its beak open and cram large quantities of corn into it. The goose squawked like crazy when it got a moment to take breath and, in between, did its best to swallow the unwanted abundance. When released, the goose waddled away with an air of injured dignity. As a result of this force-feeding, the geese developed huge livers, which furnished a Jewish-type of *foie gras*. This, together with the goose fat in which the foie gras was prepared, provided delicious sandwiches throughout the winter.

When visiting my grandparents in their new place, I was already a little older and was the terror of the cats in the house and the yard. As I used to like pulling their tails, they soon learned to scurry up the nearest tree whenever they saw me approaching. My grandparents were of course also older, and I remember my grandfather only as an old man with a gray beard, dozing in the sun, and my grandmother as a little bent old lady, with a kerchief around her head. She always wanted to kiss me, but the kerchief and the wrinkled face made me shy. When I ran away, she would follow me, offering a shilling for a kiss. That, of course, usually did the trick. The sweets I bought with the shilling in the little village grocery made an unwelcome kiss quite worthwhile.

By that time, only my grandparents' youngest daughter, Rosie, was living with them. Vienna, the glamorous capital of Austria-Hungary, had become at the turn of the 20th century a magnet that drew country people to make their fortunes. If you were intelligent and hard working, you usually could get by, and if you were lucky on top of that, you could go far. Although my mother and her brothers and sisters had usually no other formal education beyond what the village school could offer, several of them, including my mother, were very intelligent. By reading voraciously, they had developed their minds. They all were bilingual, speaking German at home, and Czech at school with the other village kids.

The oldest girl, Hanna, was the first of the girls to leave for Vienna. Her mission was to look after the oldest brother, Robbi, who had gone there earlier to find a better job than the pickled cucumber country could offer. Eventually, several others of the children made their way to Vienna, among them my mother. Robbi had by then left to take up a position with a plantation in the Dutch East Indies, a somewhat unusual development. It came about also in an unusual way. He had worked a while as an accountant but lost his job. Sitting alone in a Viennese Cafe and mulling over his troubles over a cappuccino, a stranger joined him at the table, as the Café was quite full. They started chatting, and Robbi told the stranger about losing his job and not knowing what to do. The stranger asked him whether he would be interested to work at the rubber plantation of his brother in the Dutch East Indies who was looking for someone to keep his books. Robbie thought it a good opportunity, and as in those days there was no need for visas, work permits, etc., he made the change easily. Eventually he would marry the daughter of the plantation owner and become a wealthy man.

In Vienna, Hanna ruled the family members with the same iron hand as her father – my grandfather – had used, and looked after their jobs and saw to it that they stayed on the straight and narrow. Although they were all a bit scared of her and her caustic tongue, her apartment became the monthly meeting place for the family members in Vienna until the late thirties. They came to eat her good country cooking, to tell about their affairs, to get advice and, not infrequently, to be upbraided. Of course, differences in temperament and life styles invariably developed between them as they got married and had their own families, lives, jobs or businesses. This sometimes caused rifts, and on occasions two aunts might not have been on speaking terms for several weeks. But in the end they usually made up. A basic cohesiveness continued, which was often the secret for Jewish success — family closeness and support.

My mother soon found a job with a haberdasher. How and where she met my father I do not know. It must have been during the First World War, and could well have taken place in the Viennese "Prater," the great amusement park, where the *Herr Lieutenant* on leave would have come to look for fun among the roundabouts, cafes, shooting galleries and other attractions.

My parents married during the last year of the war, 1918. It must have been a difficult year since there was little food, epidemics afflicted the weakened population, and even to the uninformed the war must have seemed lost. Then came the turbulent days of the revolution that put an end to the 1000-year reign of the Hapsburgs, and the painful periods of re-adjustment, of re-integrating the thousands of returning soldiers into a shattered economy. But my parents probably did not feel the full impact of these miseries, partly because of their happiness with each other, and partly because of the help and support that the family gave, as always, to its members.

From Czech came a little food now and then, particularly when a family member went there on a visit. Uncles and aunts helped each other to find jobs and housing.

Uncle Robbi returned from the Dutch East Indies at the end of the war, together with his Dutch wife, the daughter of the plantation owner. By using his ample means, he had been able to get an apartment in Vienna. When he moved with his family to Holland shortly afterwards, he passed the apartment on to my newly married parents.

This warm supportive family network continued until the late thirties, when Hitler dispersed them and eventually made most of them part of his final solution.

✦ ✦ ✦

Margola Levin
niftar in the late 1930's
Told by her grandson

'Grandmother was insistent; she had to have a cow'

I n the late nineteenth century the City Fathers of Chicago were building the country. They encouraged people around the world to emigrate to America and émigrés came in the thousands, from all walks of life and from all countries. Many of them were farmers. Since America has a lot of land, they leased the land for free on the condition that you worked the land yourself as a farmer; it was not possible to sell the land to someone else.

In 1895 my grandfather emigrated to America from Russia. At the time he could not afford to bring over my grandmother and the rest of the family. In Russia he had owned a small dairy, which he also started as his business in Chicago, with five or six cows, making cheese and butter.

After a couple of years he was sufficiently established to bring over the rest of the family. In those days there was no milking machinery, so the cows were milked by hand. Grandfather was a very religious man and his milk had to be cholav Yisroel. Although his dairy was closed on Shabbos, he milked his cows, since a milk cow needs to be milked twice every twenty-four hours. In those days there was no hescher, no independent supervision, and the public relied on the integrity of the person doing the work. My grandfather davened three times a day and every one knew that he was a religious man and could be relied on to follow Halacha.

Eventually the owner of the biggest dairy in Chicago came to grandfather and asked him to be an equal partner in his business, at no investment. 'I know I can trust you,' he said 'you are the kind of guy I need in the business.' Grandfather told him 'you are open on Shabbos, you do not use special feed during Pesach, and you use lard on your hands when you milk. I cannot join your business.' My grandfather could have become rich beyond his wildest dreams. Instead he made a Kiddush Hashem.

In the years around 1905 to 1910 automobiles were beginning to come onto the streets and Chicago was growing. The City Fathers had to make a decision and they changed the law, prohibiting all farm animals within the city boundaries of Chicago. An exception was made for horses, because they were still needed for transportation at that time. One of the problems was that they had to keep the streets clean for the new automobiles. A company specialising in this type of work, would go round the streets picking up the manure dropped from the horses.

Despite the new law my grandmother was insistent. She had to have a cow. She could not drink milk that was not cholav Yisroel. Dairies were open on Shabbos and they used lard on their hands when they milked the cows. Nothing would deter her and she made her way to the City Council to obtain permission to have a cow. She spoke no English, only Yiddish. She insisted that her grandchildren spoke to her in English so that she would learn the language. No one in the family knows how she obtained the permission from the City Council that she needed, but there were conditions. She had to build a barn with a double floor, one floor for the cow, and one for the manure. This she would collect in special bins and then await the arrival of the Company who would dispose of them. There were still horses and buggies being used for transport in the City, and the Company still had work to do for the City Council.

Grandmother bought her feed from the stores that sold feed for horses. A milk cow is good for a year after she has had a calf. After a year grandmother would order another cow from the farmer who raised cattle and he would bring her one that had just had a calf. Grandmother would part exchange the old cow for the new one, paying the difference in the price. Nowadays the farms are so huge, that instead of cowboys on horses, or even jeeps, helicopters hover over farms to check the whereabouts of the cattle.

The barn was located in the yard of the building owned by my grandparents. Members of their growing family were the main occupants of the apartments. There was a fence around the yard to prevent the cow from wandering. On one occasion, however, the cow escaped from the yard. The combined resources of the crowd of 200 neighbours, I was amongst them, could not bring the cow back into the yard. Grandmother went up to the cow, put her hands on the horns, said 'come on Bossie,' and brought her cow back through the gate. All my grandmother's cows were called Bossie. She usually had a cow with horns because the milk is better from this breed.

One Pesach a very big Rabbi came to Chicago for the whole week of Pesach. He needed cholav Yisroel milk for the whole of his entourage. He made enquiries and was told that Mrs Levin was the only place where he could get it. The Rabbi's aide went to see her. Grandmother said 'I am not a dairy. I only use the milk for my own purpose. Since it is Pesach I only obtain half the usual quantity of milk from the cow. The amount of milk that comes out during Pesach is much less than the twenty to thirty quarts a day that you need.'

Grandmother would usually supplement the cow's feed with bread, since hay was not available. She obtained the bread from a nearby baker, who supplied her with sacks of leftover bread. During Pesach she supplemented the cow's feed with beets.

In the end she agreed to supply them with their needs. 'I will give you the milk you want, but I will keep for my own needs, any milk produced by the cow over that quantity.' As they got ready to leave she said to them 'I gave you what you want, you give me what I want.' They asked her what she wanted. She replied 'I want an audience with the Rabbi.' Since, as a rule, the Rabbi did not speak to women, the aide said that they would have to let her know. The Rabbi told them 'of course I will see her, bring her in.' The family never discovered the purpose of her visit to the Rabbi, or the conversation she had with him. Some matters should remain only for the ears of G-d.

Belle Rabinowitz
born in 1911

'Hot bricks heated the bed'

I grew up in a huge comfortable house in the East End of London, situated on the posh end of a long street called Old Montague Street. At the other end of the street was the Petticoat Lane market where everyone came to shop, especially on Sunday morning. How I loved going there; it was so colourful and noisy.

All our neighbours were Jewish and in similar financial circumstances and I remember being friendly with everyone. Tailors, who worked on army clothes, occupied most of the houses on the opposite side of the street.

We had gas lamps for lighting, but no telephone or refrigeration. I remember that our house was the first to have electricity installed. What a blessing! We had a safe in the small yard where food was kept for Shabbos. We really had no need for a proper fridge because there was a corner shop a few doors away where fresh food was always available.

I remember that when I was quite young my father got us ready for school, while my mother stayed in bed with the latest baby. So it was father who ran to the shop and bought fresh rolls for breakfast, and then would plait my hair and send me off to school looking very tidy.

Father was a silversmith and had his own business in the bottom two rooms of the house, which served as a workshop. Since he was his own boss, he was able to take time off work to be with me when I came home from school.

On the occasions when it was very cold, father heated bricks in the fire, wrapped them in old blankets and put them in our beds to warm them. We were four girls sleeping in one room with two beds, and we slept 'tops to tails.'

Although we were not in straitened circumstances, we couldn't afford new clothes every year, so we made do. Before Pesach my mother dyed last year's dresses a blue colour and the next Pesach she dyed the same dresses yellow.

On my first day at school I ran to the back row so that I was the furthest away from the teacher. I passed the 11 + exam and was sent with three other girls to a Central school where we were taught shorthand, typing and also German.

On many Shabbos afternoons I walked with my sister and our friends to the Tower of London. It was only a ten-minute walk. What a thrill to see the ships go under the bridge! Very often we heard the bells warning the traffic that the bridge was opening and when the bridge was empty it would slowly open to allow a very large ship to sail under the bridge.

Pincus Trachtenberg
born in 1879
Told by his daughter

'So you would have another dresske in the closet?'

M y paternal grandmother was left a widow with six children. She lived in Isaslova, Russia, which is now the Ukraine, in the lower and poorer part of the city. My eventual in laws, the Greenblatts, lived in the new part of Isaslova.

The Czar decreed that Jews were forbidden to have pistols, so my father made one. His friends used to call him 'Pinnyshous', which is Yiddish for 'Pincus the shooter.' He was good with his hands and could fix anything.

The Czar's army was comprised of drafted men and my father was called up at the age of 21. The army gave him a loaf of bread once a week, which he had to sleep with under his pillow, because the other soldiers would steal it. When he wasn't in bed, he would carry it around with him. The army also provided the soldiers with soup.

The Russian/Japanese war was around the turn of the century. He spoke very little about his military service because he wanted to put the whole experience behind him. Around the time that the army was due to go to Japan, his mother came to the army camp with a bag of woman's clothing. She bribed the guards and during the night, he and another peasant soldier both dressed in women's clothing, ran away from the camp.

In those days there was a Jewish underground in the country designed to get the Jews out of Russia who wished to avoid the draft. Jews who wished to escape were told to go to a dried up river, which ran along the Polish border. The men escaped first and when they were safe made arrangements for their family to join them. On their travels my father and his companion came upon a group of women and children who were endeavouring to join their husbands. They were standing on the bank of this river, which was at the edge of a steep ravine, unable to cross.

My father and the peasant soldier picked up a child under each arm went down the bank, across the dry river, and up the other side. They came back time and again and then took the women across. On the other side they walked to the railroad station and got on a train. The underground had told them that when they got off at their stop, they should look for Moshe the redhead. When they got off the train there was a red headed man with a horse and cart.

It was the first night of Pesach and father was brought to a Chassidic home where they davened until dawn. He stayed with this family until he received his ticket to sail to America. His mother had made all the arrangements. He went steerage, which was a cheap way to travel in those days, where you took all your own food with you for the few weeks journey. A Polish Rabbi, travelling on the same boat, had his barrels of food in steerage.

When he got to New York, the immigration officials put a label on his lapel stating his name and destination, which was Boston. While he was sitting on the train, a woman handed him a banana to eat. He had never seen a banana and began to eat it with the skin on. The woman showed him how to peel a banana, and eat the fruit inside. This was the time when lots of immigrants were coming to America.

When he got to Boston a relative met him who had rented a one roomed flat for him, which had no hot water facilities. Within a year he brought his next brother over. They worked and lived in the one room together. Because he was good with his hands he learned how to repair watches and got a job with the Waltham watch company. Within two years he brought his next brother over and all three lived in the one room together. Within another two years he brought over his mother and the other children. This was all before the Great War of 1914-1918.

After making sure they were settled, he worked his way around the country for a year to see America. Then, together with a partner, he set up the Boston watch company. I can remember him saying to me that I had to get a college education, because in Russia the Jews were not allowed to go to College.

He told me once that he could have been a partner with the founder of the Elgin Watch Company. I said to him, 'Dad, you could have been a millionaire.' He said 'so you would have had another dresske in the closet.' At the age of 86 he could still fix a watch.

Moshe Zalman Feiglin
born in 1875
Told by his daughter

All Aboard Halley's comet!

My grandfather, Reb Ya'akov Zvi, studied Kabbalah and grandmother Elke helped to run the family timber business. One day, she was on her way home from a business deal in which she was collecting money from the sale of timber in the family's forest, when a bear leapt out from behind a tree and frightened her. At the time she was

Moshe Zalman Feiglin

pregnant and travelling with her maid. As a result of this encounter, she miscarried and died at the age of thirty-three in 1883.

My father was born in Gorky in the Mohilev province of White Russia and was the third son of the family. My father went to live with his maternal uncle Nachum until he was eleven years old, when grandfather remarried

At that time most people in Russia wanted to leave the country and my grandfather went to Lubavitch to obtain permission for the Rebbe to make aliyah to Israel. Finally, in 1889 at the age of forty one, he gathered his family together and with his second wife Chasya arrived in Israel.

One day, in 1911, my grandfather came home from Shul after Kiddush Levana and told his sons in Israel that he had seen Halley's comet and there was a war coming. Because he studied Kabbalah he had his way of working things out. He told his sons to leave the country. One son went to America; one son went to Australia but the eldest son, Nachum, had stayed in Russia, to manage the family's timber forests. My father stayed in Israel, where in 1912 he married my mother Bobbe Leah in Metula. In Israel the Turks exempted the eldest son from military service and my father changed the family name from Muravin to Feigelin so that he would appear to be the eldest son of the family

My father's father-in-law was friendly with the Druze. Someone told my father that the Turks were coming for him, so they say that he galloped off on a horse to the nearest port, to get away on the first boat. All boats sailed from Port Said and the first boat sailing was going to Australia. He left his wife and his children, four boys and a girl, behind in Metula.

The boat landed at Freemantle, near Perth. During the voyage the boat foundered on the Great Australian Bight, the most treacherous water in the world. The boat went under but the people were saved by another boat. News got back to Israel that the boat had foundered, but not that the people had been saved. My mother didn't know if he was alive or dead. When he landed at Freemantle he met some of his former neighbours who told him that this town was not a place of Yiddishkeit.

Thereupon he sailed on to Melbourne, where my uncle already lived. He tried various jobs, but when he turned up for work on a Monday he was told he had lost his job because he didn't work on Shabbos. He even lost a job as a bottle washer and another menial job in a rubber factory, because he refused to compromise on Shabbos.

In 1912 Australia was just beginning to develop. The Murray River, which is a very big river, runs the whole length of the northern border of the south eastern State of Victoria. It was a very fertile, well-watered country, which the government wanted settled with people working the land. The Australian government had just begun to sponsor assisted passages and advanced the cost of bringing families over. Father signed into this project along with Jewish community leaders and together, as pioneers, they decided to settle the land.

The following year, 1913, the government gave assisted passage for my mother, Bobbe Leah and her five young children. This assistance was merely a loan and I remember, as a teenager, writing out the last cheque to repay the loan. Although my father could write English, he preferred to write Hebrew.

The family settled in Orvale, three miles outside Shepparton, in the State of Victoria. My father wouldn't live anywhere unless there was a minyan. He also would not go far from civilisation without a doctor. These were the reasons for settling in Orvale and there we developed the land to produce fruit.

The main crops were peaches, apricots and pears. Trees take a long time to grow and therefore he had to find jobs elsewhere in the meantime. We grew vegetables, and kept cows, which provided milk and butter. All the family worked to milk our ten cows and prepare cream to sell to the butter factory.

In Israel my father had worked at the Rothschild's vineyards, and gained experience in working the land. This experience stood him in good stead and while he waited for the orchards to develop, he was able to obtain a position managing two farms for a Jewish family who lived in the city. He also worked as a manager in a Jewish orchard that was already developed. He cycled six miles early in the morning to manage the other farms. After five or six years our orchard was sufficiently developed and he was able to give up managing other farms.

My father was the founder of the Jewish community of Orvale. They insisted on having a shul and the government assisted by giving them half the land. He was a baal tefillah and a chazzan. On Sundays he taught any children who turned up to learn. At home he taught Torah to his own children in the evenings, after he had worked a twelve hour day. Eventually he was able to hire a melamed, a teacher, to teach all the local children.

He kept close ties with the Jewish community of Melbourne, which was basically English. It was one hundred and twenty miles from Orvale, but there was a daily train. When the community wanted a mohel, one came from Melbourne. We had no meat in the early days because it was a four-hour train journey to Orvale from Melbourne and there was no refrigeration on the train. In addition, we did not have an icebox. My father learnt shechita for chickens and was able to provide the Jewish community with kosher chickens for Shabbos.

When the melamed arrived, since he was also a shochet, the community made an arrangement with a gentile butcher and twice a week the shochet went to the abbatoir to slaughter an animal and provided Orvale with Kosher meat. The local neighbours came to our house to collect their orders.

When the orchard was developed we built a hostel in the grounds of the shul. Young people came in the summer to work during the fruit picking season, and lived in the hostel. They ate their meals in our house. We had a tennis court, which was used by all the young people.

My father was a legend in his own lifetime, because of his piety, scholarship, philanthropy and chessed. His death in 1957 was a great loss to his community.

A Lady
born in 1914

'Every family had a spinning machine'

I was born in Slovakia in October 1914 and the Great War started in November of that year. When the Russians started their march into Slovakia, the news passed from one town to another, as the people remembered other times when the Russians had come and broken everything in their path. When my parents realised that the Russians were wiping out the towns along their route, they knew it was time to leave our village, which bordered Slovakia and Hungary. The Russians wanted the land, not the people and they were killing indiscriminately.

My grandparents had an Estate with a farm, which housed horses, chickens, geese, gardens, fruit trees, a vegetable garden, and servants to take care of it – two maids and gardeners. It was like Gan Eden.

Mother had to wait another week after my birth, until she could walk. In those days women stayed much longer in bed after birth. We went on a large wagon to the big city where we took the last train out of Slovakia. I was number four in the family.

We travelled deep into Hungary to the town of Humene, and the home of my uncle. The Russians marched into the town we had evacuated in Slovakia and took it over. The Czechs came into the War from the other side, stopped the Russians and took over our town. Eventually the Czechs drove the Russians out of the town.

My grandparents stayed in the vicinity, hiding amongst the goyim. They thought they might save something of the Estate, however the Russians turned our home into stables and destroyed everything they could find. The peasants, who had absolutely nothing to lose, stayed in the town.

My father took us to Humene, and then went back to hide with his parents, because he did not want to have to fight as a soldier for Hungary in the war. My uncle also had four children and there was very little food. Since Mother was nursing me, and was surviving on very little, I have always had a small build. There was no flour, so we made bread from corn flour, and I remember that we also ate potatoes. I remember very vividly an occasion when my uncle procured an apple from somewhere. There were ten people in the house and he cut the apple into sufficient pieces so that everyone could have a very small portion. In the city of Humene, no food was coming through from the villages, so there were no vegetables and no meat. If my uncle was able to find a chicken for Shabbos, we shared it with other people who came to the house because they had no food.

When I was four we returned to Slovakia and once again lived on the Estate. The fruit trees were still there; apples, plums, pears and I also remember strawberries. There were so many apples, that we put them away and ate them throughout the winter. We kept chickens and geese, and the shochet came every week to kill chickens for Shabbos. There was a lake near the house and we had fish every Friday night. We kept cows and had milk, cheese and butter. We had everything you could want.

The peasants grew flax in the fields. They picked it by hand and laid it out to dry. When it was dry they placed it on a wooden stand and threshed it with wooden blades.

After it was threshed, the fibre became strong and very fine and they prepared it for spinning. Every family had a spinning machine and was able to make thread, which could then be woven into cloth. From this cloth the women made clothes for the family.

Since we lived near the lake, the maids took the big items, such as sheets, to wash in the water. There they beat them with a wooden paddle until they were clean. After wringing them out, they spread them on clean stones by the lakeside to dry. My mother washed smaller items of clothing by hand in a bucket. She drew the water from a well that was by the side of the house, enclosed by a wooden structure.

On the other side of the house there was another wooden structure, which concealed a very deep hole, which served as a toilet. Over the hole there was a board upon which you sat. You couldn't see anything, or smell anything. I didn't like to use it, but I had no choice.

When I was six I was sitting by the window when I heard a strange noise. Then I saw a car! It was the first car I had ever seen. I didn't know what it was but I thought it was the devil. I wanted to run away, but I was glued to my seat unable to move. I was afraid to leave the house. I wondered how it could move without a horse. We always used a horse and wagon to travel anywhere. It was two years before I saw another car.

In 1920 I was seven when my father realised that his children needed an education. My sisters were aged six and eleven; my brothers were aged five, eight and ten. The peasants did not bother to educate their children and there were no schools where we lived. The boys had to go to Yeshiva, so my father persuaded his parents to sell the Estate and move back to Humene. My father and his brothers bought real estate in Humene. The town had been taken over by the Czechs, and we were compelled to speak Czechish, not Slovak. If the teachers or the principal of the school found us speaking any language in the streets apart from Czech, we were thrown out of the school. We were even watched by the Police to make sure we only spoke Czech. When we had been in Humene for two years, I had learnt the language sufficiently well to be chosen to make a speech in the auditorium of the school in honour of the seventy-fifth birthday of President Masaryk. I wrote the speech with the help of my teacher.

In Humene my father went into business, but lost all his money. He left the family in Humene and travelled to America on his own, to my Mother's brother, who lived in Scranton, Pennsylvania. There he worked as a teacher in a Talmud Torah and as the Shammas in the Shul. He sent money back to support the family, and saved all the rest. My father went to night school, taking courses in English and American history. After six months he received a certificate, which enabled him to apply for American citizenship.

One day he wrote and told my Mother to get our passports ready, because he was coming to fetch us. I was ten when I arrived in America, in 1925. In Scranton the family had the same problem that we had in Slovakia. My sister was unable to get a job without working on Shabbos, so she moved to New York. Two of my brothers went to Yeshiva in New York. Meanwhile, in Scranton, my Mother gave birth to two more boys, and there were now eight children in the family.

In America we escaped the consequences of World War Two. Our whole family in Europe was wiped out, fathers, brothers, children and grandchildren.

Now that we were in America, I had to learn English. My American cousin suggested that I change my name to one that sounded American, however, I could not pronounce it. She told me that I could not go to school until I said my name properly. It took me two weeks. My cousin also taught me to say important phrases.

Since my English was limited I was put into the first grade with my younger eight-year-old brother. The other children in the class were five or six years old. It took one year for me to progress to my proper grade.

When I was in the seventh grade at school, the Daughters of the Revolution sponsored a history test. We had to write a composition. I was twelve or thirteen at the time. I wrote about Thomas Jefferson, and my composition was chosen as the best in Scranton. I was chosen with another boy to read out my composition at a ceremony attended by the Daughters of the Revolution. My teacher told me that I did a beautiful job, with one exception. I pronounced Thomas as Th-omas, not as T-omas.

My Mother came to the ceremony wearing a big sheitel and not able to speak a word of English. I believe it was a Kiddush Hashem that we were present at the ceremony. I never discovered what the Daughters of the Revolution thought when they realised that Jewish refugees from Europe had won the prize.

Yoel Yosef Phetersen
born in 1923

'They are not speaking Jewish, and they are not speaking gentile'

My father was born in 1898 in White Russia. At the age of nineteen, before World War One, he was called up to go into the Russian army. In those days one was in the army for many years. He desperately yearned not to go. The night before he was due to report for duty, he went out and looked at the moon. 'You be a witness,' he said to the moon, 'if the Ribono Shel Olam will save me from the army, I will become frum.'

My father didn't smoke. If he did, he coughed and choked. He thought to himself that if he coughed people would think he had tuberculosis. He stayed up the whole of the night smoking and coughing his head off. The Russian cigarette was made in two pieces. At one end there was a cardboard tube with cotton inside it that acted as a filter, the other half had tobacco in it. The next morning he went to the draft board. When they called his name he stood up with the cardboard filter in his mouth, having already smoked the tobacco. With an intake of breath he inadvertently swallowed the cardboard tube, which lodged in his throat choking him. He thought he was going to die.

As he was rasping and coughing while choking on the filter, the doctor came in and said, 'this is a sick man; he is exempt; he can go.' The army officer in charge looked at my father and said, 'he is sick? He is stronger than I am. He is going in the army.' The doctor became angry and said to the commanding officer, 'who is the doctor, you or me?'

He took off his stethoscope and gave it to the officer saying, 'here, you be the doctor' and walked away. The army officer gave in and said 'don't leave, let him go, but you stay.' There was a whole line of men waiting to be examined. My father kept his word and became shomer mitzvos.

My father married in 1918. There was nothing to eat in Russia in the early 1920's, after World War One. In the city salt and sugar were available, but no fruits and vegetables. In the small towns they grew fruit and vegetables, but they had no salt and sugar. Under communist rule, free trade was forbidden. My father would take salt and sugar and go into the country to exchange it for fruit and vegetables.

On one occasion, on his way back he was caught by two Russian soldiers, armed with bayonets. They arrested him and marched him to their officer. In those days an officer was allowed to judge a person and carry out the usual sentence of death for dealing in contraband.

My father walked between these two soldiers with his knapsack on his back singing 'G-d and His judgement is right.' Even now as I speak, I can see my father singing this song in Yiddish. The soldiers looked at him as if he was crazy. After all, he was going to be sentenced to death. Suddenly an idea came into his head and he told the soldiers that he wanted to relieve himself. They allowed him to do so, and when they saw my father, they decided to do so also. They put their rifles against the tree; my father waited for the appropriate moment, quickly disabled them and escaped with his life. They couldn't run after him because they were doubled over in pain. This saved his life.

I was born in Minsk in 1923. My father learned with the Minsker Gadol, Rabbi Mordechai Perlman. When my father became frum, he also became a ben bayis of the

Rabbi. When my mother was pregnant with me my father approached the Rabbi and told him, 'I am going to America.' The Rabbi answered, 'don't go. It's a treifeh land.' My father said 'and suppose it is a boy?' He already had two daughters. At that time it was illegal in Russia to teach Torah, although shuls were still allowed to operate. You could lose your life as well as your job. The Rabbi said, 'if this is your concern, then you can go.'

If I had been a girl they would have left immediately after the birth, because they had tickets for the boat. However I was a boy, so they didn't leave Minsk until I was three weeks old. Minsk was in White Russia. Riga, from where the boat was leaving, was in Latvia. My grandmother, mother, father, and their three children, boarded the train. We arrived at the border in the middle of a cold, snowy January night. We had to leave the train to walk to the station where they would check our papers. They deloused us with sprays us to ensure we took no lice into the country.

When we got off the train my father carried my four-year-old sister, my mother carried my two-year-old sister and my grandmother carried me. My mother had made a pillow to carry me in like a cocoon. As they were walking to the station my grandmother tripped and fell and dropped all her packages in the snow. She picked up her packages and made her way to the station. My mother saw her and shouted 'where's Yossele?' I was missing. They came back to look for me in the dark and the snow. They said to each other, 'if only he would cry we will know where to find him,' however I was sound asleep.

When we arrived at Riga the boat had already left. We sat in Riga for four months until my two uncles could arrange another passage for us. Our existing tickets were useless.

On the boat my father saw people opening bottles of soda. He wanted to open one himself and wouldn't allow anyone to do it for him. He tore his hands trying to open the bottle. He did not realise that one needed to use a bottle opener. When someone offered him a banana, this exotic fruit was a novelty. He had never seen one before and he tried to eat it like an apple with the skin on.

My grandmother was uneducated. She could not read or write. In the synagogue in Russia, she would sit next to someone who could read and who would say the words out loud. The other women who couldn't read would also repeat the words. On the boat my grandmother heard people speaking English. She said to my father, 'what are they speaking here? They are not speaking Jewish and they are not speaking gentile.' To my grandmother there were only two languages, Yiddish, that is Jewish, and Gentile, that is Russian. This is how she learned that there were many other languages.

When we arrived in America it was the 4th of July, Independence Day and people were setting off fire-crackers. My father thought he heard shooting, and said to my uncle who had come to meet us, 'what are they doing fighting here? I left to escape the revolution.' My uncle reassured him that it was only a celebration of the American holiday.

We settled in Rochester. At that time there was no cheder for young boys. When I was four years of age, my father hired a tutor to teach me the aleph bet. He remembered the promise he had made to his Rabbi, before he left Russia, regarding my education.

My grandmother was a mattress maker and, as luck would have it, one of my uncles had a mattress factory in Rochester. My father went to work for them although they were not religious. When Shabbos arrived, my father told his brother that he would not work on Shabbos. My Uncle said that he worked on Shabbos and if my father did not work on Shabbos he would not get paid. Needless to say my father was fired.

He decided to go into business on his own and fend for himself. He obtained a horse and wagon and went from house to house repairing mattresses. At the same time, because the work was not regular, he bought two boxes of the new fangled metal pan cleaners. However, he did not have the nerve to knock on doors to try to sell them. I was eight or nine at the time when he asked me to knock on the doors. Once I needed a winter coat for the cold Rochester winter, so my mother took a blue and white plaid horse blanket and turned it into a coat.

We lived near the railroad tracks. There were twenty tracks in Rochester, and the railroad station was at the other side of the tracks. The steam trains going by made a terrible racket and everything would rattle every time one would choo, choo, past. We were so used to it we didn't notice it, but our guests were always disturbed by it.

During the summer, people in Rochester would vacation on Lake Ontario where bungalows could be rented for the summer season. My father could not afford to pay the rent on two apartments, so he would give up his apartment in Rochester, move all our furniture and possessions onto a wagon and move to the bungalows for the summer. At the end of the summer he would find another apartment and move all the furniture back. He did this for several years so that we could have a holiday.

Somehow we managed. Although we were so poor and our life was difficult, it paled into insignificance in comparison with the stories of the dangers and hazards my father told me of the life of his youth in White Russia.

A pupil of Sarah Schenirer
born in 1912

'A dressmaker wants to open a school!'

When I arrived in Krakow, the first person I met was Sarah Schenirer who impressed me very much. Although she was a friendly, grandmotherly, ordinary looking woman, she had dark brown burning eyes. When I got to know her better I realised that she didn't have a shred of jealousy for other people's success. She had a short life and passed away at the age of fifty-five from cancer. No one knew her secret, even at the end.

At her school in Krakow, everything was taught in Yiddish. Sarah Schenirer was a wonderful storyteller and told interesting and fascinating stories. Besides this she taught mainly dinim, for instance the halachos of netilat yadayim, hand washing.

The seminary itself was housed in a very simple flat, where we sat and learned in a big room at a large table with long benches. Despite these conditions the teachers were excellent. Miss Eva Landsberg, from Breslau, was a descendant of Rabbi Samson Raphael Hirsch, and was a fine teacher with formal training. Apart from Sarah Schenirer we also

Sarah Schenirer

had Dr Judith Grunfeld and Dr Deutschlander who came in the summer.

Dr Deutschlander worked very hard behind the scenes for Bais Yaakov. He gave speeches across Europe to the intelligentsia about Jewish education and toiled tirelessly for the cause. Dr Grunfeld also travelled around collecting money for Bais Yaakov. It was a terribly primitive place and we quickly outgrew the flat, which housed the seminary and we needed bigger accommodation, eventually requiring a whole building. That this was even possible was only due to Dr Grunfeld and Dr Deutschlander. Without them there would have been no building.

There were some people in Poland that helped to establish the school. At first Sarah Schenirer suffered from vicious attacks. People said 'a dressmaker wants to open a school!' They even threw stones at her. After such an attack she said to her pupils 'with these stones we will build the Bais Yaakov.' It was difficult at first. Some girls slept in the big room where we learned and ate. Others who could pay a bit, slept out. We weren't interested in the chitzonius, only in learning. The whole spirit and friendship of the girls was wonderful. I had a visitor once who said 'what! Is this the seminary? The Bais Yaakov? It's so primitive!' His question surprised me, because to me it was everything. The girls didn't need gashmius, material things, only ruchnious, spirituality, and we were all very happy.

In the summer we went to Rabka, a beautiful resort in the Carpathians. It was a wonderful experience. Dr Deutschlander came and delivered inspiring shiurim in Tehillim and we sat in the meadows on the grass and listened. He was a unique and charismatic personality with a great sense of humour. Fraulein Rosenbaum, who became Dr Judith Grunfeld after she married, also gave shiurim and played games with us as well. It was the most wonderful holiday I had ever had, full of ruchnious.

When I finished seminary, I returned home to become a teacher. At the same time I travelled to different places to promote the idea of Bais Yaakov. Everywhere I went I spoke to groups of women and young girls who had never heard of Bais Yaakov. When I introduced them to the concept, they loved it. It was easy to realize what Bais Yaakov would mean to Bnos Yisroel. I loved teaching and because of this Hashem gave me a lot of siyata d'shamaya, heavenly assistance.

Bertha Gitleman
born in 1914

'I want one of you to go out to the East and create light'

Y isroel Steinpress, the well-known chazzan and composer, was my grandfather on my mother's side. He was very talented and I remember him either looking in the Gemorah or writing music. You couldn't talk to him very much, because he didn't use his words frivolously, but I learned certain songs from him, which, as a music teacher, I can say, are really music. To my grandfather, however, the Hebrew words were the important thing, not the music itself. The music is only to bring our heart closer to G-d in prayer, and whenever I taught his niggunim to someone, they became alive. The tunes were fitted to the words. Nowadays musicians take a posuk and the song rides around the same few bars of music again and again. It doesn't mean anything after a while. With my grandfather, repetition didn't exist.

As the daughter of a chazzan my mother decided that she didn't need any furniture, but she must have a piano. She bought herself a piano and taught herself to play by ear. When grandfather came to our house he sat down and played the piano.

My mother took in a piano teacher who taught me the elements of music. After this I played by myself and had no further education in music. Very soon a neighbour said to me 'you know I have a piano but my daughter doesn't know how to play, can she learn with you?' This girl brought another friend until there were seven or eight girls who liked to come, because there was nowhere else to learn.

They say "through teaching we learn". They were beginners and it was not too hard to teach them the basic elements of music. Later, when I taught in the Beis Yaakov there were always girls who would come to me in the afternoon to learn to play the piano.

We lived in Düsseldorf in Germany at the time of my birth in 1914. In 1917, when I was three years old, we left for Holland because my father didn't want to serve in the army. The nearest place to Düsseldorf was Holland. My only memory of this trip was that we went for a very long walk, through a dark wood with a Dutch woman, until we reached Holland. I was with my parents and my little sister.

Life in Holland was very pleasant. Our house resembled a hostel because it was filled with many young men from Poland who ran away. They were Jewish boys who most probably came from the same city, and because they had no money and no papers, they came to us to sleep. My mother always used to make so much food, especially meat. We had plenty of that. At that time my father had quite a nice income. He would travel back and forth between Holland and Germany selling clothing or books. He would sell whatever people wanted, crossing the border by train.

I went to first and second grade in a Jewish school in Amsterdam. We spoke Yiddish at home and Dutch at school. After three years of living in Holland we returned to Düsseldorf because my mother became ill and she couldn't tolerate the wet climate.

In Düsseldorf there was no Jewish school, only a goyishe school. I missed the school in Amsterdam very much, but I became friendly with the German girls who seemed very nice. One day a girl I used to do my homework with said 'I can't come to you to do homework anymore'. We used to do homework together in my house. I said 'why not'. She answered 'we can still be friends outside, but I cannot come to your house'. This was just a taste of the anti-Semitism that soon followed.

One day, my mother came home very excited. She had been to a lecture given by a certain Dr. Deutschlander to the women of Dusseldorf. He told them that it was now time that girls should receive Jewish education. He wanted to start a school based upon the ideas of a certain woman named Sarah Schneirer who lived in Krakow. He said it was a great zechus to meet her and he had decided to leave his 'gantzen' [great future] and wanted to help her to build up a school for girls across Germany and all over Europe.

My mother explained that this Dr. Deutschlander was going from city to city explaining to the people what he wanted to accomplish. "I want one of you to go out to the East and create light' he said. I was seventeen or eighteen at the time, and it was very unpleasant to be in school. The anti-Semitism among the girls, and the teachers too, was really unbearable. There was only myself and another Jewish girl in my class.

Dr. Deutschlander managed to gather some girls together and soon we went to Vienna, My father accompanied me from Düsseldorf to Cologne and from there I caught a train right through to Vienna. I still remember how my father ran after the train and said 'you see your father is still young, he can run. We will see each other soon'.

It was many years before we saw each other again. My grandfather Yisroel was in America and my parents were able to get papers to escape from Germany to join him there, Baruch Hashem.

After learning in the Seminary for a term, vacation time came and everybody went home, except for me because I had nowhere to go. It was decided that I should go to my grandfather in Poland. When Dr. Deutschlander heard this he said 'you must go to Krakow on your way and meet Sarah Schneirer.' He gave me his visiting card to show her that I was a student at the seminary he had started in Vienna.

When I arrived in Krakow I attended a lecture that she gave. The girls said 'you tell us we shouldn't speak lashon hora, but then we won't have any friends'. They were so open and honest confiding their fears to her as if they were talking to their mother. She calmed everyone down and spoke to everyone as a mother would speak, not like a teacher.

When the girls said goodbye to her, she turned to me and said she wanted to show me the 'crib' of the Beis Yaakov. We went through all the streets of the old city of Krakow and entered the house on the first floor. There sat an old lady. Sarah Schneirer said 'this is my mother'. Sarah Schneirer must have been around fifty years of age at this time because she passed away at the age of fifty-three. She sat me down near her mother and told me a little bit about her life and the story of the Beis Yaakov. I went home very happy and even wrote down what she had told me. I had many opportunities to relate what she told me that day. Who was I that she should take the time to invite me to her home and treat me so sweetly? I felt such a friendship and such warmth exude from her that, right then, I decided I wanted to be just like her. The time that I spent with her in Krakow was perhaps the greatest excitement I had as a young girl.

I had to return to Vienna to finish the school year. It was around Pesach time and the seminary gave a great party to which many Rabbonim came. It was wonderful that they recognized the value of the Beis Yaakov and allowed the girls to learn there. Some, however, were firmly against it; they called it "Beis Eisav" because it let the girls learn Chumash with Rashi.

At the seminary there was a dormitory where some girls slept. In Vienna I became friends with three girls who weren't from Vienna, but were the daughters of well-known Rabbonim. One girl was Hessel, the daughter of the Kapichnitzer Rebbe, whom I liked very much. The other two were the daughters of other Rebbes who were the first to send their girls there to learn. This was a great boost for Dr. Deutschlander.

At the end of the training, when everyone went home, most of the girls already had positions. Although there was a shortage of jobs, I was offered three different jobs in different places. I chose a job in Tapulcharny, a small city near the border with Germany, where they wanted a teacher who could speak German. It was the nearest place to my home in Dusseldorf, only twenty hours by train!

Upon my arrival, two very nice girls came to meet me and brought me to the home of a woman who was from Vienna and who spoke German. They told me that girls would enroll in the school just to hear my good German. We had no building and no course. We started the school in the building of the Agudas Yisroel. They already called the school Beis Yaakov and had a school song 'Beis Yaakov Lelchu venelcha b'ohr Hashem'.

They told me I could start teaching if I had ten girls. That Tuesday I met up with my friend Ilush, who said I should come and speak about Beis Yaakov. On Friday afternoon there were already signs all over the city about a new school that was opening. That night I spoke to about forty or fifty women and I told them about Sarah Schneirer.

The girls that enrolled would pay every month to a committee from whom I would draw fixed salary. First we had twenty girls, then forty and eventually we had sixty students. They had such a tremendous desire to learn. They said 'why shouldn't we also have a chance to learn?'

There is not such a nice ending to the story. I taught in Tapulcharny for six years and built up a really fine school. Then, one Friday night in 1938, soldiers came and took all the foreigners and put them in jail. I don't really recall anything of this period except that it was very hard. I sat there in jail with some of the other girls and teachers. It was Shabbos Lech Lecha. Six weeks later on Shabbos 'Mikeitz' they opened the jail and told us to get out and leave Germany.

But where to go? My parents were in America. The only country that would let us in was Holland because they needed household help. I went there and stayed with a nice family who had a kitchen in the basement. My job was to carry up heavy trays of food from the basement up to the third floor of the house. It was heavy work and I developed a hernia. I went to hospital for an operation. After this I was allowed to work at something else. This was great Mazel. I became a head teacher in Amsterdam and I had a wonderful life.

I suppose you could say that I 'missed' the war that way.

Leah Perl
born in 1906
Told by her daughter

'Mother slept on the stove'

My mother was born in a little village in Hungary called Felsha Banya. Her father was a shepherd before he married and after his marriage he purchased a large 'vinegarten', vineyard, where he grew plum trees, from which he made wine, whisky and liqueurs by hand. Mother used to work in the vinegarten as well. Her parents also owned a cotton field in Felsha Banya, where my mother, my grandmother and my great grandmother picked the cotton alongside the Hungarian peasants. They spun the cotton into yarn on their spinning wheel, which they would then weave into fabric. From the fabric they made clothes, tablecloths, curtains and anything else they needed from the cloth.

Felsha Banya was a very small community and no more than ten Jewish families lived there. We were nice to the local peasants who were not harsh or anti-Semitic people like those found in the large cities, and we depended on them to work the fields, which were far too large to handle on our own.

There were no stores or telephones in the village. If mother needed to run an errand in the next village, either to buy food from the store, or to contact her father or grandfather for any reason, she would have to run over the fields for half an hour, trying to avoid the peasant workers along the way. In Felsha Banya the family only had the vegetables and the fruits they grew themselves. They had eggs from the chickens and Zeide killed the chickens for meat. He was a shochet, but only for chickens.

My mother went to the gentile school in the next village, but for his sons my grandfather hired melamdim, Jewish teachers, who came to live with us. Zeide built a house nearby where the melamdim could teach his children.

Bubba and Zeide kept a collie dog called Bodre, who was rarely allowed in the house. From time to time, however, he did come in when it was time to taste some of Bubba's food. Zeide was not keen on inviting him into the house and he would not make a brocha in front of the dog. When Zeide was ready to eat and the dog was there, he would say 'Bodre! Nu?' and the dog would then get up and leave the house.

In the kitchen my bubba had a big stove, which was built with cement blocks at the back and stone at the front. On the top she cooked soups and stored the pans. On the bottom there were doors that opened to the ovens where she baked her cakes and challahs. In order to heat the stove, the men had to chop down trees in the nearby forest. In the winter when it was cold, the stove was alight all night to heat the whole house. When my great grandmother lost her husband, she came to live with her daughter, my bubba, who was her only child. She used to put her mattress on top of the stove to sleep. My mother would sleep there, too, next to her bubba. There were stone steps next to the oven leading up to the top of the stove.

My father was called up to serve in the Hungarian army in a war against the Russians. He went into hiding and Zeide fed him, since he refused to serve in a war with a high mortality rate for the infantry, as most of the soldiers were draftees. He remained in hiding while papers were processed for himself and his family to emigrate to America. Eventually they set sail for America in 1927.

Although Bubba and Zeide had many children, there were only five children when they left Hungary for America. The others passed away from various ailments. They arrived in America and settled in Cheyobagen, Wisconsin, where they lived for a while. It was a tiny Jewish community with very little to offer new immigrants. My sister was born there and she was very embarrassed her whole life to show anyone her birth certificate, which was printed on a postcard with pictures of farm animals, including pigs. In those days it was a real hick town.

They moved and settled in Milwaukee, Winconsin, where grandfather worked as a shochet. He was a whole community in himself. He built a mikveh in his house as well as a matzo oven. When the house was too small he added more rooms, which he built himself.

Isaac Gaba
born in 1882
Told by his son

'Well bought is half sold'

My father was a Yeshiva bochur who learned in the Telshe Yeshiva in Poland at the end of the nineteenth century. Bochurim from the yeshiva used to eat in a different house every day, known as 'essen tag'; that way they were able to keep body and soul together. In return my father taught the children of the house.

Eventually my father was drafted into the Russian army. He took the place of his older brother who was the breadwinner of the family. In those days in Russia, the oldest brother did not need to serve if someone took his place. In 1904 the army made its way to Vladivostock, to join the front of the Russian-Japanese war. My father and his cousin were amongst the soldiers. They realised that they would be killed if they went to the front so they decided to desert. When the train was in a siding they escaped and caught a train going in the opposite direction. After they acquired other clothing, they took off and discarded their uniforms, and escaped being caught as deserters.

My father was a scribe in the army and wrote letters for the other soldiers. He was able to speak and write Russian, Hebrew and Yiddish. It was a tremendous advantage in the army to read and write Russian. However if you were Jewish, you were just cannon fodder, and of course there was no chance of promotion.

My father had relations in America so he and his cousin slowly made their way to the coast. Since they were penniless, they went into towns where there were Yidden. They taught in the cheders or in the shuls, where their knowledge was sought after, to earn money for the journey.

It took three weeks for the two of them, sleeping rough, to travel across Europe to reach the port of Hamburg. My grandparents were peasants and lived in a shtetl. My father couldn't write to his parents in case the letters were intercepted. He had been away from home since the age of fourteen when he went to yeshiva. In Hamburg they were told that the destination of the boat was America. The boat stopped at London and the Captain told my father 'you are here; this is where you get off.' So he disembarked, not realising that he had not, in fact, reached his intended destination.

In London he didn't know a soul. He made his way to a very big shul that was famous all over Europe. However, the gabbaim wouldn't let him in. They did not want someone coming into the shul looking like a schnorrer. He was very upset. Having no money and no alternative he slept rough under a bridge. He found a job as a tailor, although he had no talent for sewing. The tailors sat on the table cross-legged, they didn't sit on chairs; they wouldn't sit on the floor because that is a sign of mourning and because on the table they were out of the way of the rats, which plagued the building. As he was sitting there, doing a job he hated, someone, whom he did not know, came in and asked my father where he came from. After his reply the man said he had a landsman in Wales. 'You will never make it here in London. You have a friend in Wales, go there.' Thereupon the man gave him the money to travel to Wales.

He was able to find the man who was, in fact, a friend of his. In common with many Jewish refugees who had escaped from Europe and found their way to Wales, his friend was a peddler. Every day his friend went out with a basket filled with haberdashery — buttons, needles, cotton, elastic and all sorts of notions. He taught my father the peddlers trade. He travelled on the same train as all the peddlers, and went from door to door in all the small villages. He was taught to say one sentence, 'look in the basket', when ever he was asked a question. Eventually his English improved and

A typical peddler of the period

he did well and prospered. There were no shops in the villages so when the housewives got to know him they would ask for something special and he would bring it the following week.

For years he lived in digs, shared accommodation, until he got married in 1910. At the beginning of World War One, he was called up to serve in the British army. However, he had no intention of serving in any war. He had left one country not to get killed and now he had a wife and four children. The week before his medical check up he stayed awake all night, every night. The night before his medical examination he stayed awake drinking strong coffee and smoking.

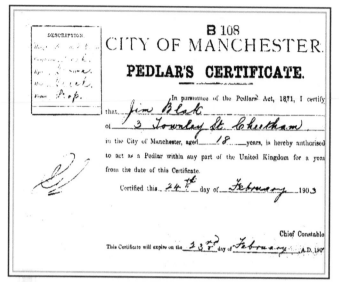

A typical peddlers certificate

In the morning, when he went to Newport, fifteen miles by bus, to the medical tribunal, he was declared physically unfit. They said 'come back in six months when you are better. Six months later he did the same thing. He never did serve in the British army, but he suffered from bronchitis all his life.

I was three years of age when my father opened a haberdashery shop in Tredegar. We lived over the shop. Since my father was still travelling, my mother served in the shop. Since my mother had come from Russia she could not read or speak English. In the shop my father used a pricing code based on my mother's name. When I was four I was able to serve in the shop because I knew the code.

My parents were Shomer Shabbos and on Shabbos the shop was closed. Since it was common practice for wages to be paid in cash on Fridays, people wanted to spend their money the following day. There was a continual knock on the door on Shabbos, which disturbed and distressed my father.

For this reason, in 1922 we moved to Cardiff where my father opened a wholesale business. He was able to close his business on Shabbos because Shabbos was a busy day for shopkeepers to sell, and not a day when they wanted to buy goods wholesale. He went to Shul every night, and nearly every evening he would bring a poor person home, because he knew what it was like to be hungry. As children we were always nice to them, although they were never clean. They would come from London and go schnorring around all the baalei battim.

There was a terrible strike in 1926. My father said to all his creditors that if they didn't make him bankrupt he would pay them 20 shillings in the pound, that is, the entire debt. He had two signs over his shop, the name of the shop which was 'The Paradise of the Small Trader' and 'Well bought is half sold'. He didn't go bankrupt and he paid his creditors in full. After the strike he moved to different premises, turning the front room into a shop.

Wales was a depressed area and never recovered from the strike. In 1936 the Welsh County Council offered land and tax-free benefits to people to work on the newly formed Treforest Trading Estate. In some cases the Council also offered a building and the opportunity to transfer their businesses for free. Many families came from Frankfurt-on-Maine. As a consequence of the Welsh County Council's offer to encourage the transfer of business from Germany, many lives were saved.

The Germans who transferred with the businesses were all affiliated with Agudah and very frum. They started a shul where my father was the treasurer of the Committee of Refugees and collected money from the town. My father was considered very honest because he didn't have sticky fingers. I remember when my father would have meetings in the front room and we were told to be discreet and stay away.

The Stern brothers came over from Frankfurt with their best workers and started a factory called Pearl Varnish. They had a formula for making very strong paint, which wasn't yet available in the country. The paint was used to coat the bottom of hulls on ships and eventually it became world famous.

When the Second World War started, the Stern family and all the Germans, who were regarded as enemy aliens, were forced to leave Cardiff and live 20 miles from the coast in the Welsh valleys where they made kehillot, communities. When they finally came back to Cardiff, they were the infusion of true Yiddishkeit. After the war, the Stern brothers took over the Chevra Kiddisha and improved the kashrus. I joined the Chevra Kadisha because of them. They were the pioneers of Welsh Jewish life.

Rabbi **Menachem Porush**
born in 1915

Guardian of the Wall

I remember Rabbi Yosef Chaim Sonnenfeld very well. It was a great merit to receive his blessings on the holidays, when everyone has to see his Rabbi. I went to see Reb Chaim. Rabbi Samson Raphael Hirsch was in Germany at that time. He was for the Jewish Kehillot, communities, in Germany what Reb Chaim was in Eretz Yisroel.

Reb Chaim had the honour of being one of those few outstanding great sages who were the right hand of the great Brisker Rav, Rabbi Yehoshua Leib Diskin. Reb Chaim set up communities of Orthodox Jewry all over Israel. He was one of those who established Torah existence in our Holy Land and built Torah life in the full meaning of that expression.

The Balfour Declaration wanted to find a solution for the Palestinians and to give a homeland to the Jewish people. At that time our great Sages wanted the Jewish community to be ruled according to the Torah. The secular Zionist movement wanted the opportunity to influence the formation of the Jewish community and would not agree. The secular movement under the leadership of Professor Chaim Weitzman wanted to take control over the ruling of Orthodox Jewry and their school system. At that time Reb Chaim raised the flag of opposition against secular Zionism and organised Orthodox Jewry to enable them to exist.

The situation in the Holy Land at that time was very difficult. It was right after the First World War, and there

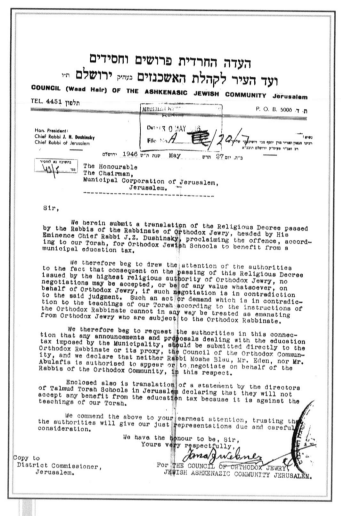

was no possibility for the upkeep of Torah institutions. Professor Weitzman said that he was willing to be responsible for the upkeep of the Torah institutions. At that time Reb Chaim brought the leadership of Orthodox Jewry together with the heads of the Torah schools and declared to Professor Weitzman that Orthodox Jewry would not give away the Torah school system. Reb Chaim stood at the front of this fight, enabling the continuation of the orthodox school system during this difficult time.

As much as is known of the strong fight from Reb Chaim against secular Zionism and Professor Weitzman, it was Reb Yosef Chaim Sonnenfeld, who was the real original Zionist. He was a Torah Zionist, who tirelessly built religious neighbourhoods and was very active in buying land from the Arabs.

The whole of his life was spent trying, wherever possible, to build our Holy Land in accordance with the Torah. At that time there was a strong disagreement with the Arabs over the ownership of the Western Wall. Looking at what has happened over recent years, we forget about the 1929 pogroms in Eretz Yisroel. At that time, in order to avoid more bloodshed, the British Mandate established a committee to find a solution for the Jews, Arabs and the Western Wall.

During the committee's negotiations, the suggestion was posed that there should be some agreement between the Jews and the Palestinians. The Palestinians claimed that the Wall was theirs, and the committee wanted an agreement that the Western Wall belonged to the Palestinians but that the Jewish people had the right to pray here. The leadership, who were the Jewish Authorities at that time, were ready to sign this agreement after securing the right to pray at the Western Wall. The committee from the British Mandate also

(Translation) GRAVE WARNING

Jerusalem
13th Iyar 5706

We the undersigned, having assembled at the residence of our master Rabbi J.Z.Dushinsky, in the matter of the attempt of persons to undermine the foundations of our Holy Torah and terribly to Threaten the very existence of our Faith by breaking the fence(of our religion) to add drunkenness to thirst (Deut.19-29), who are negotiating to receive a portion of the Municipal Education Tax for the educational institutions in Jerusalem and endeavour that the directors of Talmud Torah Schools and Torah Educational institutions (of Orthodox Jewry) should also accept from the education tax.

Now this ruthless undermining is in flagrant contradiction of the decision of all the Teachers of the Torah within the Holy City of Jerusalem, as is well known.

We therefore issue a Decree with the authority of the Holy Torah, that these persons have to withdraw their hands from this abuse.

Nobody should follow them, God forbid, and they should have pity for their souls and for the souls of their families and cease their attempts to break in the fence of the Torah, and should not flout the words of our Rabbis, which is an offence quoted in the Schulchan Aruch (Rabbi Joseph Karo's Religious Code), Yore Deah, Art. 334, to be deserving of excommunication and to be shunned by society.

He who will not heed this Warning and will accept from this Education tax, whether for himself or for others, whether directly or indirectly, or will try in any manner whatsoever, comes within the meaning of "Cursed be he that confirmeth not all the words of this Law to do them" (Deuteronomy 26-27)

God will not spare him, and all the curses..... shall lie upon him (Deuteronomy 2-29)

We are only the proxies of our ancient saintly rabbis and sages of blessed memory who in their time have declared a solemn excommunication on all who break the fence of religious instruction and education of boys and girls other than as passed to us by tradition from our forefathers.

AND NONE MAY TREAT THIS AS AN EASY OR LIGHT MATTER, FOR BITTER WILL BE IS END.

He who transgresses the words of the Rabbis, breaking the fence of religion is bitten by the serpent. Those who listen to us and heed our warning to return to the paths of righteousness will be among the blessed and their reward will be manifold.

Our words are uttered in honour of the Holy Torah and we shall make public the offence and brazenness of any who do not heed them, to their shame and disgrace all over the world.

And all who do heed our warning and listen to our words will be blessed to witness the true redemption of Israel.

Signed: Joseph Zvi Dushinsky,
Chief Rabbi of Orthodox Jewry in Palestine

Signed:
Rabbi Zelig Reuben Bengis
Rabbi Pinchas Epstein
Rabbi David Halevi Jungreiss

Rabbi Jeruham Fishel Bernstein
Rabbi Naftuli Zvi Smerler
Rabbi Israel Issac Reisman

wanted Rabbi Yosef Chaim Sonnenfeld and Rav Kook to sign.

A representative of this delegation came to Reb Chaim to obtain his signature to this agreement, but Reb Chaim said, 'I can never agree that the Western Wall belongs to the Arabs.' Then the delegation went to Rav Kook. Reb Chaim sent his gabbai to Rav Kook, ahead of the delegation, to warn him not to sign. On the way the gabbai of Reb Chaim recognised the gabbai of Rav Kook running in the street from Kiryat Moshe Montefiore, where Rav Kook was staying in a summer home. The gabbai of Rav Kook recognised the gabbai of Reb Chaim and told him that Rav Kook had sent him on the same mission. Rav Kook had said 'how can I agree that the Western Wall belongs to the Arabs.' He was afraid the Reb Chaim might agree and the two messengers were running to each other.

With God's Help.

(Translation)

DECLARATION

Whereas we have it in tradition from our saintly Rabbis and Sages handed down from generation to generation, and experience has clearly confirmed the spiritual danger of Torah-educational institutions being in any way subject to lay supervisors, except as regards matters of hygiene and sanitation, therefore, in connection with the Municipal Education Tax in Jerusalem which, according to rumour, is about to be promulgated, it is a sacred duty to warn all Torah-Educational institutions that they are absolutely forbidden to receive any benefits from the proceeds of this tax, and even more, must not contribute such taxes to the local Government Education Department.

The institutions mentioned herebelow will pass a regulation in each institution to strengthen and to give legal effect to the Rabbinical prohibition.

Signed hereunto in the month of Iyar 5705:

Signatures:

Signatories	For: Institution
Joseph Gershon Hurwitz, Isaac Jacob Vachtfogel, Yehiel Michal Mushkin	Talmud Torah & Yeshivah Meah-Shearim.
Isser Zalman Meltzer	Talmud Torah & Yeshivah Etz-Haim.
Israel Zeev Minzberg, Jeruham Fishel Bernstein, Ephraim Zalman Halperin	Talmud Torah & Yeshivah Haye-Olam.
Moshe Leib Bernstein, Samuel Spitzer Segal	Diskin's Orphanage.
Michal Shlapaborsky	Yeshivah Tifereth Zvi.
Jeheskiel Saran	Hebron Yeshivah.
Eliezer Judah Finkel	Yeshivah "Mir".
Abraham Johanan Blumenthal	Zion Orphanage.
Joseph Eisner, Samuel Spitzer Segal	Talmud Torah & Yeshivah Shomrei Hachomot.
Jacob Moshe Kurlandsky	Talmud Torah "Yavne".
Jacob Moshe Charlap	Yeshivah Merkaz Harav.
Aharon Katzenelnbogen	Talmud Torah & Yeshivah Torah VeYirsh.
Eli Slatnik	Yeshivah Heichel-HaTorah.

When I was bar mitzvah Rabbi Yosef Chaim Sonnenfeld had been invited but he caught the flu and was unable to come. The next day my father took me to his house to ask for his blessing. On that occasion my father brought to Reb Chaim a letter from Rabbi Yaakov Rosenheim and asked him if he should answer. I remember, even now, Reb Chaim putting his hands on the table and saying to my father 'Reb Moshe, write to the Holy Agudas Yisroel.'

There was a custom in the secular schools on the 15th Shevat, the Rosh Hashanah for trees, to parade in the streets before planting trees. Reb Chaim saw the students marching and said 'G-d shall make thousands like you' even though the leaders of the secular schools were his mortal enemies. He was sure that these children would become baalei teshuvah, return to learning Torah, therefore he gave them a blessing.

Yetta Bloch
born in the late 1890's
Told by her daughter

'It never rains here, so you don't need a roof'

B efore the turn of the century my grandfather brought my father to South Africa from Lithuania to help establish him in a business. My father opened a store on the edge of the Bush Veldt in the Transvaal, which was in the back of beyond. He did not succeed in his business and he returned to Lithuania when he was in his very early twenties.

Upon his return, my father was strolling in the park one day when he noticed my mother. Because my father was a very handsome man, she also noticed him. Despite the fact that my mother lived in another town, feelers were sent out and arrangements to meet were made. My mother's family thought he must be a rich man from South Africa. After all, only a successful man would wear a gold chain and carry a pocket watch. They arranged for my father to marry my mother without a dowry, which was unheard of in those days.

It was only after their marriage that my mother realised that father was not a wealthy man. He could not succeed in making a parnossa living in Lithuania and decided to return to South Africa and build a new future there. By this time my parents had a son and a daughter and my mother was pregnant with a third child.

Father went to South Africa alone hoping to send for mother and the children later on and he started ranching with cattle in the Northern Transvaal. However, World War One broke out and travel became impossible. My mother and the children were obliged to live with relatives, moving from one family to another. My mother was a simple, uneducated woman from Lithuania, who spoke Yiddish, a little Russian, some Polish and a bit of German. She had very little money, just the jewellery she received upon her marriage, and when the War ended she decided to take the children and join Father in South Africa. Father did not know of mother's intentions.

From Shauli, a town in Lithuania they had a three-week journey by train to Vladivostock, the port city where they could catch a boat. During those three weeks, at every stop she rushed off the train, with her basin, to buy whatever food was available such as eggs, milk, rolls and bread. At night she hung up a sheet that was sprinkled with camphor to avoid infection and disease. On the journey she met many interesting people and picked up various folk remedies.

When they arrived at Vladivostock, they took a boat to Yokohama in Japan. To get around difficulties with language, she negotiated with hand signs and was fortunate that other people helped her. In Yokohama my mother took a boat to Durban, South Africa.

She had only enough money to buy a third class ticket on the boat, which meant sleeping on a mattress on the lowest deck with only the Japanese poor for company. She was the only European woman on the boat travelling third class. The Captain took pity on her and gave her permission to drag the mattresses on to the upper deck every night. However she had to wake up early every morning so that the Japanese sailors could swab the deck. She fenced off a corner of the deck with a sheet for privacy. In the morning she woke up to a ring of Japanese sailors waiting for them to move so they could clean the deck.

As they drew closer to the port of Durban, she sent a telegram to my father announcing their imminent arrival. She had visions of a comfortable home and an established business waiting for her in South Africa. She was unaware of what awaited her because the outbreak of the War had made communication between them impossible.

My father received the telegram and came to the port in time, but waited in the wrong place. Consequently, my mother waited for hours in the boiling hot sun and the children were fainting from the heat of the sun amongst the piles of luggage. The meeting was full of reproach instead of the joyous one it should have been. She said to my father 'let's just go home.'

They travelled by train for hours eventually arriving in Johannesburg. My mother asked my father 'is this where we are going to live?' 'No', he said, 'we have to travel on another train.' They travelled and travelled until they reached Pretoria. 'Is this where we are going to live?' my mother asked hopefully. 'No,' said father, 'we are just changing trains here.' They took a train to Pietersburg in the Transvaal. It was a small town, smaller than Johannesburg or Pretoria, but still acceptable. 'Is this where we are going to live?' asked mother. 'No' said father, 'from here there is no train we must take a horse and cart.'

They travelled through wild veldt, open veldt, then dry hot veldt with grass and more grass with only an occasional thorn tree, or hill and valley for variety. They travelled for hours in father's horse and cart, and finally, in the distance mother saw a tiny little house. It was roughly built with a tin roof held down by big pumpkins and rocks.

She got off the cart and waded through the tall grass into her living room. My father showed her the kitchen, which was outside and had no roof. 'Why is there no roof?' mother asked. 'It never rains here so you don't need a roof,' father answered. 'When it does rain' he added, 'you will be so glad you won't worry about the kitchen.'

Typical building with pumpkins on the roof

She asked 'where will the children go to school?' My father said 'we will arrange for them to board with a Jewish family in Pietersburg.' My mother said to herself, 'we are not going to be here very long because I am not going to be parted from my children.' She had just travelled with them in a tight family group for weeks and weeks and she had no intention of being parted from them in order to send them to school.

I was born in South Africa in 1919 and we eventually moved to Brits in the Transvaal where my father opened a store. He also had cattle on rented ground. Mother did not think that the school in Brits was good enough for my brother as it was too countrified. She drove him to school, in their Ford car, to Pretoria 32 miles from Brits. It was a big thing to have a Ford car, so they must have been doing very well.

My mother wanted my brother to play the violin so she drove him to Pretoria for lessons. When my brother turned thirteen, he boarded with a Jewish family in Pretoria because Mother thought he was now old enough to live away from home.

Because mother developed her ability to treat illnesses with folk remedies, I remember as a child seeing a row of black people sitting outside the house every morning waiting for my mother to open the door and treat them. The blacks came with empty bottles to fill with her mixtures. She healed wounds, heavy chests and other problems without regard for the colour of their skin, because she harboured no prejudices.

On one occasion when my mother was in the General Store, attached to the house, she saw a man outside. He was dressed in multicoloured feathers and beads and was shaking a string threaded with bones. He was prancing around trying to put the fear of G-d into the blacks who were standing around the store. My mother listened to the peculiar sounds that were coming from him and watched his gestures but these made no impression on her. What she noticed was the running sore that he had on his leg. She asked my father who he was. My father told her that he was a witch doctor. My mother replied, 'a fine doctor he is, look at the running sore on his leg.' She went into the house, made a mixture up and gave it to him

I remember one child had epilepsy that mother controlled with one of her mixtures. When my brother became a doctor, he told me that he remembered that mother put mustard in the mixture and that one of the medications then currently used by the medical profession to treat epilepsy contained mustard.

This simple uneducated woman from Lithuania had become educated in the school of life.

Rev. **Shalom Camissar**
born in 1918

'It cost five shillings a week to go to Yeshiva'

After Succos in 1933 when I was fifteen years of age, I made my way from London to Gateshead Yeshiva. In my mind I imagined the Yeshiva as massive, but the building was not imposing and did not live up to my expectations. It was a simple corner house on Berwick Road, which was also utilised for meals. There were several rooms on the upper floor used for sleeping accommodation. At that time there were around forty bocherim, who had been sent by their parents from Germany to escape from the Nazis. All of them came from religious families.

My mother came from Poland and my father from Russia and they settled in England before the Second World War. Life was difficult in those days and parents were only too eager for their children to help with the family budget. However, my parents wanted me to learn in Yeshiva and were prepared to support me. My father was a tailor and my mother was a felling hand, which meant that she finished off garments by hand sewing. In those days it was unheard of for women to go to work.

On the first night after my arrival, there was no accommodation for me in the Yeshiva, so I slept in the home of the Rosh Yeshiva, Rabbi Landinsky. At that time I could not speak a word of Yiddish. Although my parents spoke Yiddish, and I understood it, they discouraged me from speaking Yiddish in order to help me get around in English in their new home country.

That first evening in the home of the Rosh Yeshiva whilst waiting to go to bed, the Rebbitzen asked me in Yiddish, 'where do you come from?' I answered 'London.' She was perplexed and said in Yiddish 'London? I have never heard of London. Perhaps you mean Lundun. When I came from Lithuania I passed through Lundun, so that's how I know it.' She was surprised that I spoke no Yiddish.

It cost my parents five shillings a week to send me to Yeshiva. My mother would post a postal order every week.

On Shabbos I had essen tag [an eating day] with the Secretary of the Yeshiva, Lonty Suffrin. He was paid three shillings for all the Shabbos meals.

We learnt in Derwent Water Road where there was a shul called the Blechener Shul, because it had a tin roof. Blechen is the German word for tin. It stood on the embankment by the main railway line, and every time a train passed it would shake the building to its foundations. During the course of the afternoon we looked forward to seeing the 'Flying Scotsman' making its way to Scotland from London. Because it was a famous train, it was a special event for me personally; it was the Concord of the 1930's.

The shiurim had three levels and took place in the main shul. One in the main shul, one at the back of the shul and one in the ezras nashim, which was a room adjoining the shul. I came to the Yeshiva as a complete beginner in the Talmud and could not enter a class where the tuition was entirely in Yiddish. The use of English was strictly forbidden. I had individual tuition in Yiddish and Talmud given by the shochet of the community, Rabbi Dovid Dryan. Rabbi Ephraim Fine also tutored me and after six months I had reached the stage where I could join the main class.

In the morning we davened in the dining room of the Yeshiva where there was an Aron Hakodesh. The Rosh Yeshiva would stand by the door and if a bochur tried to walk in late he would push him out. The tefillin were kept in the Aron Hakodesh, so the bocher would have to wait until the service was completed to retrieve them, which meant he also had to forego breakfast. After davening, we trudged along to the shul, which was ten to twelve minutes away.

The regime was very tough. We were banned from reading newspapers or any secular book, and no bochur was allowed to go to the cinema. To make certain of this, Baalei Battim would volunteer to take up a position outside the cinema before the film ended. The cinema was in the same street as the Yeshiva, and once I went to see the Charles Laughton film, the Private Lives of Henry the Eighth. At the end of the film we left the cinema by the back door, in order to avoid the guard. If a bochur was caught it meant instant dismissal. Because I was a filmgoer in London, I wanted to see this famous film, which had won many awards.

Those who slept in the Yeshiva found it difficult to go to the cinema because, at a certain time, the Yeshiva door was locked. In order to get back into the Yeshiva, it was arranged in advance that the bocherim who slept there would open up a ground floor window. Rabbi Landinsky would personally station himself near the open window to catch any bochur climbing in.

I used to order a newspaper, the Daily Express, which I brought with me from my lodgings. On one occasion, during breakfast, the Rosh Yeshiva put in an appearance. He saw me reading the newspaper, which he tore out of my hands, ripped it into shreds and threw it in the fireplace. In those days we had coal fires. The Rosh Yeshiva said 'in Yeshiva one doesn't read newspapers at Shulchan Hashem. One should have a sefer mussar while sitting and having breakfast.' I learned my lesson and never brought a newspaper to the Yeshiva again.

At the beginning of the term there was sufficient food for the bocherim because funds were available. Later on when the money ran out, food was very sparse indeed. One evening the bocherim were so hungry that they went into the kitchen to make chips in the chip machine. When the Rosh Yeshiva came in he said it was the equivalent of stealing.

During this lean and hungry time, during the break in the afternoon, a non-Jew passed by with a sack of lettuces, which he sold for one penny. I bought one and shared it with another bochur. It was one of the most magnificent meals I have ever had.

Sometimes when we were hungry we would go to the fruit shop and buy fruit. Three bocherim would give a penny each and we would buy an apple, an orange and a pear. We would cut it in portions so each bochur could taste some of each fruit.

There were times when we could have done with more food. Because funds were scarce, we took it for granted that that was how it was if you wanted to learn. In spite of everything we had no complaints. On one occasion the mother of one of the bocherim sent a cake from Germany. I was offered a slice, but I refused it on account of the fact that the Nazis could have poisoned it.

We learnt until 7.00 p.m., davened Ma'ariv, then went back to the Yeshiva for an evening meal. Since the shul had a tin roof and it was impossible to sit and learn in the building on those occasions when it was exceedingly hot, we were allowed off for the afternoon. On those hot days the bocherim spent the afternoon at Whitley Bay. The return fare was six pence. When it was cold in the shul, there were enough ovens to heat it.

At the end of zeman, the term, we had to overcome the difficulty of finding the ten shillings return fare to London. There were day excursions from London to Newcastle where the day return fare was the same price as a single ticket. One of the bocherim would go to the station and ask passengers if they were returning to London the same day. If not, could he buy the ticket for one shilling? The passenger was only too pleased to sell it for that amount, and the bochur could travel to London that day.

The only obstacle was the ticket collector who, when seeing the boys come onto the platform later on in the day, would remark, 'I don't recall you coming from London this morning.' But he would let them on anyway.

A Gentleman
born in 1925

'So the Rabbi tied his peyos
to the ticket counter'

M y mother, brother, sister and I arrived in Eretz
Yisroel on a Friday before Shavuos. Father had come
over the year before. It was a great relief to stand on dry
land after fifteen days and nights on a boat and we all felt
relaxed after the experience when we lost our sea legs

We needed to get settled so we went to an uncle and
aunt who lived in Battei Warsaw in Jerusalem. There I
went with a cousin to buy wine in Meah Shearim and I
saw all the people dressed in white Chassidic clothes in
preparation for Shabbos. As this was not our custom in
Europe I asked him 'what is the matter, is it Yom Kippur?'

My father said to the children when we arrived 'kinder,
you know where you are. This is the land of our fathers.
Here we are going to live.' He had a job at Bikur Cholim
hospital and that night we davened Ma'ariv there with
him.

My father was a follower of Rabbi Yosef Chaim
Sonnenfeld who was committed to keeping Eretz Yisroel
firmly rooted in the Holy Torah. I went with my father to
see him and I received a Brochah from him to learn Torah.
Despite being a talmid chacham he was not aloof and
personally involved himself in many disputes between
people and in situations where the honour of the Torah
was at stake.

I remember one incident concerning the opening of the
Edison Cinema on Shabbos. Rabbi Sonnenfeld, who was

tall and physically imposing, tried to persuade them to close the cinema on Shabbos, but to no avail. He then tied his peyos to the bars of the ticket counter so that people couldn't buy tickets.

A British Minister once met with the Rabbi, who asked him 'tell me what were you impressed with? What influenced you the most in Israel?' The minister replied 'the blue heaven of Yerushalyim and the blue eyes of the people who live here. Elsewhere you don't see those deep blue eyes.'

DISTRICT COMMISSIONER.
JERUSALEM.
PALESTINE.

JERUSALEM MUNICIPAL CORPORATION REGISTRY.

Date: 14 MAY 1945

File No. A

10th May, 1945.

Sir,

I wish to congratulate Your Worship, and through you the inhabitants of Jerusalem, for the magnificent display of flags and bunting which decorated the city in honour of Victory Days. Considering the short notice and the lack of materials available I consider that the inhabitants of Jerusalem have every reason to be satisfied and proud with these visual manifestations of their relief and joy.

I would also like to express my appreciation of how the Municipal Corporation of Jerusalem reacted to the occasion with good spirits, good temper and general cheerfulness.

I have the honour to be,
Your Worship's
obedient servant,

DISTRICT COMMISSIONER.

HIS WORSHIP
THE ACTING MAYOR OF
JERUSALEM.

In the Beis Din of Meah Shearim when it was the divorce day, they pulled down black curtains at the window when they wrote a get, because it was a black day.

My father had bought an apartment for us in Givat Shaul. At that time only two or three families were living there. Bermans Bakeries was in existence then and they distributed bread. We bought vegetables from the Arabs in the Old City or from the Machane Yehudah market. We obtained milk from an Arab from the nearby Arab village of Dir Yassin on the edge of Har Nof. We didn't order it; the Arab just came round with his goat and he

C O P Y .

MUNICIPAL CORPORATION
OF JERUSALEM.

9th May, 1945.

Your Excellency,

On the occasion of Victory Day in Europe
I offer to you on my own behalf and on that of the
Corporation of the City of Jerusalem our hearty
congratulations on the successful termination of the
war in Europe. To you personally the event must be
particularly happy when one remembers the early period of
the war and the magnificent though distressing circumstance
culminating at Dunkirk. For this reason it is the greater
pleasure to me to have this opportunity of submitting this
message with my most sincere good wishes for an early and
successful termination of the war against Japan and for
a speedy return to peace and prosperity.

I have the honour to be,
Your Excellency's obedient servant,

Sgd. D.Auster
His Excellency   A/MAYOR OF JERUSALEM.
Field Marshal the Right Honourable
Viscount Gort, V.C., G.C.B.,C.B.E.,D.S.O.,M.V.O.,M.C.,
Government House,
J e r u s a l e m .

squeezed milk out of the goat into our pot. Mother became paralysed as a result of the contaminated milk. She had a stroke, which caused the paralysis and was taken to Bikur Cholim hospital. Mother was in hospital for a year. I remember walking from Givat Shaul to Bikur Cholim hospital to visit her.

I went to the Etz Chaim cheder, which had a branch in the Zichron Moshe neighbourhood not far from Givat Shaul. Rabbi Aryeh Levine was the Mashgiach of the cheder at that time. He welcomed each student into the cheder as his own child. When I arrived he gave me a Siddur and on one occasion put drops into my eyes.

Eventually the family moved to Geula. One brother was a butcher. Another brother was a builder. He built the Mirrer and Navardok yeshivas in Jerusalem. I went to the Chevron yeshiva in Geula. A cousin of mine was also learning in the yeshiva. One day an Arab came into the building and stabbed my cousin in the leg. He survived, but his leg was badly injured. I remember the blood splattered all over the walls.

For a while I trained with the Haganah in Neve Yaakov. It was mostly gun training. We helped with the cooking as a contribution and in exchange for the lessons. If the British discovered us, we pretended to learn.

While we were with the Haganah I remembered my father's words. 'Kinder, you know where you are. This is the land of your fathers. Here we are going to live.'

Jacqueline Philips
born in 1924

Growing up in the Netherlands East Indies

I was born in The Netherlands East Indies, which was a colony of The Netherlands until after World War Two. In 1948 the country was renamed Indonesia when it received its independence from The Netherlands. During the time that we lived there we spoke Dutch.

My parents on their wedding day

My father was born in The Netherlands where he served as an auditor in the army. When there was a vacancy for a similar position in The Netherlands East Indies he applied, not only because of the exotic nature of the post but also because of the extra money and benefits the job offered. After marrying my mother in 1920, they set off for the Islands where we lived until I was nine years old.

We had a beautiful villa where there were annexe buildings in the back for the servants. We had a gardener, a cook, and a maid to do the dusting and cleaning. Each servant had a room of their own. We had electricity, a telephone and an icebox, luxuries by anyone's standards, at that time. There was a room just to do the washing and ironing. The bathroom had tiles on the floor and you stood next to the waist high concrete tub or well to take a bath. You drew cold water from the well, which you threw over your body. There was no hot water, but since the temperature outside was hardly ever less than 30 degrees, you were able to manage with cold water.

There was no public transport except the trains, and nobody had a car. There were no local shops and since it was too far to walk to the market my mother used to go by bendi. This was a little cart pulled by a horse. Passengers sat opposite each other in seats behind the driver, who sat at the front. Bicycle carts later replaced bendis. Two passengers sat in the front and the driver pedalled the cart from behind. When my mother wanted to go to the market she told the servants and they would go to the local people, who in turn would tell the bendi driver in the kampong. When you needed a doctor, you went to his house. All this seems primitive now as I look back, but we were used to it then. I didn't know anything different.

The Europeans lived in stately villas, which were lined up along wide streets. The locals lived in their own neighbourhoods called kampongs. Their houses were made of bamboo with only leaves for roofs.

Jewish life didn't really exist for us and there was no synagogue. One day, when I was six, I came home crying, asking my mother, 'why do they say I am not one of them, because I have black curly hair and a bent nose?' My mother didn't answer as she comforted me.

One day I saw my mother at the sewing machine, sewing something big and white. 'What are you doing?' I asked. 'An old Jewish man has passed away,' she said, 'and he needs a burial shroud.' Only one or two of my parent's friends were Jewish, there was no real Jewish community.

I went to a European school for Dutch speakers, which was a twenty-minute walk each way. I went with a friend. No way did parents take you to school or pick you up. You walked. I don't think the local children went to school at all.

In the East Indies there was rich vegetation and lush rain forests. I remember visiting a farm, when I went on an outing, where they had Dutch cows. The cows could only live on that farm because it was high in the mountains, and the air was cool. Otherwise they would die in the tropical heat.

We left The Netherlands East Indies when I was nine years old. Since service in that country was regarded as a hardship posting, the years he served in the army were counted as double. My father was only forty-eight when he was obliged to retire to Holland on a pension.

When we left The Netherlands East Indies, I remember standing next to my mother on the boat watching the country becoming smaller and smaller in the distance. She said 'we will say goodbye to the East Indies'. 'Will we go back?' I asked. 'We are going to live in Holland now,' she replied. 'Perhaps you will marry a man who wants to live in The Netherlands East Indies, and you will return,' which, eventually, I did.

We stopped at Port Said, Egypt, where my mother bought winter clothes. Alongside the ship came the three or four metre boats of the peddlers. People would stand at the rails and place orders at the ship's side. The goods were then hauled up by rope. Money was lowered down

My parents, my brother and myself

in the same way. I remember that my mother bought me a set of five thin bracelets.

After the stopover at Port Said we travelled for, what seemed, weeks and weeks, but was actually six weeks in all. There were classes on board the ship for the children, together with games and plenty of entertainment. I remember doing basket weaving.

At Genoa, Italy, we stopped again and disembarked for an outing to the cemetery, which was also a tourist attraction. The graves were decorated with statues of the people who were buried there. The statues indicated the profession or work they did in their lives. It made a lasting impression on me.

In Italy we disembarked and took a train to Amsterdam. We travelled through Switzerland and I remember being impressed by the Alps, which I had never seen.

When we arrived in Holland we rented an apartment. On a Friday night, we sometimes visited my mother's father, whom we called Opa. He lived with his two unmarried daughters who looked after him. Their living quarters were behind the haberdashery shop, which they ran. I can still remember the smell of the meat and vegetable soup, prepared specially for Shabbos. While we waited for the meal to start we sat with Opa in his grandfather chair. He wore a hat and had a little beard and I wore my black chiffon dress with white lace collar and cuffs.

When my brother was going to be Bar Mitzvah I saw my mother knitting something. I asked her what she was making and she told me that she was knitting an arba kanfos, a four cornered garment, for my brother's Bar Mitzvah. After six weeks we found a house near The Hague and my brother got ready for his Bar Mitzvah. For the first time ever I saw Hebrew letters and I learnt the alef bais along with my brother. My brother suffered with his eyes and in his Bar Mitzvah photograph he is wearing his monocle.

Our Jewish life in Holland was a slight improvement over life in the East Indies. When I was ten I was invited to a Seder night with my mother's family. However it was too expensive for my parents to pay the travel expenses for me to go. I once went to a Chanukah party and I saw candles, but I didn't know what they were.

Up to the age of sixteen I lived the life of a Dutch girl. In the winter when it snowed I remember that we put sleds behind the car and were towed through the streets. At the age of sixteen everything changed. I went into hiding because the Nazis had arrived in The Netherlands.

Claire Rose
born in 1923

'One knife,
which everyone shared'

I n 1937, at the age of fourteen years and three months I
came to Israel with my parents from Bratislava,
Czechoslovakia. In my part of the world there was no
anti-Semitism, if it existed it was 'underneath'.

We travelled on a train to Trieste and from there took a
boat to the port of Haifa. As we sailed in the
Mediterranean Sea, I wondered if the boat was seaworthy
because the tables were always at a slant in stormy
weather, but we landed safely. My sister Esther, who was
now married, had settled in Israel in 1929. My sister Ruth
had arrived in 1933 and lived in Kfar Hess. When we
landed at Haifa I saw a city where everything was white
and the sun was stronger than I had been used to in Europe.

My brother-in-law met us at the port and took us to
Kibbutz Hephzibah. Once there we went straight to the
communal dining room, where people ate after working.
Eight to ten people were sitting at the table eating bread,
salad and tomatoes. Everyone received a fork and spoon,
but there was only one knife, which everyone had to
share. I remember the occasion when Yosef the Yemenite
boy took the knife to make a salad and everyone had to
wait until he had finished using it. There was also Leben
and cheese on the table. Later in the day we had a meal
consisting of bread and jam. Once a week we had chicken.

I looked around the kibbutz and noticed that there were
very few houses. People slept in huts or tents. The day

that we arrived, a scorpion that was hidden behind the rocks bit a seven-year-old boy and unfortunately he died. It was such a tragedy for the kibbutz.

I soon started working in the fields taking out weeds from amongst the carrots, and thinning the carrots so that the remaining plants could develop properly. When it was time to pick grapes we started at four in the morning and stopped work at noon, because it was too hot to work in the vineyards later in the day. We packed the grapes in boxes and they were sent to Tnuva. I didn't get paid for this work.

The Kibbutz also kept agricultural chickens that laid eggs and also cows that they milked. They sold all their products and did not keep anything for the kibbutz.

When it was mealtimes someone would take a stick and hit a large piece of metal that was hanging next to the dining room. All the people working in the fields heard it and stopped work.

When we arrived, I had only a blouse and a pair of shorts. When I needed any other clothes I went to the person in charge of clothing and told her what I needed and eventually I received it. I also received a towel. If a member of the Kibbutz wanted to go into the city, or get married, they put in a request for the relevant clothing. The person in charge of the clothing washed everyone's clothes. There was a tag on all the clothing to indicate to whom it belonged.

The children were housed in the children's house and a member of the Kibbutz took care of them while the parents worked. The children ate and slept together in this house. The parents only saw their children after work.

My sister and her husband lived in a house made of stone and when we arrived their son was three years old. I slept in my own bed in a wooden hut with two other girls.

The heat was unbelievable. There was a shared shower room and toilet. My parents had their own room in a stone house. Many of the girls in the kibbutz were refugees from Europe and had no parents. They adopted my mother addressing her as 'mother'. Those of my parents' generation helped each other. My father worked as a bookkeeper.

After six months we moved to Kfar Hess. My sister Ruth lived there with her family as well as my sister Bracha. Bracha and I worked in the orchards picking citrus fruit, oranges, grapefruit and lemons. We packed each fruit separately in paper and it was sent all over the world. A member of the Kibbutz had the job of writing down the name of everyone who worked, and you only got paid if your name was written down. My name was not written down for two days and I did not get paid. When it rained we went into the forest to pick mushrooms, which we ate.

The toilet was in an outhouse, which was literally a hole in the ground. When it got filled up someone took a shovel and took out the contents and put it on the fields.

I remember one incident when I was standing in my bedroom and my sister Esther saw me standing next to the window. 'You can't stand near the window,' she said. I didn't realise that a window meant danger, because the Arabs used to shoot at us from the open orchard. The Kibbutz had a watchtower with a searchlight, which encircled the kibbutz, and someone always on watch. The kibbutz itself was surrounded by barbed wire.

There were always battles between Jews and Arabs at Kfar Hess and the Arabs used to put mines in the open orchard. I was fortunate that I never stepped on a mine.

Speranza
born in 1922

'n'egg n'arf f'r apenny'

In the 1920's, 30's and 40's television was in its infancy and the wireless was an important lifeline to the world beyond the home. A weekly wireless programme about London was introduced to the strains of the 'Knightsbridge March.' The voices over were those of the, then perennial, flower sellers seated on the steps around the statue in the middle of Piccadilly Circus, calling 'vi'lets, lovely sweet vi'lets'. They were a familiar sight with large baskets of violets standing beside them from which they sold small, bound posies to the passer by. They were perhaps the best-known traditional street vendors and helped the streets of London between the wars become a cacophony of sounds and colourful sights

Women from the surrounding countryside walked the London streets with baskets of lavender on their arms, calling 'lavender, sweet lavender! Who'll buy my sweet lavender?' In summer came the strawberry sellers, but all year round the gypsies came with hand made clothes pegs and little bunches of heather 'for luck'. 'Cross my palm with silver,' they would cry, in an attempt to tempt you to ask them to foretell your fortune.

Cheerful Breton onion sellers, wearing blue denim and black berets, with shining golden onions festooned about their bicycles, vied with Italian ice cream vendors whose sales cry was 'hokey pokey, hokey pokey.' Eventually the street sales of ice cream were made with bicycles that had a freezer attached, that announced their presence with the ting-a-ling of a persistent bicycle bell. One could also buy hard-boiled eggs announced by the cry 'n'egg n'arf f'r apenny.'

Craftsmen, not able to afford the cost of premises in the lean years between the wars, plied their trade in the streets. As a child, I watched entranced as the itinerant chair menders plied their trade. Cane seated chairs were then in popular use and the craftsmen arrived with a small handcart or a large bag containing tools and materials, calling 'chairs to mend, chairs to mend.' Householders brought worn or damaged chairs into the street and the chair mender settled himself on the granite kerb at the pavement's edge, feet firmly in the gutter, with the broken, cane-seated chair in front of him. The demolition of the old woven seat, then its replacement with new cane, as near as possible to the colour of the original, and exactly replicating its original pattern, seemed miraculous to me.

'Old knives to grind, knives to grind' was the signal for all and sundry to bring out their knives to be sharpened in the street. The knife grinder pedalled his trolley, which had a small metal canopy attached to it by metal corner struts, which projected over the seat at the rear. This canopy sheltered the equipment and the knife grinder from the rain. Suspended vertically under the canopy and turned by a pedal operated band, was the wheel, the rim of which provided the sharpening surface. I loved to watch the knife grinder sitting under his canopy, skilfully applying knife blades to the wheel. I can still hear the song of the wheel as the knives made contact. Best of all, I enjoyed the sparks flying from the point of abrasion, like miniature fireworks.

One could also purchase food in the street from the hot pie vendors or from the muffin seller who peddled muffins, announcing their approach with the call of 'muffins,' followed by the clang of a sizeable hand-bell. The muffins were carried, on the head, in a flat rectangular tray covered with a clean white cloth. There is a children's song, 'do you know the muffin man who lives in Drury Lane?'

The head was also the means by which the vendors of second-hand clothes carried a pagoda of three or four hats, in addition to their other wares drawn by horse and cart. Also drawn by horse and cart was the tinker shouting 'any old iron? any old iron?' Old zinc tubs, no longer needed by householders with newly installed indoor plumbing, could be thrown on the cart, together with old bedsteads and other metal objects.

Milk was initially sold house to house from metal churns, transferred to customer's jugs by a metal measuring ladle. They traditionally heralded their approach with a yodel 'milk-o!' Milk was eventually delivered, in horse drawn vans with the milk sold in foil-capped bottles and left in a shady spot near the door of the customer's home, still with the old traditional 'milk-o!' yodel. The birds soon discovered it was easy to peck open the foil tops and have an early morning breakfast of thick cream from the top of the milk. In the winter, when the temperature was below freezing, the milk froze, pushing the foil top up an inch above the top of the bottle.

As the milkman advanced up the street from house to house, the horse ambled gently forward. My route to school took me along four different streets and four different milk rounds. I fed the horses with apples or carrots on most school days, and knew them all by name. I was whinnied and snuffled at in friendly daily greeting to the sound of four different yodels.

One morning, in the street where my school was, I gave my favourite horse one carrot instead of the usual two, the second being lost in the depths of my school bag. As I searched, I heard the 'first bell' ringing from school. The 'late bell' would soon follow, so I had to run. The pupils' entrance was at the end of a narrow passage between two high brick walls. When I had almost reached the door, I heard a grinding noise behind me. Not wanting to be marked late I ran into school without looking round. The horse had followed me up the narrow passage and got stuck. Neither the police nor milkman could move it backwards or forwards!

One lovely June day, in 1929, we heard a street vendor calling 'ripe strawberries.' My mother took money from her purse and said to me, 'give this to Cook and ask her to go out and buy three punnets.' A little while later Cook returned with the money. 'I'm sorry, madam, your 'ripe strawberries' were 'live tortoises.' The sale of live animals is now illegal, as are the violet sellers, banished from Piccadilly Circus by the passage of time and the Authorities.

London has now lost most of the voices that so vividly enhanced its street life, and they are only kept alive in song and rhyme. In the following rhyme the word 'tell' means to count. The clerks in the bank were called 'tellers' — the one that counted the money.

Old knives to grind, old knives to grind!
If I had the money that you could find
I never would cry old knives to grind.

Old clothes to sell, old clothes to sell!
If I had the money that you could tell
I never would cry old clothes to sell.

Old chairs to mend, old chairs to mend!
If I had the money that you could spend
I never would cry old chairs to mend.

Ruth bat Frumet
born in 1925

'Juden Unerwuenscht' – prohibited to Jews

My grandmother's name was Rosalie Tedesco. In Italian this name means 'the German.' At some point in time the family had been chased out of Germany and settled in Italy, hence the name. My grandmother came from an affluent family, while my grandfather came from a small hamlet in Bavaria called Budenweisen. Upon her marriage in the 1860's, my grandmother refused to move to Budenweisen unless grandfather built a house for her. Since she also refused to travel there in a horse and buggy, he arranged a continuation of the railroad to be built from a nearby hamlet to take her there.

My father, Yomtov ben Raphael Benjamin worked in the seforim store in Frankfurt-a-Maine, owned by my mother's father. In the course of his work, father met my mother and they decided to become engaged. When her father heard about this he refused to allow my father to continue to work in the store. However father refused to give in and he and my mother became engaged in 1914. My father refused to get married before the war since he couldn't face the possibility of leaving my mother a widow.

My father served as a soldier on the front line on the German side in World War One. A story that he was fond of telling us concerns an occasion when he was davening the Shemoneh Esrei by the front door of the bunkers. As he was davening the soldiers heard bombers coming overhead. The other soldiers ran into the underground bunker yelling to my father, 'komme, komme.' As he was stepping backwards at the end of the Shemoneh Esrei, a bomb hit the bunker and he was the only one who was saved. My father always told the family that he was saved because he was doing the ratzon of Hashem.

After the war, in 1918, he married my mother, and once again worked in the store. After my grandfather passed away he inherited it with my grandmother.

Four of my siblings were born before me and one was born after me. Our home was a mixture of east and west. In Germany if you wanted to be a guest you had to be formally invited. There was no such thing as the door being open. Everything was stiff and formal, but our home was a combination of both formality and openness. When poor commercial travellers that came to the shop my father brought them home for meals.

When I look back, even the school system was affected by this formality. We had an English teacher who supported a caste system. He put on one side of the scale the daughters of lawyers and doctors and on the other side of the scale he put the daughters of storekeepers. You were not measured by who you were but who your family was. Therefore in English language I never obtained a pass mark. It was a stigma not to come from a prestigious family. The teacher of French was different, and in French I got A grades.

I remember our shoemaker; he was an old Yid, with a long beard, a big yarmulke and a leather apron. When we took our shoes to be mended, he would take a handful of little nails and put them in his mouth. His sefer was next to him, and when he wasn't busy he was learning.

Our family owned no car, telephone, washing machine or refrigerator, nevertheless we survived beautifully. Four families lived in our building, and in the basement there was a cellar for coal, a cellar for laundry and a cellar for preserves. On the top floor was the mansarde where each tenant had one or two storage rooms. We used one such room for the maid. There was no light in her room; except for the kerosene lamp she carried upstairs in her hand every night. Next to her room was a small room, which was a toilet. One sat on a board, which had a hole in it that took up the whole room, with a pull chain for flushing.

We only had one sink and that was in the kitchen. I slept in the bathroom with my sister. The bathroom was large, big enough for our beds, two chests, a closet, one table and chairs and my doll's carriage. The bathtub was covered over with a drape to hide it when it was not being used. Once a week, the water was heated with coal briquettes for everyone to take a bath.

Every night we filled a pitcher with cold water in order to wash ourselves in the morning in the accompanying bowl. In winter when I woke up my windows were painted with ice flowers, but the water in the pitcher did not freeze.

In the family living room there was a table, a desk, seforim, a sofa and a chest of drawers. In the corner was a stove with a chimney. When we wanted to make a fire, we went down to the cellar and shovelled coal eggs into a large metal coal jug and then brought it upstairs and put the coals in the stove. In the winter we put a bowl of water or the teakettle on top of the stove to heat it in order to have hot water for washing as we had no running hot water, only cold.

Our laundry woman came every two weeks and she took care of the laundry. The maid's job was to go into the cellar to start the fire before the laundry woman came.

She boiled the clothes in a huge kettle, which stood on the coal fire and she stirred it with a stick as if she was cooking. The laundry woman then rinsed the clothes in the

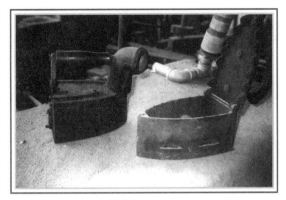

Irons of the period

sink with cold water and hung them outside to dry.

Another lady came in to do the ironing. The big pieces such as sheets and tablecloths were not ironed, but put through two rollers to straighten them. The iron was a coal iron. You opened it up, put in burning coals with a pair of tongs and then shook the iron. You let it stand for a minute and then ironed the clothes. A third lady would come to the house once a month to do the mending.

We had wooden floors and parquet floors. The floors were washed then waxed and then an iron weight was rolled back and forth on the floor to polish it.

The refrigerator was only used in the summer time. It was a little like a closet in the centre of which was a metal insert with a lid on top, into which the man put the ice block when he delivered it. It had two compartments, one for milchig and one for fleshig, and there was a spigot on the bottom which you opened when you wanted to drain the water into the bowl underneath. In the winter we stored food in the cellar in order to be able to cook fresh food every day.

To make ice cream we had a little wooden bucket with a metal insert and a blade. Over this were a lid and a handle. My mother cooked the mixture and put it in the metal container. Ice chips were put in the wooden bucket together with a special orange and red salt called viesaltz, to prevent the ice from melting too quickly. Our biggest treat was to lick the blade. This treat would go to the child who churned the handle until the mixture became ice cream, which usually took about half an hour. Generally we had the ice cream on a Friday night, so that we could eat it before it melted.

In the mid 30's, a law was passed in Germany, requiring families to have a one-pot meal once a week in order to conserve food. One could not have side dishes on that day. Our family, who lived in Frankfurt, at that time, had our pot meal on a Wednesday and this was soup with vegetables.

Growing up in this period gave us an uneasy feeling of being different. We did not feel secure walking the streets. Hitler youth ran after us throwing stones. On the park benches and in the shop windows there were signs 'Juden Unerwuenscht' [prohibited to Jews]. It was not a time to be in Germany.

A Lady
born in 1920

'We had no telephones and no lashon hora'

I have lived in Jerusalem all my life. My parents were born in Batei Hungaria, a neighbourhood of Meah Shearim built with money sent by the Jews of Hungary a hundred years ago. My grandmother came into an apartment when it was new. I lived with my grandparents in their apartment until I got married at the age of fifteen and a half and moved into my own two-roomed apartment close by, where I still live. My ten children were all brought up in this apartment.

When I first moved into the apartment there was no water in the house, and we fetched water from the well in the courtyard below. Every building had its own well and on the roof of each building there was a pipe that directed rainwater into the well. Three or four families shared a toilet in the courtyard. The government rationed the water according to the size of each family with every soul receiving a bucketful twice a week.

The well in Meah Shearim today

We took the water from washing the dishes and used it for the lavatories and other things like washing the floors and managed with difficulty.

In every neighbourhood there was someone responsible for giving out the water and no one could just take it because there was a lid on the well.

Food was difficult because there was very little. We didn't have a first course and a last course. Whatever there was we ate. Our meals during the week consisted of bread, green beans or barley soup and every one had the same. A chicken was considered a luxury with one chicken for Shabbos divided among the whole family. Despite the hardships we were happier then than we are now because we knew that there was nothing else to get. We were happy with what we got. We never got a banana as fruit to eat; it was used as a spread on bread shared among a number of children.

When we wanted milk we never went to the Arab's house, in case they gave us milk from the horse. So when the Arab lady came round with fifty goats, each family bought half a litre. There was no money for more. Every family bought their own jug, which

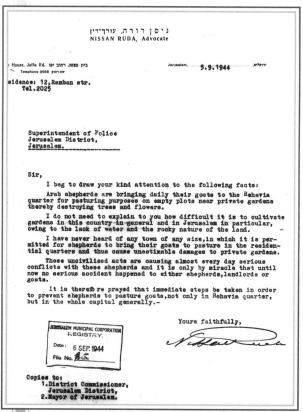

was filled with milk for the baby's porridge and for morning coffee. We had a primus stove, fuelled with paraffin where we boiled the milk and did any other cooking. Half the quantity of milk was used to make cheese.

There was a factory close by that provided ice. We put the ice in a bowl and round the ice we put perishable food such as the milk or fish, or the chicken for Shabbos. An icebox was a luxury and came later. When there were two days of Yomtov, or Yomtov followed Shabbos, the factory would open for a short while on Yomtov in order to provide fresh ice. Over the ice we placed a towel; each type of food was in its own container with one towel kept specifically for this purpose. We were much more particular then about cleanliness than people are today. Today everyone eats food from the Shuk. There was not so much food then. In factories today there are flies and mice. We made our own food and cooked our own jam.

Once during the week we baked our bread, taking it to the bakery to be placed in the oven. For an extra payment the baker would pick up the bread and deliver it when it was ready. We prepared thick flour, made the dough with

---

Q/15/49

26 July, 1943.

Gentlemen,

I wish to make a special appeal to you for your assistance in a matter with which I feel sure that you will sympathise.

2. As you know efforts have been made to plant as many trees as possible along the streets of the City. There are few people who realise how difficult it is to bring trees to maturity. They and their tree-guards are constantly being damaged and destroyed unwittingly or through carelessness and sometimes by wanton measures.

3. It has been observed that the carts which take round paraffin for sale from house to house are not infrequently the cause of damage. The drivers either tie their animals to the trees or tree-guards with the result that the trees are eaten and the bark damaged. Sometimes the drivers do not tie their animals at all but leave them in the street without applying a brake or other means of preventing the animal moving. In such cases as soon as the driver is out of the way the animal moves forward to the nearest tree and damages it.

4. I have received information from members of the public confirming the reports of municipal officers. Note was recently taken of cart No.71, but I am not mentioning this in order that the driver may be punished but merely to quote it as an example.

5. I should be most grateful for any assistance that could be given by instructions being issued to your employees to prevent any form of damage to trees.

I have the honour to be,
Gentlemen,
Your obedient servant,

TOWN CLERK.

Messrs The Vacuum Oil Co.,
Jerusalem.

```
                    C O P Y

G/15/49               9th September, 1944.


Sir,

        I have the honour to refer to letter of the
5th of September, 1944, a copy of which was transmitted to
me.   I am in entire agreement with the view that the
Urban Area is not a suitable place for the grazing of
flocks and herds.  The amount of damage done to trees by
human beings is only exceeded by that done by goats,
sheep, cattle and camels.  It would I think be worth while
considering whether it would not be advisable to
prohibit flocks and herds being within the Municipal.
or Town Planning Area save under special conditions
and along special routes.  On the other hand there
would be no advantage in making by-laws to this
effect unless there were reasonable possibility of
their enforcement and I should be grateful to
receive your views on the matter.

                I have the honour to be,
                        Sir,
                Your obedient servant,

                    (Sgd.)  D. Au

            A/ MAYOR OF JERUSALEM.

Superintendent of Police,
Jerusalem District.

Copy to: District Commissioner ref. Nissan Ruda's letter
                            of 5.9.44.
```

water, then laid it flat to dry. After that we rolled it up to make noodles.

For lighting we had a paraffin lamp. Arabs would come with their horse and cart and ring the bell to let us know that he had arrived. My father wrote a big book on astronomy by the light of the paraffin lamp.

The Arabs came round from the Old City selling apples. They wore a kafiya on their heads and carried the apples in boxes on their heads. Watermelons and other fruit in season were sold from carts, although not every day.

We used the oven of the neighbourhood bakery to cook the cholent for Shabbos with each family's name on their pot. The pots were covered so there was no problem that it was in the same oven as the bread. The owner of the bakery opened up on Shabbos for us to collect our pots. We paid him on Friday. On Shabbos we davened in the morning and in the afternoon we visited family or read stories to the children.

We bought our eggs from the shuk. Some people bought little chicks and grew them on. When they were big they took them to the shochet. I don't know if it was cheaper than buying a fully-grown chicken.

The Joint distributed clothes according to the size of the family. In those days we took old clothes and remade them to fit another child. We did not have as many clothes as we have today. Sometimes we would buy material and make clothes.

I went to school in the apartment of the Rebbitzen. We learnt how to read and say Berachos and she told us about Shabbos. Before the Chagim we learnt about each festival and we went through the Siddur. We learnt about honouring our parents and she taught us that we should try to emulate our mothers. We took our Siddur, Chumash and our half size notebook in a bag that our mothers made from potato sacks. We learnt for an hour or two every morning. We learnt how to write the aleph beis with pencils.

We played with stones, they call them jacks today, or greggers made out of wood by the carpenter or we skipped with a rope. The boys made things from wood with a hammer and nails. When we weren't playing we were helping mother or sewing clothes.

C O P Y

MUNICIPAL CORPORATION OF
JERUSALEM.

G/15/49   23rd September, 1944.

Sir,

I have the honour to refer to your letter 106/21/JD of the 15th of /9/ September, 1944, and note that you would find it difficult to enforce such by-laws at the present time. Having regard however to the long delay which always occurs in enactment of by-laws, I think you will agree that no harm will be done in their preparation for which I shall welcome your advice and assistance.

I understand that a fatal accident occurred recently at Talpioth when as a result of goats grazing a Mr. Kornberg tried to intervene with a result that the shepherds threw stones at him one of which struck him on the head. If this is so the need for the by-laws would appear to be emphasized by actual experience.

I have the honour to be,
Sir,
Your obedient servant,
(Sgd.) J. Ausin
A/MAYOR OF JERUSALEM

Superintendent of Police,
Jerusalem District.

The children washed their own clothes with water carried from the well and wrung them out with their hands. In those days we didn't need physiotherapy. In those days we never said we don't have the energy, money or time, nor did we say we had nothing to wear. We had no telephones and no lashon hora.

There were shops in the neighbourhood selling food, material, gold and silver, but most of the men learnt in the Yeshiva. The men received money from the Yeshiva, and no one had cheques that bounced. If they had money they bought. If they didn't have money they didn't buy.

If a girl asked for a dress, mother would say 'your father learns in the Yeshiva' and she wouldn't ask again.

The British were not good to the Jews. They caused the Arabs to initiate pogroms by saying that the Jews want to steal your land.

Nevertheless, all the difficulties of life at that time helped us to pull together and establish a unity between us that today's modern world could never hope to achieve.

Solomon Joseph Cohen
born in 1893
Told by his daughter

A diamond's true worth

T he wall was quite wide, and was built from mud and stones, but because I was so young I never realized how much hard sweat and labor it took to build that wall. As a small child, my family occasionally went to visit my father at the "Diamond Diggings" where I loved to sit on the river bank; or on the wall if it was not too dangerous and I had permission. I watched the workers as they brought up the large flat baskets, which held the gravel, onto the riverbank, so that my father could sieve through it for uncut diamonds.

When my father, Solomon Joseph Cohen was six years old, in 1899, he came to South Africa from Ponevezh, Lithuania, with his parents and three brothers. Like many other immigrants his family opened a general dealer's store in the country near to the City of Kimberley, where they made a decent living until in the 1930's when the "Great Depression" descended on the world with all its wrath and destruction, bankrupting our family store.

The City of Kimberley is famous for its diamond mines, which produce millions of dollars worth of diamonds. The De Beers Consolidated Mining Company owns the mines, and all the mineral rights. There are also places near Kimberley on the riverbed of the Vaal River full of diamonds waiting to be plucked from the earth. These diamonds are called "alluvial diamonds". The deposits on the riverbed of water-borne clay, sand and gravel are caused by the swift stream of flowing water against the

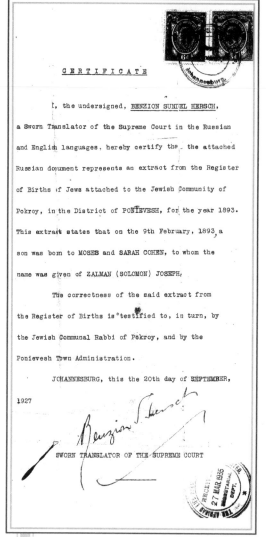

riverbank and contain many alluvial diamonds.

With the Depression, my father, and many other people who were out of luck, went to "dig" for diamonds in the Vaal River. They were called "diamond diggers". The whole operation was run by a few powerful and rich men who would hire the diamond diggers and supply them with a small part of the equipment and labor needed for the operation. In those days all the work was done by hand with a pick and shovel.

Each diamond digger was responsible for building his own "breakwater" to keep the water out of the riverbed. The diamond bearing gravel, the result of repetitive grading and sorting on the riverbed by the digger and his workers, was then brought up onto the riverbank and sieved by the diamond digger.

It's hard to imagine how the breakwater was built. The area of the Vaal River near Kimberley has a very low rainfall. The riverbed is often dry and the diggers would use the opportunity during the hot summer months to build the breakwater with the help of the workers. The breakwater consisted of 2 walls each approximately a meter wide running parallel to each other about 70 to 100 meters apart along the width of the river. When it rained and the water level rose, the walls kept the river water out leaving the riverbed dry. These walls required quick construction and constant inspection for holes and leaks. Unfortunately there were more failures than successes.

As soon as the breakwater was complete, there was no time to lose in digging up the riverbed. It was very hard to dig the rocks out of the clay and remove them until there was only small gravel left. The gravel was then brought up onto the riverbank in flat baskets so that the digger could carefully sieve through it to see if there were any diamonds.

It was quite common for a few diamond diggers to stake their claims next to each other, pool their resources and build a breakwater together sharing in the meager profits from the sale of the uncut diamonds to the owners.

My father had a faithful employee or servant as they were called in those days, called 'Sibi', who worked for him in his general store. I remember him as a short, black man who always had a big smile for me. He worshipped my father and worked for him at the diggings. Every Monday morning my father, Sibi and their little terrier dog called 'Scampy', would drive out in my father's grey Nash motor car, to the diggings and come back Friday afternoon. There was always much excitement when they came home on Friday. I would hover around to hear what tales they told about the week's happenings... an accident occurred to one of the workers while he was digging up the ground and he was very badly hurt ... it was so cold he couldn't sleep at night ...it was so unbearably hot with no light breeze to break the heat ...once more the breakwater wall came crashing down ...

A typical diamond digger of the period

When it rained, the breakwater walls crumbled more frequently, and the water from the river came pouring in, destroying all the hard backbreaking work in a few minutes. On one occasion, I remember my father telling us that during an inspection on a very cold, stormy and rainy night, he stopped the wall from crumbling by putting the coat he wore in a hole that started in the wall and holding it in place in the pouring rain for eight long hours while those around him worked feverishly to fill the hole – just like the dykes in Holland.

The work at the diggings was not easy. There was no electricity and food was cooked on a primus stove or an open fire. The men lived on the riverbank as close as they could to the river, where the breakwater was in the process of construction. They slept in corrugated iron shacks and tents, which had no ventilation, and which were extremely hot in the summer and surrounded by mud. In the winter it was unbearably cold. They got up at dawn and went to bed at sunset after a hard days' work.

The breakwater required inspection throughout the night in case of leaks in the walls and to prevent other damage from occurring.

The diggers received a very small percentage from the sale of the diamonds, hardly enough to exist. At the end of the War in 1945 most of the diamond diggers, including my father went back to the towns to make a better and easier living.

After the Second World War the diamond diggers who remained used bulldozers and tractors, reducing the amount of labor needed and making the manual work much easier. Many old-time diggers preferred to work out in the open countryside despite the hardships and lived on the riverbanks until they died.

Alluvial diamond diggings also took place in other parts of South Africa along the Vaal River and the Orange River. To this day the diggings still attract many prospectors, and places like Barkly West, a small town on the Vaal River near to Kimberley, has become a tourist attraction.

Not many Jews became diamond diggers. My father had no other option and as I've grown older and I am better able to appreciate exactly what he was up against, I am proud of the work he did to save his family.

Rabbi **Yehuda Braver**
born in 1891
Told by his daughter

'Aleh leben, schtizeh neitik'
All are alive, support needed

Rabbi Yehuda Braver

My father was born in Lithuania and learned in the great yeshivas in Telshe, Volozhin, Ponevezh and Vilna. He was eight years old when he left home to go to Yeshiva. He slept in the Beis Hamidrash and ate 'teg.' He went to different families to eat every day. Sometimes he wouldn't go to eat teg, but instead he bought a loaf and a piece of herring and divided it into three, and that constituted his three meals that day. When he ate teg, sometimes he felt that he was looked on as a kind of beggar, and it wasn't kavodik for bocherim to be treated in this way. Despite economic poverty and the physical limitations of life, the bocherim were able to attain a high spiritual level. Their deveikus, clinging to Hashem, raised them above their physical limitations.

Communal meals and dormitories came into existence in the 1920's. The Rabbi of Lublin, Rabbi Meir Shapiro, said that eating teg damaged kavod, and he raised money for his Yeshiva in Lublin to provide sleeping and eating facilities in the building for the bocherim.

My father would say that nothing could compare to Yeshiva davening, which was on such a high spiritual level, that bocherim reached heights which were not possible when davening with the Ba'alei haBatim.

In 1913 while he was still a Yeshiva bochur, he was drafted into the Czar's army. There was no kosher food, therefore he was unable to eat anything, and his bed was a bag filled with straw. He had made arrangements to meet his first cousin, Rebecca Itzikovitz, on the border of Germany and Poland, and escaped from the army after one night. They were married in August 1913, in a little town on the border, and three days later were on a ship sailing from Hamburg that was bound for New York, via Ellis Island.

World War One dispersed the Yeshivot in Europe from their original locations. There was very little communication, no shipping or transportation, and the only air traffic was military. For the duration of the war my father had no contact with his parents. The Jewish rescue organisation, HIAS, tried to trace families, but for a long time they had no word as to whether their parents were alive or dead. Eventually, in 1919 after the end of World War One, my parents received a telegram, 'aleh leben, schtizeh neitik.' 'All are alive, support needed.' These were the first words that my mother heard about their parents and she would repeat them all the time.

From the ship, my father made his way to an Aunt's house, where, within a matter of days, a cousin informed him that a small Jewish community in Akron, Ohio, was seeking a Rabbi. He obtained his semicha shortly before he left Europe and by Rosh Hashanah he was appointed

Rabbi Yehuda Braver with his wife and sons Benjamin and Hyman in 1921

the Rabbi of the community. There were around a thousand Jews in Akron, mostly immigrants from countries in Europe, and their common language was Yiddish. Akron was a tyre manufacturing centre and the unskilled labourers did not need to know the English language, thus making it the perfect centre for Jewish immigrants from Europe to settle.

My father could speak Russian, Lithuanian, German and Yiddish and was able to converse with all his congregants. Three million Jews were leaving Russia at this time due to the pogroms and the economic situation. Since my father had learnt in Telshe in Europe, he was one of the very few poskim in the United States at that time. Between 1914 and 1919 it was not possible to correspond with the poskim in Europe, and he became a Torah pioneer in America. The Rabbis in Europe regarded the United States as a treifeh medina, and did not encourage bocherim to go there.

After he had served the community for ten years, in 1923 he accepted a position in Kansas City, Missouri, where he became the Rabbi for Kansas City and Greater Kansas City. In 1935 my father established a Yeshiva in Kansas City, which was supported by the community.

Only four years later, World War Two broke out in Europe, and although the United States had not entered the War at that time, it would after the 7th December 1941 when Japan attacked Pearl Harbour in Hawaii. The American people wondered how Japan, such a small power, could be so brazen as to attack America. The government were enlisting and drafting the young people into the army, and the bochurim left the Yeshiva in Kansas City to volunteer in the war effort. As the Yeshiva's enrolment dwindled, it lost the financial support of the community. Because it was in the Mid-West, and not in the large cities, which were the centres of the Jewish population, the Yeshiva faded away.

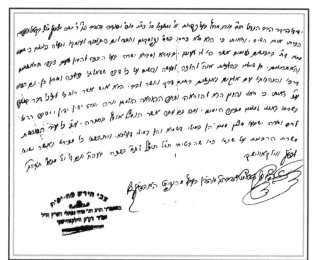

Rabbi Yehuda Braver's Smicha

In Mexico City, the beginnings of a Jewish community had been started twenty-five years previously. The community invited my father to be the Rosh Yeshiva of Etz Chaim Yeshiva in Mexico City. In the summer of 1944, my parents, my youngest brother Joseph, my twin sister Miriam and I, went to Mexico City. My sister and I were 17 years of age and had just graduated from High school. My older brothers were drafted into the army, and one was killed in a training accident. He had just completed his navigator's course when he volunteered to take the place of another navigator who had not turned up for a training exercise. The plane crashed and he was killed with the rest of the crew.

General Franco was in power in Spain and many intellectuals who disagreed with him escaped to Mexico, which granted them immediate citizenship.

Mexico City was still in its formative period and my father increased the membership of his Yeshiva by inserting notices in the Yiddish newspaper, which also announced his talks to the community over Rosh Hashanah. Yiddish was the language of the community because the members were mostly refugees from Europe. The community became large since most of its members were religious Jews with a large number of children. They were generally well to do and had established textile and leather factories. Since they were Zionists they were generous to Israel.

We came from a large community in the United States to a small community of 20,000 people, concentrated in Mexico City. We were in a new land with a new culture, a new way of life and a new language, Spanish. The original dwellers in Mexico are the Aztec Indians and we enjoyed visiting the huge pyramids, which they had built and were now a tourist destination.

My sister and I were exactly the right age to go to College. The United States government issued a Bill of Rights, known as the G.I. [Government Issue] Bill. Boys who had had their education interrupted because of the war were given a monthly stipend to go to College. Mexico City College had an agreement with Ohio State University that their students could come to Mexico and get full credits.

When my sister and I were in that student body, it was suddenly flooded with boys and women who came to take advantage of the courses, which were held in the language according to the registration of students. G.I.Bill students could live very well in Mexico, because the rate of exchange of the dollar to the peso favoured the dollar. The students had an apartment and a native Mexican maid. We had two maids in the house; that was the way of life. Those with small children had a nanny. The apartments in Mexico had staff accommodation built on the roof.

Mexico had a restrictive immigrant policy and it was necessary to prove that you would not be taking the job away from a Mexican. However, during the war, the President of Mexico made a special dispensation, in order that families could be reunited, and survivors from Europe were allowed to join their families in Mexico. Some of these young people became my father's students.

My mother would go shopping in the market, where the shochet had a booth with cages filled with live chickens. My mother would choose a chicken from a cage and the shochet would shecht it on the spot. My mother then took the chicken to a boy in the market and he 'flicked' the chicken; that is he plucked off its feathers.

Ba'alei haBatim came to my father with their sheilos, questions. Of these two stick in my memory. A couple had fled from Belgium and had left behind their ketubah. Since, according to halachah, the couple could not live together without a ketubah in the wife's possession, my father reconstructed the details and asked a sofer to write a new ketubah. The second case concerned a man with a mentally ill wife. The halachah allows a man to remarry, in the lifetime of his wife under certain circumstances, although this is not a common occurrence. My father arranged for the man to have a heter meah Rabbanim, permission from one hundred Rabbis, and he remarried.

Mexico City has an altitude of 3,000 feet above sea level and this altitude took its toll on my father's health, and he developed high blood pressure. In 1948, after three and a half years in Mexico, we moved on to Los Angeles, California.

My brother Joseph was 12 years old and I took him to Cleveland to learn in the Telshe Yeshiva. The son of Rav Bloch had escaped the Shoah, the Holocaust, and he laid the foundations of Telshe Yeshiva in Cleveland. It began in a basement apartment, with a minyan. Gradually, he had community support and the Yeshiva was revitalised on American soil.

In Los Angeles my father did not have an official position, although he had a private minyan in the house and he was a kashrus supervisor. He was niftar at the age of 65, may his memory be for a blessing.

Max Oestreich
born in 1909

'Mother, if you buy from the Jew, I shall report you'

I had only a very short time with my father because he passed away when I was 9 years old. He was a cattle dealer and we lived in a farmers' village in Germany, one of four Jewish families among a population of 700. Before the First World War it was called Langstadt, but when the village was taken over by Russia the name was changed to Babenhausen. Eventually all the little surrounding villages were absorbed into Babenhausen, and presently there is a population of 45,000 people. Babenhausen is an old city, in existence since 1295, and is considered one of the most forest rich cities in South Hessen.

Before the First World War there was no electricity or water in the houses. I lived twenty metres from the well where we pumped our water. In those days if someone needed water they took two pails to the well, filled them up and carried them back to their home. There was always clean water in the well.

Each family had a big house with plenty of room. We had a cooking oven in the kitchen and an oven for heating in the living room, both of which burned wood. Every year the burgomeister of the village would organise the cutting of the trees for fuel. These trees belonged to the village and after the trees were cut down the forest was replanted.

Every family had animals; chickens, cows and geese. Very few families had horses, except for the big farms, which needed the horses to work their large fields. The small farmers put cows to the plough and goods were brought from the fields by wagon pulled by cows. Every family had fields where they grew everything they needed, such as corn, potatoes, wheat and food for the animals. We baked our own bread.

Whenever we needed help to work in the fields we asked one of the farmers. We waited for rain, as there was no other way of watering the fields.

Every farmer had a big hole in one of his fields where he collected and stored animal waste and urine. When fertilizer was needed on the field, the farmer pumped out this liquid fertilizer by feeding a line into the hole and pumping the liquid manure into a barrel, on a wagon, for distribution onto the field. The toilet outside the house in the yard was located near the hole. The waste from the toilet was collected in a small hole, which had a pipe connected to the big hole. This was also mixed with the animal manure. Everything was used, nothing was wasted.

I went to the school in the village. Although the children, generally, didn't work, sometimes the farmers found work for us to do. We could take the animals on the plough and walk them up and down.

In 1918 my father succumbed to the influenza epidemic. After father passed away my mother, my sister and I were alone, so it was arranged for someone to help us in the fields.

I remember the day the First World War started. It was Shabbat and we were taking a walk in the fields. There was a declaration that the War had started. As we passed City Hall, we saw, posted outside, the notice announcing the War. I remember that someone had been killed and that had precipitated the outbreak of fighting.

We were prepared for it. The younger boys were called up for service into the army. As children we enjoyed watching the soldiers march through our village as they went from place to place. The soldiers were kind to us. In those days nothing was motorised, horses pulled everything. Because my father was a cattle dealer, we had a big stable where we were able to stable the horses for the soldiers.

When the army came through the villages they brought everything with them. They carried their own food and also food for the horses. They had their own kitchen, which was a big cauldron, on a wagon pulled by horses. They stayed only two days before they moved on. Although the soldiers had tents, some of them slept in the houses. The large houses of the farmers had plenty of room to accommodate the soldiers. We were always happy to see them.

In 1922 the stock market crashed and all the money people had in the bank disappeared, forcing them to start again. We didn't worry about food because we grew it. In addition we had chicken, eggs, and milk. When we needed to shecht a chicken someone went on a bicycle to the next town and asked the Rabbi for a kosher shechitah. Every year we schechted a cow, which provided us with meat and sausages for the entire year. We smoked the meat in the oven to preserve it. The rear, the treifeh part of the cow, we gave to the treifeh butcher to sell.

We had a nice life and were very happy. G-d gave us sunshine and he gave us rain. No one bothered us and the goyim respected us and the way we lived.

We had a shul where originally, at the end of the 1800's, there were 25 members. As the young people gradually moved away there appeared to be no future in the village. By the beginning of the twentieth century the world had changed. It was the same situation in the next village, a forty-minute walk away. In order to have a minyan for Shabbos every week, one Shabbos we went there, the next Shabbos they came to us.

On Rosh Hashanah we had our own minyan because the young people, who had their own businesses in the next town, came home. Usually they were apprentices in the textile stores where people bought all their necessities.

My mother's brother and his wife had no children and lived in a different town, which had a better school. In order to attend that school I went to live with them and slept away from home.

In 1938 the war against the Jews started and people were forbidden to do business with them. I was in the textile business peddling cloth. I remember the day that I went to a customer who used to live in my village. She asked for some material to make a dress. As we were talking her 9 year-old son came in and said 'Mother, if you buy from that Jew I shall report you to my teacher.' The teacher was the head of the party. I said to the customer, 'Katrina, forget about it,' and put my samples together and walked out.

On another occasion I was with my boss peddling textiles when a Catholic woman, whom we knew, saw us in the street. She called out 'you shouldn't go home. They have put the synagogue [in the next big town] on fire.'

We went home anyway and the Police came and took us in. They put us in jail that night and the next day we were sent to Buchenwald. At that time if you had papers that you had applied to emigrate you were released. We had applied to emigrate to America and my wife went to the main offices of the Gestapo to show them our application papers. Although I was released after exactly four weeks, it was some time before we were able to set sail to America.

In our village we had a burgomeister who was 'a piece of gold' and not a Nazi. In the village there were two other Jewish fellows. After I was released from Buchenwald in 1938, the burgomeister gave the three of us a jobs cutting down trees in the woods, so that we could make a living.

In 1939 my wife and I left for Frankfurt. The Jewish organisation that we were registered with sent us a letter that we had should go from there to Berlin where we were to join a group going to Lisbon. From Lisbon we set sail to America.

✦ ✦ ✦

Editors Note: On June 28th 1914, Archduke Franz Ferdinand, the heir to the Austria-Hungary Empire, was murdered in Sarajevo, Bosnia by a Serbian national. Although many Serbs lived in Bosnia, it was annexed by Austria-Hungary in 1908. The Serbian nation and the Serbian nationals, who lived in Bosnia, were very angry about this annexation.

Austria-Hungary accused the Serbian government of being behind the murder of the Archduke and with German support declared war on Serbia on July 28th 1914. A local war started, which soon turned into a general war.

Rabbi **Ya'akov Baker**
born in 1914

'The Jewish people in my village had a wonderful Pesach that year'

Rabbi Ya'akov Baker as a cantor in America

I was born in Yedwabne, Poland, a few months before the First World War started. Yedwabne was near the German border, and was in the war at the beginning.

After the war, when I became Bar Mitzvah, I would walk to the yeshiva in Lomza, 19 kilometres away, in order to save a zloty and my parent's income.

The villagers were kind and used to invite me to have a drink, or give me an egg, which was considered kosher because it has a shell. I found the villagers pleasant and was surprised that, later on, many of them became holocaust murderers. As I walked through the woods, I found berries, mushrooms, and fruit such as apples. I took them with me to the yeshiva, to share with the other bochurim.

In 1935, Madame Prostorowa, the Prime Minister of Poland, passed an order forbidding kosher shechitah. At that time the Jews were ten per cent of the thirty million population of Poland, which meant that there were three million Jews. The meat in Poland was mainly supplied by the Jews. The Poritz wanted to do business with the Jews because they sold us the animals. We killed them, and since we eat only the front of the cow, the hindquarters could then be sold back to the Poritz very cheaply. In 1933, when the Nazis began to rule Germany, they wanted to take the meat business away from the Jews and spread anti-Semitism in order to win over Eastern Poland. There was plenty of anti-Semitism there already.

When I was twenty the Rabbi of Yedwabne came to the Lomza yeshiva and said, 'we need to save the town from starvation.' The main shochet was watched by the Secret Police, twenty-four hours a day, so the Rabbi came to me to teach me shechitah. Eventually the Secret Police discovered that I, also, knew the work. It was close to Pesach and we needed to supply the town of Yedwabne with meat. The Jews of the town would not use milk products on Pesach because there was a question of whether the cow had eaten chometz before and during Pesach.

We devised a plan. In the middle of the night the butchers came with their horses and wagons on a back road, and I jumped out of the window into the wagon, to avoid the Secret Police who were watching at the front.

The butchers knew that the Secret Police would go after them; therefore they followed the advice of the Rabbi who told them to leave their wagons at the home of the Poritz of the village, which was seven kilometres from Yedwabne. We walked another three kilometres to the barn where the animals had been prepared for shechitah.

We started at three o'clock in the morning; and by three o'clock in the afternoon all the work was finished, and the meat divided up for each villager.

Meanwhile the Secret Police found the horses and wagons at the estate of the Poritz. He had stacks of corn, which could easily hide people. The Secret Police dismantled every stack. The Poritz cursed them and told them to restack all the bundles. When the butchers went back for the horses and wagons, the Secret Police put them in jail but there were unable to find the meat since it had already been divided. The butchers had a moment of joy as they cursed the Secret Police who were hooligans, and the Jewish people in my village had a wonderful Pesach that year.

Shortly before the Seder I heard a knock at the door. It was one of the seven butchers who had been given the meat to divide amongst the community. The butcher had forgotten to leave meat for himself and his family. He brought with him a note from the Rav, addressed to me, and a little calf, which he wanted me to slaughter. The note, written in Hebrew, advised me to prepare the calf in the stables attached to the Police station. The Rav understood that the Police would not look for the calf in their own stables. The Rav added that the Police would not catch me if I am engaged in the mitzvah of saving people's lives.

My bubba and mama were in the house and cried as they heard the story. On the one hand the butcher had nothing to eat for Yom Tov and on the other hand I was being sent to the Police stables. I was on the point of going to America and needed to pick up my visa from the Police station.

Eventually my bubba and mama said 'go, it's a pity for this man to have Pesach without food. Hashem will save you.' I went to the Police stables and slaughtered the calf. The Police heard the bleating calf and went to every stable except their own. I returned to the Seder.

Another butcher bought a heifer in the market on the Wednesday before Pesach, and kept it in his basement. He wanted me, or the old shochet, to slaughter it. The Secret Police knew he had it and knew the voice of the cow. I was going to the synagogue to learn, and had to pass the basement, which housed the cow. The Secret Police were sure that I was going to slaughter the cow so they prepared to stop me. When they saw me passing by they ordered me to stop and put my hands up. Convinced that I was carrying the shechitah knife to slaughter the cow, they searched me thoroughly, but didn't find it. It was an offence to carry a knife with intent to slaughter an animal. I had the knife in a wooden box up my sleeve. As I raised my hands I prayed to Hashem to save me, and the fact that I raised my hands to their order, meant that they did not find the knife.

Aleksander Kwasniewski

Paying homage to the inhabitants of Yedwabne

R abbi Baker, Honourable Rabbi

I would like to thank you for your words and the present that you sent to my address.

Your words meant a great deal to me, Rabbi, since you are from Yedwabne, and they come in spite of the horrible crime that took place through our common neighbours.

Allow me to express my deep acknowledgement to you, Sir, for your words in connection with the crime that took place in Yedwabne.

As a representative of the surviving remnant of the generation who bore witness to this very horrible crime on your nation, you

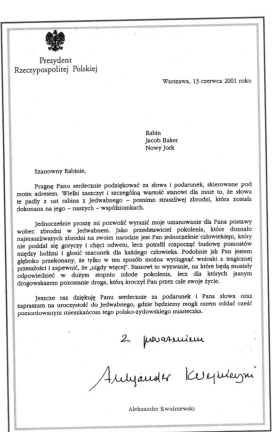

Rabbi Ya'akov Baker with the President of Poland in 2001

are, in spite of this, a human being without bitterness or thought of revenge, but you are able to start and build a bridge between people by maintaining a positive attitude to every human being.

Exactly like you, Sir, I am deeply persuaded that only in this way, in spite of the tragic past, that only this attitude can ensure that this will never happen again.

This attitude requires a major effort by the new generation to show them the brightness of the direction that you chose for yourself.

Again I thank you for your present and your words and I invite you to the event in Yedwabne where together we can pay homage to the inhabitants who were murdered in this small Polish town.

Aleksander Kwasniewski

✦ ✦ ✦

Editors' Note: On the 15th of Tammuz 5701, [July 10th 1941] all the Jews in Yedwabne were ordered to go to the market place. There they were forced to put on their tallaisim and tefillin and to dance and to sing. Then they were locked in a big barn, near the Jewish cemetery, which was splashed with benzine and ignited. All the Jews were burned alive. After the murder the Beis Hamidrash in the centre of Yedwabne was partially destroyed. The new generation of Jews found the mass graves and there were still witnesses from the old generation to verify the events that took place in Yedwabne on that day.

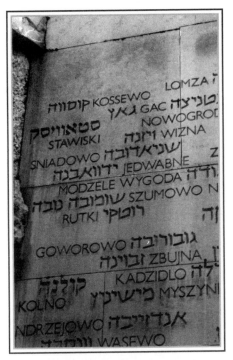

In the valley of the communities in Yad Vashem

Miriam Pollack
born in 1903

'How can you see a girl if your cufflinks are different?'

M y parents had a beautiful house in Hungary more than eighty years ago, with a sink in the kitchen and a toilet in the garden, which every two or three months professionals came to clean out. In those days indoor plumbing was a luxury that only wealthy people could afford.

My father was regarded as a wealthy man and sold refurbished second hand clothes. He travelled by train or autobus to the market in Budapest, where he purchased clothing with missing buttons, stains or ripped seams. He put on new buttons, cleaned the spots, sewed up the ripping, pressed the garments and put them in his store. Since father bought the clothes for almost nothing, he was now able to sell it at the price of a new garment; he made a lot of money from this business.

We lived in Kisvarola, which had a large Jewish community. I went to a Jewish school where I learnt both Yiddish and how to read and write.

The 1914-18 War was far away from us and did not affect us. My in laws to be, however, saw the clouds and said they didn't look like rain clouds, only war clouds, so they fled to America. They stayed there for three years and two boys were born there, before they returned to Hungary. They never told the children that they were born in America because, in those days, it was a shameful thing. My husband was Bar Mitzvah before he found out.

The reason it was kept a secret was that he who didn't work on Shabbos could not make ten cents, so they worked on Shabbos.

I had a grandmother who was a smart woman. When I started going out on shidduchim she said 'who is going to be lucky enough to get you for a wife?' She had to see all the boys herself because she saw more than I could. She said 'this boy is not for you.' I asked, 'Bubbie, why?' 'His cufflinks weren't the same,' she said. 'How can you see a girl if your cufflinks are different?' Another boy she rejected because his handkerchief was dirty. 'A young man who wants to see a young lady should have a clean handkerchief when he takes it out of his pocket to blow his nose and not have to search for a clean place. I remember one boy whose face, she said 'did not look healthy'. 'He died the same year. She saw things that I did not.

I was twenty-one years of age when my husband came to see me, and he was twenty-two. My grandmother said, 'Miriam, this is your choson.' He had a pimple on his forehead that he hid with his hat pulled down low, but nevertheless, he was a handsome man and lived to a great age. He was ninety-four years old when he passed away.

I was twenty-five when I left Hungary. We felt something coming in the air. My husband made a decision. 'Now I am going to take out my papers.' He was referring to his American papers. He went to the American consulate. The woman behind the counter said 'what are you doing here? Take your wife and children and go to America right away.' In the consulate they knew what was going to happen. I paid forty dollars for passports for my children. I was very heavily pregnant and my baby was born on Shabbos four days before my husband had to go to America. They forced him to go. It was nine months before my papers were approved and I could join him.

I left Hungary with four children on a boat for seven weeks and couldn't have had a nicer time. It was a French liner where the ship staff took good care of the children and stopped at every country.

I didn't recognise my husband when he came to meet me at the dockside. When I disembarked I didn't believe that it was my husband talking to me. My Uncle accompanied my husband, and it was he whom I recognised. In the taxi I said to myself 'this man is not my husband.' Only the voice was his. Two different worlds had separated us in only nine months.

It was 1928, the year of the Great Depression in America. Things were so bad that he had to take off his beard otherwise he couldn't get any work. He changed his clothes and got a job on the railroad, where he worked very hard. He was a yeshiva boy and that's what he had to do.

I went to sleep hungry every night. Whatever I bought with the money my husband bought home, I gave to the children. I accepted that that was what my husband was able to do. Every night I prayed that I could return home to Hungary, where I had had a dry goods store and a nice little house. I wouldn't miss America at all. There was no work during the depression and my husband could not earn enough for food, medication or a pair of shoes. Even though he was still working on the railroad, he did not work on Shabbos.

I needed to work, but with four small children I could only work in the house. We bought a sewing machine so that I could sew neckties at home. I went to the stores with my baby carriage to try to get work.

The workers were on strike outside the stores because there was no work and they had been laid off. I worked for half price. The shopkeepers put the merchandise for me to sew in the baby carriage. The striking workers would have killed me if they found out that I was taking any available work.

I lived on the third floor and the woman under me didn't like me because her apartment shook while I was working on the sewing machine. She told the authorities that I was working at home and they came with the Police who took away my merchandise. I went to another store and offered to make expensive hand sewn neckties, work I could do without a sewing machine. I had no alternative. I had to help bring in more income because my husband could not earn enough.

How many times I wanted to go back to Hungary, but the authorities in America wouldn't let us go back, they knew. My husband worked for seven or eight years on the railroad.

I was cut off from my family in Hungary. Slowly we found out what was going on. My grandfather was lucky; he passed away before the troubles. My grandmother, father, mother, five sisters and two brothers all went to Auschwitz. I would have gone to Auschwitz if I had not been in America. My two brothers survived Auschwitz, but I lost the rest of the family.

The human brain cannot fathom Hashem's ways.

My brothers found each other and were happier than words can describe. My two brothers were staying together and one said, 'Yossi, you stay here, I will get us something to eat.' He went away and never came back. No trace was ever found of him.

After the war, the newspapers advertised that they would help people locate lost relatives and friends. I wrote and told them I was looking for members of my family. Someone told Yossi that I was looking for him. Information was passed from one person to another as people looked for their lost family members. I sent Yossi papers to come to America. He now lives in America with his Hungarian wife and they have a beautiful family. My husband took him into our business, a self-service grocery store. It was a nebech with the big stores, they were open on Shabbos.

Joan Sklan
born in 1928

'At what time would you like your order delivered?'

One day, as we sat over tea, I recalled to a friend my memory of the lamplighters. 'Lamplighters?' my friend enquired, 'what are they?' As I am a few years older than her, I told her what I could remember.

He did his round an hour or so before dark. An elderly gentleman, sometimes two, appeared at the tall lamppost on the pavement outside the front of our house. He reached up to the top of the lamppost using a long pole, which he grasped with both hands. He linked the end of the pole with a small chain, which hung down from the light and pulled it down, and lo! the gas gradually lit up the pavement. He moved on to the next one and the one after that, until the whole street glowed with an eerie light.

There was a song about the lamplighter from the mid 1930's, which went something like this:

A moment after dark,
around the park
an old fashioned gent goes parading.
Dressed in funny clothes,
and singing as he goes,
his lamplighters serenade.
His snowy hair seems so much brighter
beneath the candle glow,
the old lamplighter of long, long ago.

I only remember these verses because, as a child, I loved to sing and listen to music. I'm sure I would have had piano lessons if there had been two shillings and sixpence to spare. When my mum was feeling affluent, I was treated to a two-penny sheet of printed verses without the music, sold by an elderly man by the roadside.

I listened to the music on the wireless and learned the words from these badly printed sheets. Sometimes words would be missing, so I made them up instead, often misinterpreting the original meaning of the song.

In the evenings our parents told us stories, which we never tired of hearing, from the time before we were born. Mum told about how they moved from London to Brighton during the 1914-18 War. One brother was in the army and was so badly gassed that he had to be discharged. I remember him as a sickly man who nevertheless married and produced three children. Another younger brother died in the terrible flu epidemic that raged around that time.

Before the Great War, one of my mother's sisters married a South African and lived there for many years, paying visits home every few years. Before she was married, to test whether she would prove a competent and satisfactory wife, her future mother-in-law gave her an enormous bag of wool and cotton reels all tangled up in a dreadful mess. She spent many an hour unravelling it without losing her temper, thus winning over her in-laws.

On the day of her wedding she whitened the front doorstep to the house, before she donned her wedding gown. This was done with a white stone, then scrubbed with a hand brush and finally rinsed by throwing buckets of water over the step.

Every summer she sent a huge crate of the most gorgeous peaches from South Africa. We would sit eating them letting the delicious fruit, full of juice, course down our cheeks and mouth, not caring if some of it found its way onto our newly washed clothes.

My father came to England, with his parents and older brother and sister, around 1898, by boat from Russia to escape the Pogroms. They travelled for weeks and finally arrived in London where they rented a room. As resourceful new immigrants they had a makeshift stall in an East End market, where they sold fruit and vegetables, which earned them a meagre living. As the family increased the older children looked after each other, while the newest baby was placed in a wooden orange box under the stall, so that my grandmother could feed and change the baby during market hours.

Things were also different during my childhood. I remember watching the milkman arrive at the top of four flights of stairs, carrying a huge metal milk churn with a little iron jug hanging from a chain attached to the churn. 'How much will you have today?' he asked my mother, as he stood at the door gasping for breath. The jug was dipped into the churn many times, and came up dripping as the milk over-flowed over the stone floor. Most days, mother filled two or three pretty jugs to the top, which we used up before the milkman called the next day and the whole process was repeated. The little iron jug dangled, un-washed, against the side of

the churn. No one thought about germs then and in spite of the unwashed utensils, we all survived.

Then the baker called too, arriving with an enormous wicker basket filled to the brim with fresh rolls and bagels. I can smell them, even now!

We used to walk to the nearby railway station where my mother would order coal to be delivered. After returning home, we heard the clip clop of the carthorse and the loud voice of the deliveryman as they arrived in the yard. Each flat had its own neat little shed, where the coal was emptied sack by sack. The coalman was covered in coal dust; his face and hands were as black as ink and the dust rolled off the thick waterproof hood and cape that protected his raggedy clothes underneath. Dressed thus, he climbed the four flights of stairs to collect the payment.

As a child I would watch in delight as the butcher and the fishmonger weighed, cut, gutted and chopped as they chatted affably to their customers. Most of all I loved the grocery shop. Sugar, beans and other dry items were weighed on scales. A piece of greaseproof paper was wound into the shape of a funnel, into which the contents of the scales were poured, and these fell into a bright, thick blue bag which was then neatly folded to seal the contents inside.

I can still smell the pickled cucumbers and pickled herrings that filled huge wooden barrels. The shopkeeper bent over the barrel, hauled up a few cucumbers and dangled a few choice herrings, which were then wrapped into sheets of greaseproof paper.

Butter sat on a huge marble slab and was shaped into an almost perfect rectangle between two wooden bricks with handles. When we bought eggs, we were sometimes given thirteen for the price of twelve. I was allowed to count them from the stall outside the shop. I placed them in a wooden basket, and then carried them carefully inside where the grocer would pack them in a box. There were high chairs on our side of the counter, where customers would sit as they gave their order to the shopkeeper. 'And what time would you like your order delivered?' we were asked if we had bought too much to carry home ourselves.

Sometimes we heard that shoes were available in the shoe shop, and we queued outside from seven o'clock in the morning. There were always other shoppers in front of us and when the shop opened at nine o'clock only around a dozen people were allowed in at a time. The choices were almost nonexistent, but if we wanted new shoes we would settle for a size smaller or larger, if they were more attractive than those of our own size. No wonder that females of my age have oddly shaped and painful feet.

Everyone followed the rules of the blackout. No lights were shown after dusk so that enemy planes had nothing other than their own ability to find their targets. Curtains had to be lined with black material and the windows were taped tightly to prevent them from breaking if bombs fell nearby. When we went out after dusk, we carried torches fitted with a round piece of black paper with a small hole in it, which allowed only a pinhole of light to shine through. We unscrewed the top of the torch and inserted the paper against the glass.

When I started going to school at the age of five, my mother gave me a half penny or a penny with which to choose a treat at the corner shop, a short walk away. There were little stools for small children to stand on and sometimes my sister would lift me up so that I could make my choice. There were lots of things we could buy for a farthing, a quarter of a penny, so if we had a whole penny there were many choices to make. No one hurried us or ushered us out quickly. My favourite treat was a four-inch milk chocolate flake that I could buy for half a penny, which I crumbled up as finely as possible into a paper bag, threw my head back and sucked the mouthfuls of delicious chocolate. By applying this method I could make my half penny last a long time! At home there was drinking chocolate in a tin, eight inches high. The chocolate inside was shaved into very fine flakes, and for a treat we were allowed to dip a teaspoon inside, scoop up as much as we could, and very slowly we would enjoy emptying the spoon. When sweets and chocolate rationing began in World War Two, confectionary was sorely missed. Ration chocolate, the War substitute, had a horrible taste.

Eggs were very few and far between and we were introduced to powdered eggs, which could only be scrambled or made into an omelette.

We queued for practically everything. Whenever we saw a queue we automatically joined it. You marked your place by asking the person in front of you to mind it for you and then you went to the front to ask what the queue was for. Often the merchandise would run out just before you reached the front and a sign saying SOLD OUT would appear.

There were no combs to buy, so most women, old, young and in between, would tie scarves around their heads in imitation of the women called up to do war service in the munitions factories. Their hair could not come near the machinery, so they wrapped turbans around their head, which became a fashion statement during the war. There was much competition between women to find the prettiest square scarves. This was not easy in those days, when coupons were required for all types of clothing. On days when one tired of the turban, we would take an old stocking, wrap it around our heads and roll our hair round it until no stocking was visible. It was a lovely hairstyle and those of us who wore it felt very fashionable. It wasn't possible to buy stockings very often, so instead we painted a very fine straight seam down the back of our legs with a dark pencil or a fine brush.

We took great care of the underwear we had. If the elastic gave out we were out of luck as it was impossible to find any. We even queued for that if we heard of a shop that was selling it!

Zipporah Hess
born in 1921

'Until the Olympia
they left the Jews alone'

M y parents came from Frankfurt-am-Maine where my grandfather was the shammas in the main shul there for 40 years until Kristalnacht. I was born in the modern city of Berlin. Because of the difficult economic situation in Eastern Europe many people migrated from Poland and Russia to Germany and settled in the Northern section of the city. In 1918, my parents moved into a building with electricity, an elevator and central heating. There were two shuls and each one had its own hospital and Jewish school.

In 1936 Berlin hosted the Olympia, which was good for the Jews. We made sure to see the opening ceremony with the flags. Until then they left the Jews in Berlin alone. We had no problems, but after the Olympia they began to oppress us. My father was an insurance broker and one day the company sent him a letter which said 'we do not need you any more.' After this he sat and learnt and I went to work. I was a teenager at the time and I don't know how we managed financially.

After the Olympia everything had to be reported to the Police. I remember the Oneg Shabbaton our shul organised every four weeks with thirty people attending. Each time we went to a different house for two hours. When it was at my house the Nazis came to check but everyone had gone home. If we organized a meeting at night, we hired a goyishe watchman to watch the building. He would sit at the entrance and look through the window to see who was there, but he refused to work after 8 p.m.

It was at this time that my father tried to escape with the family to America. We had a relative, an uncle on my Mother's side who wanted to marry a goya and was thrown out of the house. He went to Texas and married a goya there. He gave six affidavits for six different people and re-

My parents, my sister and myself on the left

fused to give one for us because he felt he had given enough. We promised we would not bother him, or go to Texas, or ask for money. Another cousin of my mother also intervened and finally in June 1937 he gave us an affidavit. Two days before we received it America established a quota system. Our quota number should have allowed us to enter America in January 1939, but we were put off a full year because America felt it had too many applicants.

In 1938, I could not get a degree because the Germans would not award them to Jewish applicants. I worked in an old age home for a few months and then as a dietician in a hospital belonging to Agudas Yisroel. In the 1930's in Germany, kosher shechitah was forbidden and the old age home changed to 'new kosher', which was a different way of killing the animals. For this reason I left the old age home. My family did not eat meat shechted in Germany and we imported our meat from Holland.

On the night of Kristalnacht in November 1939 I was at home with my father and sister. Mother was visiting her parents in Frankfurt. At three in the morning my father got a phone call that our shul was on fire, and when he looked out of the window he saw a Nazi on horseback riding towards the shul. We lived across the street from another shul that was more conservative, but that shul was not attacked, since it was in the middle of a yard surrounded by a lot of houses.

There was a teenager living with us whose family lived in a small town in Germany without any schools. They sent her to Berlin for her education. In the morning of Kristalnacht, my father received a phone call that her father had been murdered. A Nazi had rung his bell and when her father opened the door he was shot.

Kristalnacht was even more dangerous during the day. My sister was a dressmaker and worked with a lot of people. When the Jewish boss heard that the Nazis were coming he hid all his workers in a room. The Nazis destroyed the place but my sister came out alive.

In the afternoon the Gabbai of our shul came and told me to tell my father to see what had happened to the shul and to go into hiding. He said that the Nazis were rounding up the men and boys. I searched for him in the street but I could not find him. As I walked home I saw the Nazis destroying stores. When I arrived my sister and father were there. I was overjoyed because I thought they had taken him. He wouldn't leave to go into hiding until my mother came home the next day.

My mother had trouble leaving her parents because Grandmother lived over the shul and didn't want to leave. My mother begged her and said 'if you don't want to leave I will leave.' So she did. She went to the train station to travel to Berlin, which was an eight-hour journey from Frankfurt. She was alone and afraid and felt terrified sitting on the train with Nazis.

As soon as Mother came home my father ran into hiding at the home of a gentile family he knew, leaving my mother, sister and I in the flat. We were the only frum people living in this building. The Nazis came but they left alone the men renting rooms in our house.

The synagogue in Frankfurt

The Nazis went to the shul and took out my grandfather. They took him across the road to the park before they ignited the shul. Grandfather was then taken to the place where all the men they had rounded up were gathered. Grandfather was born in 1880 and was sixty years old. Someone, my grandfather doesn't know who, told him to leave and he just walked out of the building. No one stopped him. There were no police and no one watching. He went home and no one came for him.

My uncle in Frankfurt was fortunate enough to move his business to England. He sent his son to Yeshiva in England and got permanent visas for my grandparents in the winter of 1939. He arranged temporary visas for us to go to England as long as we didn't work until our quota number came up to go to America.

After Kristalnacht I worked in the kitchens of a hospital. Eventually I received a visa, which entitled me to go to England in May 1940. My parents' visa was for a June 1940 departure. However my Uncle wrote that it was too dangerous to wait and we should as soon as possible. Fortunately our quota number for America came up in January 1940 and in March 1940 my parents and I went to America by boat. My sister had left earlier and gone to Ireland. When the war broke out she went to America. Fortunately we were all saved.

Esther bat Leah
born in 1925

'In the goldene medina you had to be American'

M y mother's mother was almost one hundred per cent American. She was the oldest of her siblings and was brought to America when she was two years old a short time after the Civil War. She and the rest of the children were educated in American schools and the family language was English. Even her parents spoke English to the children. She and my Grandpa lived with her when we were children, during the height of the depression. I called her grandma, not bubby. Most of my friends had bubbys who came from Europe and spoke Yiddish as their native language. My father's mother died a month before I was born and I am the first of the cousins to bear her name.

In the early days of the twentieth century we had indoor plumbing, but the toilets were outside the apartments in the hallway and shared by several families. I remember in the kitchen we had a double sink, which not only separated between milk and meat, but also served for washing clothes and bathing the children. A large portable basin was brought in to the kitchen for the adults to sit and bathe.

Grandma would tell me of the times when they first had electricity in their apartment on the Lower East side of New York City. At first of course they only had gas light, which was efficient but not the best, and was unreliable when it went out at the wrong time. When electricity first became available for apartment dwellers, there were no

*My mother born in 1904
with my Aunt Feygi and Aunt Blanche*

central units. Each household had a meter into which they dropped a quarter. Like the gaslight it would stay on only for the length of time that the meter indicated.

We did not have a telephone until 1948. We had to go down five flights of stairs to use the phone or take a call from our neighbour's phone.

Almost everyone was poor, and the hardest thing was that the men had to work long hours in what were called sweat shops at that time, sewing clothing. These sweat shops were mostly owned by non-religious Jews, who required that people must also work on Shabbos. Most families were shomer Shabbos and this was very hard. If they didn't come in on Shabbos, on Monday they were fired from their job. This made it very important to find work with a religious Jew or to open a business of one's own, or work at home. Many families did sewing and other small jobs from home where the whole family, including the mother and the children, helped with the work.

My grandma owned a grocery store on the Lower East side. In those days the 'Blue Laws' of New York State did not allow shops to be open on Sunday, because it was the official day of rest. Those Jews who had shops on the

Lower East side were closed on Shabbos and if they wanted to open on Sunday they were fined and had to close. Many, many years later this changed, and Sunday became a very big shopping day on the Lower East side.

Now, however, there are very few Jewish shop owners, as the area is mostly oriental. There was always a Chinese and Italian presence

My great grandmother in Lower East Side in the late 1900's

but the Chinese stayed mostly to themselves, however there was a lot of friction between the Italian and Jewish inhabitants. There were street battles, with one side or the other claiming some streets. One did not venture into the streets claimed by the other side. This did not prevent some of the Jews becoming gangsters along with their neighbours in the Mafia.

We did hear tales of the hardships that the depression caused to most of the immigrants that came from 'the old country.' As a child I remember thinking that this was part of Russia at the time. In later years we were thankful that being in America had spared our families from near certain death.

My grandparents lived long before the advances of the things we are used to today. Not having much money, everything was done on a very simple scale. Sometimes weddings were held in people's homes, with the most limited amount of people. Certainly no Bar Mitzvah reception was held anywhere but in a home. I remember my mother telling me stories of how, when they first married, in someone's home, when they entertained their guests they would take one small cake, about three inches in diameter, and divide it into six pieces. No one ever ate outside the home in a restaurant. When they visited family, even in the evening, the children went along. We did go away for the summer to somewhere in the mountains. I also remember how exciting it was when my uncle took us for a ride in his car.

My parents took in family members who came from Europe before the holocaust. As far as I know we had no one left in Europe. One of the reasons that there were not many grandparents was because of the immigration quotas. Only those who could work, or were young, or who could be vouched for, could enter the United States.

We were kept absolutely uninformed about the real goings on in Europe regarding the holocaust and what was happening to the Jews. We did see and hear war news of course, but only what was written in the papers and what we were told on the radio. It was not on the newsreels in the cinema. The government and the established Jewish community hid most of the news of the holocaust from the public. It was only after the war that the full extent of what happened came to light. The Jews were expendable. Wiesmandel begged them to bomb railroads leading to Auschwitz; they could have done it. We were totally ignorant of what was going on. A Polish non-Jewish diplomat told them the truth.

Because we were unaware of what was really happening to our fellow Jews, life went on more or less normally with only a few restrictions. Nylon stockings were very rare and cigarettes were rationed. The Broadway shows and the musicals went on as usual. There was rationing of gasoline and some foods. However, I no longer had to wear hand me down clothing from my cousins who were better off than we were. I wore shoes without cardboard in them to cover up the holes in the soles. My parents both had jobs and we moved to a better apartment.

In an office where I worked down at the waterfront, I saw the ship, the Queen Mary, loading soldiers to go to Europe. They would go to France and England, not Poland, Rumania and Hungary. In my mother's generation there were no boys; they had all been drafted into the army.

The Jews in America in 1939 were just coming into mainstream America. When the Jews came from Russia, the Jews in America were already in the mainstream. Those in the reform movement did not want to make waves and risk their hard earned status as 'loyal Americans.' They encouraged their Jewish brothers to throw off the symbol of their Jewishness. When the Jews came to live in the Lower East side from Eastern Europe, they were told that they couldn't talk Yiddish. They were told to take off their yarmulke and their tzitzis and be American. As they came off the boat they threw their tefillin in the East River. If you dredge the river you will find them. In the goldene medina you had to be American.

Rabbi **Yisroel Orlansky**
born in 1925

'The Steipler would take me out of my crib to quieten me'

My father's parents lived in Dabrwa, near the big city of Gradna, which was originally in Russia. One of their children went to England in the 1880's to escape from the poverty. My grandfather was a tailor and a very pious Jew. He was a young boy when his father passed away and he learnt to sew in order to support the family.

Until the First World War, my father, Reb Yitzhak Orlansky, zt'l, was a yeshiva bochur in Slobodka where Rabbi Nosson Zvi Finkel, who founded the yeshiva in Slobodka, was the Rosh Yeshiva. My father learned there for two or three years. While he was in Slobodka he was present at the Chasunah of the daughter of Reb Moshe Epstein and the son of Reb Nosson Zvi Finkel.

My father
Rabbi Yitzhak Orlansky

When World War One started everything was interrupted and the yeshivas closed down. Since he was still a young boy, he returned to his parents thinking that maybe he should learn a trade. If he had experience working as a tailor, maybe this could be his parnossa in the future.

His father started to teach him how to use a needle and

as they worked he noticed that his father had tears in his eyes. Crying, his father said to him 'you will be a schneider?' [a tailor]. When he saw his father crying for his forsaken learning he made up his mind to go back to the yeshiva.

During World War One, the doors of the Navardok yeshiva were open to everyone. Rabbi Yosef Horowitz, the Rosh Yeshiva, was the head of Navardok, and my father went to learn there. During his time in Navardok my father became very close to and attached to his Rebbi.

During World War One, poverty was very great. My father only had the clothes that he stood up in. The Rosh Yeshiva told him that he couldn't go around with torn pants and a coat 'that he didn't know was how old.' Before Yom Tov, the Rebbi made an effort to obtain tzedakah to purchase a new suit for him. The Rebbi wanted to spread Torah to every town, and to build new yeshivas. He sent bochurim out to find new students who would learn in the new yeshivas.

The bochurim did not have suitable clothing. The Rabbi said to my father 'they cannot go with old clothes, let them have your suit. You will get it back.' My father hesitated and spoke to his Rebbi about 'my' suit. The Rebbe said 'my suit?' 'How can you say my suit?' and gave him a lecture. 'Everything is from Hakodesh Boruch Hu. A person should not be attached to his possessions and feel that it is theirs, if another person needs it. Don't become so attached to your things.' The Rebbi in Navardok worked very hard with the bochurim to encourage them to be attached to Torah and Mitzvos. My father gave his suit to another bochur and wore his old clothes again.

In 1920/1921 the communists took over Russia, and Poland was established as an independent country. There was no future for Torah in Russia and by degrees the

Russians closed the batei Midrashim and the chedarim and it was forbidden to go to a shul or a yeshiva. There was a young Jewish group in Russia, known as Yevseckzia, an abbreviation for the Jewish section of communists. This group thought that communism would relieve Jews from poverty and prejudice and there would be paradise in the world. With the power of communism behind them they destroyed everything concerned with Judaism.

When it was time for my father to return home to Poland, which was now a free country, he needed to leave communist Russia, which had closed the borders with Poland. The yeshiva organised the border crossings, which were now illegal. To cross a border at this time you went to the little towns and paid a goy who knew all the places to cross because border control was weak. This could only be done at night. A lot of the bochurim of Navardok were arrested and were unable to return home to Poland. Even when they crossed into Poland they faced the possibility of arrest. The Poles thought that the bochurim were communists and were coming to plant the seeds of communism in Poland. 'You came to spy' the bochurim were told. They would show their tzitzis and say 'we are religious. We are running away from Russia to come to Poland to find a free Country. We want to be able to practise our religion and establish yeshivas.'

Immediately upon his return to Poland my father became involved in establishing yeshivas. The Steipler was in Navardok for many years and was one of the boys who crossed from Russia into Poland. After his marriage, my father, who was very capable, influenced many boys to go to yeshiva. He became a menahel of mussar in the great Navardok yeshiva in Pinsk, Poland. At the same time the Steipler became a Rosh Yeshiva in the same yeshiva. Rabbi Shmuel Weintrob was the head of the yeshiva and a disciple of the Alter of Navardok.

My mother was fond of telling me that as a bochur, the Steipler would come to our home where my mother would serve him food. If she was in the kitchen and I was in the crib crying, the Steipler would take me out of the crib to quieten me so that I would stop crying. My mother told me that the Steipler would be so deeply engrossed in his learning, while he was walking from the yeshiva to our house, that he did not notice the street lamps, and bumped into them. When I was six or seven, I went to the Steipler for Chanukah gelt. My mother and his Rebbitzen were friends. He had a handkerchief in which he had coins. He would untie his handkerchief and give me gelt. My mother admired him greatly.

I learnt in the Navardok yeshivas, and later in Meszreitch, a big yeshiva under the auspices of Rabbi David Blacher, a disciple of the Alter of Navardok. In 1939, when I was fourteen years of age, the Second World War broke out and my learning ceased.

Poland was split. Eastern Poland was taken by Communist Russia and western Poland by the German Nazis. Although we were caught in between, we had a little relief. The city of Vilna and the area around it remained independent. It was returned to independent Lithuania. Latvia and Estonia, the Baltic States, were, at that time, also independent.

In 1938 there was an agreement between the Russian and German Foreign Secretaries, Molotov and Ribentrov, that they would split Poland. In the pact there was a little clause in small letters that said that at the time that they split Poland they would return Vilna to Lithuania. For 400 years, Vilna had belonged to Lithuania until the Poles took it after World War One. They were trying to make a good impression on the world to correct the injustice done to Vilna by the Poles.

When Rabbi Ozer Grodzinsky realised that Vilna would become part of Lithuania, he sent messages to all the Rosh Yeshivas and told them come to Vilna with all their bochurim. In Poland you were either part of communist Russia or German. Twenty-two yeshivas took advantage of this agreement, and, with the great scholars of Poland, they settled in Vilna. The borders would be open for a certain period of time and then they would be closed. My family went to Vilna, as did other great people such as Rav Shach and Reb Aaron Kotler.

Yeshivat Mir came to Vilna in its entirety, with hundreds of bochurim who were issued exit visas. After nine or ten months the Russians decided to take over Lithuania and closed down the embassies, making it hard to leave Vilna. However, before that event, thousands of Jews were able to arrange their escape. When the Russians took over, all the people in Vilna that had requested an exit from Vilna to overseas were suspected of being enemies of the communist system and they were sent to Siberia. Although this was a harsh edict it saved many from perishing in the fires of the holocaust.

The communists looked for my father, since his name was on their list. The names of my mother and the children were not on the list. They only looked for Yitzchak Orlansky. When my father went to shul to daven on Shabbos, he didn't come back. He stayed in the shul. On Tuesday night I joined my father in the shul and that night the Russians broke into the shul, arresting both my father and I. In June 1941, together with hundreds of yeshiva bocherim and fellow Jews, we were transported to Siberia.

My father and I travelled for two weeks on a train in cattle wagons, until we came to Barnaul, a big city in

Siberia. From the train we went on a cargo boat on a river for a thousand kilometres, arriving at a forest. In the forest were huts where we were to live. There was a big wood industry in Siberia, and our job was to cut down and saw up huge trees.

The Shofar my father made

In the train my father made a decision that he would do his utmost not to desecrate Shabbos. The Russians had a rule that anyone aged over sixty could not be forced to work seven days a week. It was 1941, and my father was aged forty-three. Since he was a Rabbi and had a beard, it was not difficult for him to look sixty-five. I was aged sixteen but with the short pants my father asked me to wear, I looked thirteen, and as a young person I, too, was not obliged to work. Anyone who did not work received only half a portion of food. We happily accepted this. All my friends were forced to work on Shabbos.

We arrived in Siberia close to Rosh Hashanah, but we had no shofar to blow for the numerous Jews. My father looked around in all kinds of places to see how he could make a shofar. In a nearby slaughterhouse he found a head. Although he had no tools, he took the shofar from the head, and with a big nail that he found, started digging in the shofar with the nail to hollow it out. For several days he alternately held the nail in a fire until it was red-hot and then dug and dug with the nail until the shofar was hollow. We used this shofar every year until 1946.

By the end of 1941 a Polish exile government had been established in London who was able to make an agreement with Moscow that all Polish citizens taken to Siberia were not prisoners but free Russians. We could now leave the forest and go and live in Barnaul. We had to fulfil all Russian demands, but we didn't work on Shabbos.

In 1943 my father was caught teaching religion, which was forbidden. He was arrested, tried and sentenced to five years in prison. I was now alone. I wrote lots of letters to Molotov and to the authorities in Moscow. After intervention from America, my father was released after one and a half years.

A week after we left Vilna, the Germans proclaimed war with Russia and occupied the town. My mother, my brother and my sisters remained in German occupied Vilna in the Ponar ghetto. The Germans dug huge graves in a forest outside Vilna, brought thousands of people there and shot them. In 1945 we discovered that my family's fate was to die in these graves.

Selma Kaminetsky
born in 1918

'Brother can you spare a dime?'

M y father was born in the 1880's in Vilna. After his Bar Mitzvah at the age of thirteen, his grandmother sent him with his father to America in order to earn sufficient money to bring the rest of the family over. In America they opened a button factory and later a pleating factory, which at that time were in fashion. In due course they earned enough money to bring over the rest of the family.

My mother was born in 1898, the year of the Spanish American war and the year the United States annexed Hawaii. She worked on one of the pleating machines in the factory and at the age of eighteen she married my father.

I was born on the East side of New York where the religious immigrants began to flood in. The pressure to work on Shabbos was so great at that time that it is hard for us in our day now to understand it. Many observant newcomers to American shores succumbed to it in order to support themselves and their families. My parents did not work on Shabbos. My father forbade us to play with anyone who was not religious and my mother forbade us to talk to them.

We had a bathtub in our tenement but the toilet was in the hall outside our apartment and was shared by all the families on our floor. We had a leather chaise, which we called a 'lunch.' We did not have electricity and therefore there was no refrigeration. We had an icebox in the kitchen and I remember having constantly to empty the basin of water under the icebox. The lights were gas jets.

We washed diapers by hand in the tub, but other laundry was given to the laundry service. It was cheaper if the laundry was returned wet, but those who could afford it had the laundry returned washed, dried, ironed and folded.

When my grandfather died, my father closed the factory and became a butcher in Boro Park. My father made sure to wash the meat every three days even though this made the meat dark, and he needed to sell it within a day or two. Many butchers, who claimed high standards of kashrus, did not wash the meat, since they could not sell meat that became dark.

My mother bought chickens from the chicken market and plucked the feathers out by hand. I remember that there was a telephone in the corner of the store, which was directly across the road from us. Although we did not have one in our house, our neighbour had a telephone. She received our calls and came to tell us that a call was waiting.

My sister remembers her first day at school when she was five years old. She asked our mother to go with her, because she knew that all the children went with their mothers. Mother said to her, 'don't be afraid, you can go alone because Hashem is watching.'

After Shabbos my mother enjoyed going to the silent movies as a weekly treat. There was no such thing as baby sitters and the children went with her. When I was barely able to reach the ironing board I would spend the whole of my only free day, Sunday, ironing.

This was the time when a person with a fever was placed in a tub of cold water. In order to avoid contracting polio, one put camphor balls around the neck. Burns were treated with butter. Doctors made house calls, but people did not go regularly to the dentist and eyeglasses were not usually worn. You had buckteeth and you couldn't see.

During the depression, families were barely able to make ends meet. Every family had a ration book. I remember having coupons for an Hungarian dish called mamaliga and coffee. I had never drunk coffee before, but when it became available on coupons, I started to drink it. I saw men selling apples in the street and waiting on breadlines singing 'brother, can you spare a dime?' However, because everyone in our neighbourhood was poor, we did not see rich men throwing themselves out of the window. My Uncle Phillip, who was single and owned the prosperous Boston Post lumber company, used to visit us every month to pay our grocery bill.

My mother refused to allow us to play cards or to use bad language. A red bar of lifebuoy soap was kept to wash out the mouth of any child who used bad language. At a time when few people had cars, my mother bought a car. There were no traffic lights and policemen would stand at the intersections directing traffic. My neighbourhood was on the policeman's beat. He knew everyone as he walked round.

During the Second World War, I heard stories of atrocities committed by Hitler, but in common with other Americans, I could not believe them. I believed that the Jews would be persecuted in America as they were in Europe. The city went dark as the lights went out. If your lights were on without blackout material, the Police would fine you.

We listened to President Roosevelt, every week on the radio as he told us what was going on with our boys in the European and Pacific theatres. He told us where the army was, but we never got the nitty gritty of why they were there. We never knew the extent of the atrocities of the holocaust, until the refugees came over and told us. President Roosevelt didn't tell us the truth.

Oscar Mareni
born in 1907

'For years the Governor preserved old Jerusalem'

On Tisha B'Av in 1934 I arrived in Jerusalem from Czechoslovakia. In those days there was always trouble at the Kottel. The English forbad the blowing of the shofar at the Wall and made every effort to find it. The English Police stood along the narrow streets of the Old City looking at the passing girls to see who had the shofar. They could only look; it was forbidden to search them. For this reason it was normally hidden by girls.

The Kottel was wonderful at that time and even more impressive than it is today. The space between the wall and the Arab houses was only two feet and you had to look up to see the big stones. The effect was awe inspiring and it made more of an impact than today when you have the space in front. There was no separation between men and women; they stood together without a mechitzah and sitting down was forbidden. When the Jews wanted to introduce benches at the Kottel, especially for Tisha B'Av, the English Police denied their request and fights broke out between them.

The Jews tried for years to remove the W.C., which was situated on the way to the Kottel about twenty metres away in a narrow road on the corner. Sewage from the toilet flowed all the way to the wall and fouled the air. The British Authorities refused to move it and it remained there until after the formation of the State of Israel.

The house in which I was born in Czechoslovakia

Jerusalem at that time was a very small Capital since all the surrounding suburbs we see now did not exist. At that time Egypt was under British Colonial rule. The first Governor of Jerusalem was an English Official who came from Egypt. For years he preserved old Jerusalem. He promulgated a law that within a circle around the City, no changes could be made without the agreement of the government. This was a significantly historical event because the first mayor of Jerusalem was ready to destroy all the walls of the Old City.

There were never elections in Palestine until the autumn of 1934 when a law was promulgated forcing municipalities to elect leaders. Before 1934 there was an Arab burgomaster for Jerusalem appointed by the English government. This burgomaster was sent into exile to an island in the Indian Ocean for his political activities against the English.

At that time the temporary English Military Authority had an official gazette called the Palestine Gazette. They wanted to transfer its ownership into private hands and put it up for sale. I knew the man who bought it and turned it into the Palestine Post. Subsequently it became the Jerusalem Post.

When I arrived in Israel in 1934, the economic and political situation was very bad. It seemed as if nothing existed. As an unskilled worker working in construction, I was frequently unemployed. During the period of immigration from Germany there were Doctors working on construction sites. Politically, the English government and the Jewish people of Israel had different views about the direction of the Country. The Jews from other Nations tried in every imaginable way to reach Palestine and the English did everything possible to prevent it. This caused friction. Illegal ships arrived, and they were redirected to Mauritius in the Indian Ocean. They were not allowed to dock in Israel.

During the troubles between 1936 and 1939 the Arabs positioned themselves against the English. In 1911 Jaffa was mainly populated by Arabs, so most of the Jews left Jaffa and founded Tel Aviv.

I knew some of the founders of Tel Aviv. Akiva Weiss had the idea to found a Jewish city. He bought the first house in Tel Aviv, constructed on the corner of Herzl Street. The town's first name was Achuzath Bayit.

In 1935 the Arabs attacked the remaining Jews in Jaffa, and killed a few of them. I had moved to Tel Aviv and together with other residents of that town travelled to Jaffa to burn down the City. However the Haganah prevented us. The English Police did not want to fight first and stood behind the Haganah. If the Jews had gone past the Haganah the Police would have been forced to act. In the Middle East you can't remain silent when something is done to you without losing face.

As a result of the troubles in Jaffa the Arabs wanted the Jews to die of hunger. At that time the port at Tel Aviv did not exist and all shipping came through the port at Jaffa. All port employees were Arabs so enacting their plan was not difficult. They stopped all ships coming into the port at Jaffa and they refused to carry any goods addressed to Jews and Jewish institutions.

In those days the Jews were heavily dependent on Arab merchants and agriculture. The Arabs sold their goods so cheaply that all the Jews bought from them. As a result Jewish agriculture hardly existed. When the Arabs declared their boycott on providing food and goods to Jews in order to force them out of Eretz Yisroel, everything changed.

That was a blessing for the Jewish settlements that had been unable to compete against the cheaper and better-established Arabs. The kibbutzim were so poor that they only had one knife and fork on the table and these were attached to a chain. They sold what they produced and only left a minimum for themselves. The Arab boycott enabled the kibbutzim to produce and sell their produce without competition. In one day it became a sellers market. This was the beginning of the flowering of the kibbutzim and the settlements.

It wasn't long before the Jews imported goods from Egypt and Syria and this went on until World War Two.

In 1936 war broke out between Italy and Ethiopia. The English fleet stood in the Mediterranean ready to attack Italy over Ethiopia. As the daily threat of war loomed closer the Jewish sector made preparations to stockpile goods. The Jewish Agency warned everyone to buy food and established a line of credit for Jewish importers to buy more foodstuffs. Everything was very cheap at this time.

We were worried about the Jews in Europe because the situation was very dangerous and the outbreak of war appeared certain. The Jewish Agency sent a number of volunteers to help the Jewish communities in Europe. We had the impression that the Jews in Europe didn't realise that their lives were in imminent danger. The Zionists in Europe had a different attitude. In 1934 I left my family to go to Eretz Yisroel. Only one of my brothers survived the war from my entire family. I was certain that Hitler would do as he said he would do. The majority of Jews in Europe said that as soon as Hitler would become the ruler of Germany, he would speak another language. He would be interested in the businesses and industries of the Jews, and nothing would happen. It was only talk, and in any event there would be pressure from America.

In Palestine there was a different attitude because we were certain he would do what he said. We did everything legally and illegally to get Jews out of Germany. At the same time we prepared ourselves economically. The Jewish Agency was prepared to give money to small industries to buy materials and machinery from Europe. We were absolutely certain that war would break out.

On Mt. Carmel we prepared a place of last resistance and this is where the Haganah would fight in Palestine. I was in the Royal Air Force serving in East Africa during the Second World War. I did not see my wife for two and a half years. The war situation looked very grim. General Rommel, who led the German army, was near Alexandria and the whole of North Africa was in his hands. He wanted to join with the Balkans but Palestine was in his way. Syria was French and was in his hands.

El Alamein was where the Germans were finally stopped. General Koenig came from Africa and the French joined with the English under Montgomery. The Germans were forced to leave Africa and retreat to Italy. I was discharged from the army in 1944.

When I came back to Palestine things had changed drastically. Palestine had been a poor country with nothing to offer to the Jewish sector. Now it was rich because the whole of the British Empire bought whatever Palestine could produce. A friend of mine produced zips, which he made manually with primitive machinery. The British army was ready to buy everything he made, and he became rich. The English were ready to bring machinery to serve the immense army including Australians and New Zealanders, but transport was complicated and dangerous. German U-boats were in the waters. It was imperative to produce as much as possible in Palestine and not rely on transport.

After the war, the war offices were dismantled and hundreds of Jews employed in the military offices were discharged and the offices closed. Palestine was a hinterland for the army. A great number of people were

now without an income. In addition there was friction between the Jewish population and the English government, who did everything to prevent the immigration of even a single Jew.

The Jewish military organisations started to become active and waged a real war against the English military. One of their most notorious military victories was the explosion of a wing in the King David Hotel where the government offices were situated, and English government officials working in them were killed. There was also an explosion in the Income Tax office. It was then the English took illegal counter action and introduced explosives into the Jewish Agency compound.

At that time the Arabs were passive and happy to see the English and the Jews fighting each other. Therefore they felt there was no need for them to do anything. The next English attack changed the face of the war with an explosion in Ben Yehudah Street, the main centre of Jewish commerce. At six o'clock in the morning, when everyone was asleep, the English blew up the Palestine Post.

After that the look of Jerusalem became different. In all strategic areas the Jews put dragon teeth in the road. This type of cement construction meant that the cars were now under the control of the Haganah. In Rehov Jaffa there was a pit over which there was an iron plate that could easily be removed. The Haganah now had full control over every passing car. Up until that point the English had been in control. The English now only passed in convoy and with permission of the Jewish military Authorities. This was in the winter of 1947/48.

I was in hospital for eight months at this time so I didn't take part in the declaration of the State of Israel. I was standing on an island in Zion Square, which no longer exists, when the English threw incendiary bombs. Both the feet of my wife were burnt and although a passer by threw her down and put out the fire, she was still burnt on ten per cent of her body. My son only had a burn on his shoe. I received third degree burns on eighteen per cent of my body. I was an old soldier and I knew what to do to save my life. I threw myself down and started to roll. In my left hand I had a thick book of the United Nations Palestine Commission reporting on the situation regarding the partition, which I had just bought. I put it against the lower part of my body and with my right hand I was able to put out part of the fire. My shoes and trousers were on fire but passers by came to help me.

At that time there were quite a number of incidents. If the siren sounded to start the curfew everyone had to remain at home.

In 1896 Theodore Herzl wrote a book, called Judenstat, which became the foundation of the Zionist movement. The translation of the Hebrew name of the book is Tel Aviv. Recently, when I met the President of the State of Israel in his official residence, I presented him with a copy of the book written in Gothic German for his library. I said to the President, 'without this book written by Herzl you wouldn't be here.'

Speranza
born in 1922

Holidays, lazy days and spies

I t was in 1938 that the Prime Minister of Great Britain, Neville Chamberlain, went to Berlin to negotiate peace with Adolf Hitler. At home, nevertheless, Britain prepared for war.

My father, a volunteer Air Raid Warden, had a steel helmet with A.R.P, Air Raid Precautions, on the front. He spent his free time fitting and distributing gas-masks to the residents of our neighbourhood, the St. John's Wood catchment area of London.

The government decided that in the event of war, all children would be evacuated from London. In that eventuality, my family would transfer to our tall, later Georgian terraced house by the sea in Sussex, our holiday home. This so delighted my brother and me that I felt positively guilty that war could bring me such delight. I had always wanted to live there permanently.

Mr Chamberlain returned to England with the hoped for outcome — 'Peace in our time.' The nation was overjoyed. The family remained in London during term time.

However, war preparations, including accelerated Territorial Army manoeuvres, continued. 'The Terriers', as they were known, were part-time soldiers who bivouacked annually under canvas with their military regiments, for military exercises.

During one of our holiday stays in Sussex that year, my father rode his horse as usual over the South Downs. I rode, like my mother, gently through the local fields and bridle-paths, or along the beach. My father had forgotten the presence of the Terriers.

On this occasion, he collected the horse from stables in Arundel and, riding on the Downs, found himself on a woodland ride, blocked at its end by a locked farm gate. Instead of obeying the 'No Entry' sign, he turned his horse for a run-up and they leaped over the gate into a woodland glade. There they were ambushed by a group of men in Arab dress. The horse was seized and my father was handcuffed and taken for interrogation.

The officers before whom he stood congratulated him on his wily infiltration into their camp as an enemy spy and asked to see his papers. My father explained that his civilian identity card was in his locker at the stables in Arundel. Amid howls of laughter, the Commanding Officer said 'nice one!' and put him under guard as an enemy prisoner. Only with the help of the local police did mother finally secure his release — and that of the horse.

My pocket money did not stretch to much riding, so I spent much of the summer holiday in 1938 working at a local hacking stable. Grooming, mucking out, drain clearing, feeding, watering, exercising and turning out to pasture paid partially for my rides. One day, a young man, who had booked his ride by 'phone, walked into the stable yard to pick up his mount. He was tall, with cropped fair hair and wore a military style black shirt. Such a garment was worn by Sir Oswald Moseley's virulently and violently anti-Semitic British Union of Fascists, 'the Blackshirts.'

The young man mounted the horse saying that he required no escort since he was an officer in the German cavalry. 'You are welcome to ride alone' said Mrs Gordon, the stable manager, 'when you have removed those spiked spurs. They are not necessary and they are cruel.'

'Nein' he answered

'Kindly dismount and remove your spurs before you ride, Mrs Gordon insisted.

'Nein, Nein' he shouted 'Heil Hitler!' and turned to ride away. The usually even- tempered, red-headed Scotswoman, Mrs Gordon, smacked the horse on its hindquarters, and, as it shied, grasped the man by arm and ankle and hauled him from the saddle. Surprise yielded success and as he got up from the cobblestones, she grabbed a pitchfork and saw him off the premises.

It was during that holiday that our friends next door had added a new cook to their domestic staff. 'A wonderful pastry cook' said Mrs B. to my mother, a week or so later. Mother asked Mrs B. whether Hitler's plain cooking was as good as her pastry. 'Why do you call Maria, Hitler?' asked Mrs B. 'Mother said 'as a Jewess I am hypersensitive about Germany because of the persecution of Jews in Germany.' 'I do understand and sympathise. It's intolerable, replied Mrs B., 'but Maria is doing no harm.'

'Are you sure?' retorted Mother, 'how does a domestic servant acquire crocodile handbag and shoes and a silver fox fur, all of which she wears on her afternoons off.' 'That is interesting, isn't it,' laughed Mrs B. uncomfortably.

My brother and I loved the top room at the front of our house. From its dormer windows, on a very clear day, we could see the coast of France. Outside the windows was a narrow gully, running in front of all the houses in the terrace, between the house wall and a window sill height stone parapet. I was gazing out to sea, as usual, when my brother came into the room and dared me to crawl along the gully past the adjacent houses. I was just too large, so he went alone, but quickly returned and climbed back into the room.

'Listen,' he whispered, 'what can you hear?'

'Seagulls' I said, and waited. After a few silent moments I heard a sound I could only associate with films, black and white in those days, about spies. Morse code transmission! The sound was repeated at intervals and we were sure that we had defined it correctly. My brother's knowledge of Morse code and my school room German were not equal to the needs of the moment.

We discussed our next move. During the past two years we had played detective and had twice caught real life thieves. The second, which we had reported to the police, had resulted in their having rounded up a gang of antique silver thieves. For us it had yielded a police warning to keep out of danger and leave police work to the police.

'We had better tell Mother, once we have found out whether this is 'Hitler's' bedroom and the most usual times of transmission' I whispered, as we closed the window.

It was indeed 'Hitler's' room. We logged transmission times and reported to our mother, who rang the police.

Some days later we saw Maria, wearing her silver fox fur in midsummer, being escorted away by two police officers. We never saw her again. Our neighbour, Mrs B. so hated shop made cakes.

In 1939 war was evidently imminent. Instead of returning to the sixth form, prior to university entrance, I remained with our household in Sussex and enrolled at the West Sussex school of Art to prepare for a teaching qualification.

Heavy guns were mounted along the sea front and windows were criss-crossed with adhesive tape to prevent shattering by blast. Roads leading inland were barricaded with old bedsteads and discarded farm machinery, laced and secured with barbed wire. We spent a lot of time helping to fill sand bags on the beach, to fortify the sea front, between the gun emplacements fortified by the military. The Home Guard was formed, but armaments did not arrive, so they were armed with sporting rifles and pitchforks, the fiercest available weapons.

On the day war was declared, Dr Alexander had been called to see my feverish, itching brother, and he joined us to hear the Prime Minister's broadcast declaration of war on Germany. On declaration of war, our doctor was to report to the hospital in Chichester. Prescribing medication for my brother before leaving, his parting words were 'a fine time to have German measles!'

In the summer of 1940, the army decided that our first floor balconies were ideal machine gun posts. Every resident in the terrace was given ten days notice to leave.

Our Rabbi and his family were spending their summer holiday nearby. They had relatives in Lancashire, now Merseyside, where they decided to go for the duration of the war. Our Hebrew teacher, who travelled from London to teach us, would now have some difficulty, and with no home to live in, our parents were persuaded to travel to the North-West. My brother was accepted in a school and I was accepted in the College of Art.

Thus it was that we were severed from the clear sunlight, gentle hills and coast of Sussex and lost a much loved home, but we all lived to give thanks, at its end, for having survived the war.

Rabbi **Yehudah Broyde**
born in 1918

'I still daven in the Mir minyan, but there are only two or three of us left'

I went to the Mir Yeshiva in Poland in 1933 at the age of fifteen, as my father wanted me to learn in an environment away from New York, where I was living at the time. I joined my brother, who was already learning there, together with many American boys who had their Bar Mitzvah in the Mir Yeshiva.

I travelled to Mir on my own, although there were other people travelling to Poland, on the 'Olympic', a boat owned by the Cunard White Star line. Kosher food was served in the kosher dining room, with its own mashgiach, for passengers who wanted kosher food.

The boat landed at Sherbourne, where I was met by a man from the Cunard line and escorted to the international train. We travelled for two days through Germany to reach Poland and although my mother had given me some toasted honey cake to give to my brother I didn't have any other food with me. That was my food on the train. I saved a few slices for my brother so that he should taste food from home. My brother met me at the station and we travelled the sixteen kilometres to Mir in a horse and wagon. I shared his room for six months until we had separate accommodation.

My Rosh Yeshiva was Rabbi Lazer Yehudah Finkel and the mashgiach was Rabbi Yerucham Levovitz, considered one of the greatest men in Mussar at that time. The mashgiach gave shiurim on Gemorrah, yireh, bitachon and

*In Mir, Poland. I am walking behind
Rabbi Chaim Shmulevitz
and Rabbi Yeruchalm Levovitz*

Avodas Hashem. Rabbi Yisroel Salanter had started a yeshiva in Lithuania and his group of bocherim, which at that time included Yerucham Levovitz, were known for their piety, ethics, and scholarship. They devoted their studies to Avodas Hashem and discussed moral issues.

The yeshiva was one tremendous room that had no pillars supporting the ceiling. There was special construction in the attic to keep the ceiling up. Four hundred people sat and learned in the room. We sat, nine to a bench, but everyone had their own shtender and their own Seforim. The yeshiva had a library of commentaries of the Rishonim and the Acharonim.

The schedule was unchanging apart from a half an hour difference in the time of Shacharis between the winter and the summer. In the morning at seven thirty we davened for about an hour, and then individuals had their own seder, either by themselves or with a chavrusa, until nine o'clock. Groups of five to ten boys would eat together in the house of one of the townspeople. We paid the lady of the house every month to shop, cook and serve three meals a day. I paid thirty-five zlotys, around seven dollars, for a month.

For breakfast I had bread, butter, eggs and coffee. In the summer we were given small berries with smetana. After breakfast the seder would start at ten o'clock until noon, learning with a chavrusa. From noon until two o'clock I learned with my Rebbe, who was one of the older boys in the yeshiva, whom I paid. At two o'clock we learnt mussar on our own and at two thirty we davened Mincha. The boys then usually went for a walk before going to their respective houses to have lunch.

For lunch we had a little soup and chicken or meat. Around four o'clock we went back to the yeshiva and then I had a second Rebbe, again one of the older boys, for two and a half to three hours. I then learnt with a chavrusa, after which we learnt mussar for half an hour and davened Ma'ariv. The seder finished around nine-thirty. Since I was still a young boy I usually had supper before Ma'ariv. The bocherim were usually still fleishig at suppertime and could not eat milchig. In any event it was a light meal served with cocoa.

On one occasion when my father sent me money, I bought a goose for six zlotys in order to have something differ-ent to eat. The woman of the house had it shechted for one zloty and then she plucked out the feathers. She sold the down feathers for one zloty, which

The library in Mir, Poland.
Rabbi Benish Finkel is seated in the middle at the front. He was twenty years old and eventually became the Rosh Yeshiva of Mir. I am standing on the ladder at the back.

Sitting on the bench in the middle is Rabbi Shimon Shkop with his son-in-law Reb Feivel and Reb Boruch Ber on either side

were used to fill pillows. The fat of the goose, the schmaltz, she used for cooking and sold the rest for making candles. The bones she sold to make fertilizer. From the meat ten people ate well for two days. Since there was no refrigeration the meat had to be eaten quickly. Every part of the goose was used.

Every three or four weeks I discussed my learning with the Rosh Yeshiva. Twice a week, on Sundays and Thursdays he gave a gemorrah shiur to the whole Yeshiva and on Tuesdays the Rav of the town would give the gemorrah shiur. Every week the Mashgiach gave a mussar shiur to the whole yeshiva.

Since I was an American boy I heard the stories that were told about Rabbi Yehudah Davis's brush with the goyim. The goyim did not expect anyone to stand against them and after the incident with Rabbi Davis [see his story] they made a complaint to the Police. Rabbi Davis was told to leave the country, so he went and learnt in Telshe yeshiva. We all had problems with the goyim.

In 1939 the Germans were constantly threatening the surrounding countries and the Polish government decided to mobilise the soldiers. My cook's uncle was the town wagon driver and he delivered goods, such as material and shoes, for the townspeople to the train station and back to the village. Half of the house where I ate was the stable for the horse and the way into the house was through the stable. When the soldiers were mobilised they slept on the hay in the stable.

The people of the town became used to the threats by the Germans and eventually didn't take any notice of them. The soldiers were constantly mobilised by the government and then disbanded. This went on for half a year and the Poles in the town were not frightened of war, or of anything happening because the coming and going of the soldiers was routine.

Just after Pesach, and just before Germany would invade Poland, my parents sent me a ticket to return home. I went to discuss the matter with my Rosh Yeshiva, Rabbi Finkel, who said that if my parents had called me I had no choice but to go. After six years of learning in the Mir Yeshiva in Poland I returned to America.

After the war we started a Mir minyan in Brooklyn. I still daven with that minyan, but there are only two or three people left who learnt in the Mir in Poland. The minyan also comprises those individuals who joined the Mir yeshiva in Shanghai from the other European yeshivas. One of the members of the minyan is a fellow who was born in Mir, Poland, whose brother went to the yeshiva in Mir. He told me the following story.

After the Germans invaded Poland, the townspeople experienced the fever of war. The town of Mir was a

I am walking with Rabbi Chaim Shmulevitz in Mir in Poland

Jewish town with a population of five hundred families and the goyim lived on the periphery of the town. When the Germans entered Mir they rounded up the whole of the Jewish population, and led them out of town into the woods. The Rav of the town spoke to everyone when they were rounded up and he told them to have faith in Hashem, encouraging them as much as he was able.

The Germans then shot the whole town and threw them into ditches. This fellow threw himself into the ditch without being shot, but acted as if he had been. Several other people also did the same thing. At night, after the Germans had left the scene, they crept out of the ditches.

As soon as the Germans invaded Poland the whole yeshiva moved to Vilna, although some of the bocherim went home and never returned to the Yeshiva. The Russians invaded Vilna and when there was a threat that Vilna was going to be given to Poland, the yeshiva moved on to Lithuania. The bocherim learned in different shuls and when the Germans came closer, the Yeshiva went into Russia and travelled to Vladivostock. Some of the bocherim remained there but the bulk of the yeshiva, together with bocherim from other Yeshivas went to Japan. The Japanese consul in Vladivostock gave them exit visas to Japan in contravention of the orders of the government. Eventually, after many years in Shanghai the Mir yeshiva went to East New York.

I was twenty-one when I returned to America and I lived in Manhattan and learned in the local yeshiva. The Vaad Hatzolah in New York tried, in every way, to raise money for the refugees in Lithuania and Vilna. They needed to raise money for visas and transport in order that the refugees would be able to travel. There were times when the Rabbis even travelled to Washington on Shabbos in order to help the refugees. The American government gave a few visas, but not many. Agudas Rabbonim got together to do everything they could for their fellow Jews in Europe, but tragically the American government did not support them.

Cissie [Simcha] Flegg
born in 1924

My father handed over the Shul
to the Mir Yeshiva

My grandfather, Avraham ben Yechezkel, was born in Iraq in the middle of the 19th century. He eventually moved to India and settled in Bombay.

At that time the Sassoon family controlled the franchise for the opium trade in India. To strengthen their business, the Sassoons gave a tremendous amount of money to the British Crown. In return, when China closed the borders of Shanghai to the Sassoon family because opium was killing so many people, Britain went to war with China around 1880 in order to reopen the borders.

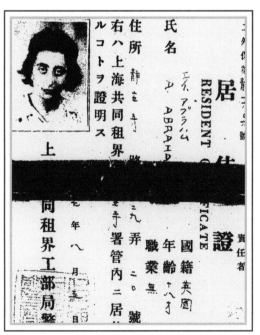

My Shanghai Resident's Certificate

China was defeated by Britain and the borders of Shanghai became internationalised. Once the borders were open, Jews migrated to Shanghai from the Yemen, Iraq, India and other surrounding areas in the near and far East. Shanghai required a mashgiach to supervise kashrus for the growing Jewish population, so the Sassoons asked my grandfather to assume the position. My grandfather moved from Bombay to Shanghai in the year 1896, and became mashgiach.

Both my parents were born in India while Queen Victoria was Queen of England and Empress of India, thus making them British citizens. My father, Moshe Hai ben Avraham was born in Bombay in 1890 and needed a passport in order to travel to Shanghai. Under British Law he needed a surname, which was not the traditional surname of the son of the father's first name. He dropped the word ben and adopted the name Avraham, his father's first name, as his surname.

I was born in Shanghai in 1924 amidst a very colourful Jewish life. There were, at the time, only 2,000 Jews at most, amongst millions of Chinese. These small numbers did not deter Jews from flocking there to do business. There was no anti Semitism whatsoever. The Chinese were afraid of the non-Chinese, however, especially in the side villages in the countryside,

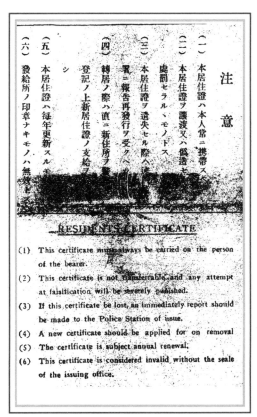

注意

(一) 本居住證ハ本人常ニ携帯ス

(二) 本居住證ハ讓渡又ハ偽造ヲ處罰セラル、モノトス

(三) 本居住證ヲ遺失セル際ハ速ニ署ニ報告ヲ再發行ヲ受ク

(四) 轉居ノ際ハ直ニ新住所ヲ登記ノ上新居住證ノ支給ヲ

(五) 本居住證ハ毎年更新スルモ

(六) 發給所ノ印章ナキモノハ無

RESIDENT'S CERTIFICATE

(1) This certificate must always be carried on the person of the bearer.

(2) This certificate is not transferable and any attempt at falsification will be severely punished.

(3) If this certificate be lost, an immediately report should be made to the Police Station of issue.

(4) A new certificate should be applied for on removal

(5) The certificate is subject annual renewal.

(6) This certificate is considered invalid without the seale of the issuing office.

where they regarded the non-Chinese as the white devil.

In Shanghai we had a private house with servants wherever we lived. The servants had their specific tasks. One servant washed the clothes; another cooked and served at the table, yet another accompanied my mother shopping, which was done at the local market. Mother walked there with a Chinese boy and after making her purchases, loaded them up on a rickshaw. Rickshaws were carriages with two wheels drawn by a man who would run if he was taking passengers, but who walked with my mother and the boy while carrying her shopping.

The price for the rickshaw was determined beforehand by arguing first. You didn't get into one without bargaining, because the drivers felt cheated otherwise. This was their way of life. If you didn't haggle over the price, they felt that they had undercharged.

We didn't have a refrigerator, only an icebox. At the end of each day left over cooked food was never kept. Every evening at least six beggars were outside the door waiting for food. The cook or a boy emptied out the perishable food from our pots into their cans, which they brought with them. There was always a lot of poverty in this densely populated country.

When we walked to school it was common to see dead bodies on the way. A truck drove around and the driver threw all the dead bodies into it. Disease was evident on the people, wasting away, lying in the streets. They had no homes, only hunger and starvation

I was fourteen years of age when a friend took me to see an opium den. The strong, sweet smell of opium hung in the air as we approached. I peeped inside and saw living skeletons either sleeping or smoking opium. All they did all day was to smoke opium, doze off, then smoke opium again, day after day, until they died. I asked my father, 'how can people trade in opium?' My father said that people needed opium for pain, if they used it as a drug, it wasn't wrong. It was not a sin to misuse opium. I couldn't agree with him and I never went near an opium den again. The sight of it nauseated me. The opium smokers used every cent they could to buy opium. They weren't suffering; they just wasted away. They were decaying, slowly rotting, then leaving this world.

In 1937 Japan occupied part of Shanghai. By 1940 they occupied the whole of Shanghai. We were living in a part of Shanghai that was not safe. August 15th 1937 was Bloody Saturday. My parents stayed at home to watch the house while the children walked to a safer area. We walked for an hour and a half. The occupation had taken its toll and we saw bodies hanging from wires as a consequence of the battles.

We made our way to my father's first cousin who had moved to Shanghai from Iraq, where he was the watchman for the tomb of Ezra. The tomb was known as a place where you could go and pray for a cure for an illness, and then you would recover. Even the Moslems recognised the sanctity of the tomb and also prayed there.

Japan entered the war against the United States and Britain, and all citizens of those countries were restricted in their movements. We were compelled to wear a red armband; on mine was displayed the number B [for British] 2215. In addition we were obligated to carry a resident's certificate at all times, and could not go into public places. At the whim of the Japanese, roadblocks were set up, preventing pedestrians from crossing the road until the siren sounded.

At this time my mother was heavily pregnant with my brother. She thought that roadblocks would prevent her from reaching the hospital and took the precaution of applying for, and receiving, the necessary permit. I was walking with my mother to the hospital, carrying a bag with all the necessary baby clothes when a roadblock was set up, and we were not allowed to cross the road. My mother showed the permit to the Japanese guards but they refuse to allow her to cross, threw the bag and its contents onto the road and pointed their bayonets at her stomach.

At that moment a man approached my mother and said, 'don't worry; don't pursue it. I am a doctor; I can help you. There is a hospital on this side of the road.' At that moment the siren went and we reached the hospital in time.

Germany was applying pressure on Japan to eliminate the Jews. While this was going on, over 15,000 German Jewish refugees came through the open border into Shanghai. We couldn't help them because our bank account was frozen.

Ever since Bloody Saturday, families abandoned the area where we lived. My father was the Chacham, the Sephardi Rabbi, in the big synagogue built by Mr Hardoon, from Iraq. It had three floors, the ground floor was for weddings and receptions, the next floor was for the men to daven and the top floor was for the women to daven. It had its own kitchen and mikveh.

By the time the Mir Yeshiva arrived, the shul had not been used for a long time. My father had leined in the shul, had blown shofar, was the shochet, but now he handed the building over to the Mir Yeshiva. We were British, and there was no reason for us to stay in the area. This area was Honkew, an area for stateless people like the bochurim who had been made stateless by the war.

In April 1943 we were interned in the Lungwah camp, an abandoned army base, on the outskirts of Shanghai, but not before the Japanese had entered our home and labelled all our furniture 'the property of the Japanese.' During the next few years they re-entered the house and removed all the metal, the door handles and the plumbing, anything that could be used as armaments for the war. Two and a half years later, when we returned, the furniture, minus the metal was still there, as we had left it.

In the internment camp everyone was assigned camp duties. My father arranged kashrus for the 48 Jews who required it, out of 17,000 British, American and Dutch internees. I worked in the sick bay, while my mother did her weekly share of cooking. Each hut had either 30 single men or single women; my parents had their own room, which they shared with the younger children. You were supplied with a bed and a shelf, where it was not uncommon to find a dead rat. The water was so hard that when you washed your hair it was impossible to put a comb through it. We were allowed occasional parcels, but otherwise we were not supplied with clothes or shoes, we had to manage with what we had. We put paper or straw in our shoes when the soles wore out. A cigarette ration was given to each person and it was possible to barter with these.

After the Second World War everything changed and the communists took over. The capitalists had their heads chopped off publicly if foreign currency was found on them.

I was a Britisher, so I left Shanghai in 1946 and travelled to England. I worked my passage over as a nurse on the ship. In Britain I was a student nurse and took all the exams until the final exam fell on a Shabbos that was also Yom Kippur. I went to the nursing supervisor and told her that I was sorry, but I could not take the exam for religious reasons and I would take them the next time round.

The nursing superior told me that she would allow me to take the exam, on my own, the Thursday before. I sat in the classroom, on my own, with access to all the textbooks. From time to time someone would come in to check. When I gave in my papers I asked the superior how she felt able to trust me. She said 'if you are willing to forgo the exam for your religion, you can be trusted.'

✦ ✦ ✦

Editors' Note.

Another contributor remembers what life was like in Shanghai during this time.

I came to Shanghai with the Mir Yeshiva and once I stayed in the home of a Chinese man. The floor was black mud and in the middle of the room was a big table, which was pure white. They were making cheese and milk from Soya beans. I remember the contrast between the black and the white.

On the roof was a barrel, which served as their toilet facilities. At three in the morning I awoke to the sound of the cleaning lady cleaning out the barrel. For five years we did not drink water from the tap without boiling it because you could catch Typhus from the water.

People died in the street. I saw a Chinaman fall down and right away another Chinaman came and stole his shoes. If you went to the Police they told you to bury him, so no one went to the Police. Eventually someone did it.

There were no horses. The transport was big wooden boards on wheels, pulled by two chinamen at the front and one or two at the back to steady it. As they went by, the poor people slit the sacks of rice with a knife to steal the rice, or crack the jugs of oil. They caught the oil in their hands, put it on their hair, and squeezed it out of their hair when they got home.

There was a river with a million people living on the boats. There they are born, they get married and then they die, on the boats. The water on the river where the people lived was poisonous and unusable.

Devorah Weinberger Tamari is the daughter in law of Julius Weinberger, who was the administrator of a refugee camp in Shanghai during World War Two. Julius told his daughter in law how the shul in Shanghai came to be built. He told her that Mr. Hardoon had a recurring dream of his father telling him to build a shul in the district of the International Settlement in Shanghai.

After the third dream he spoke to his friend Victor Sassoon, who had moved from Baghdad and was now one of the leaders of the community who funded the settlement of refugees in Shanghai. Refugees leaving Germany were allowed to depart with only ten Marks. However, in order to enter Shanghai one needed one hundred pounds sterling. The Sassoons, together with other wealthy Jews, funded the entry of refugees as well as providing food and shelter.

The Sassoons funded the building of the shul, even though at the time the Jewish community wasn't large enough to justify building such a structure. The instructions in the dream were very explicit, even to the amount of seating and what to put in the kitchen. When the Mir Yeshiva came to Shanghai they moved into the shul.

When the communists came into power in Shanghai, the Jews settled in Hong Kong. In the 1980's Devorah went to Hong Kong and stayed in the Mandarin Hotel, which was owned by the Sassoons. It was there that she met Ernest, son of Victor Sassoon, with whom she discussed this dream. Ernest confirmed that indeed there had been a dream and the shul had been built because of it.

A Lady
born in 1917

'I have seen nothing
but war in my life'

Just before World War One my parents came to Copenhagen from England to visit an Aunt and Uncle who lived there, and they could not leave Denmark when war broke out, nor when the hostilities ended. My father was a tailor and as new immigrants to Denmark we settled in Copenhagen where most of the Danish Jews lived.

I was born during that war the third in a poor family of six children, and I have seen nothing but war in my life. I came to Israel in 1977 because Israel was a place that was always present in my mind. It didn't bother me that there was perpetual war in the country. I was accustomed to it.

We lived in a three-roomed apartment, which included a workshop. After my father died in 1940 my mother continued to run the workshop together with my two brothers. I remember the poverty of my home life as a young girl. I had no bed of my own. We used sofas that we pulled out at night and pushed back during the day. Some of the children slept in my parent's bedroom and some slept in the lounge. We washed in the kitchen because we had no bathroom, only a toilet. Once a week we went to the public baths to have a proper shower.

My Jewish education was minimal. When I came home from school I had to help my mother keep the apartment clean, which was a hard job with very little space and six children.

There was a room in the building downstairs where we did the washing. There was a cauldron on the gas to wash the clothes but first we scrubbed the clothes clean with a metal scrubbing board, a brush and brown soap. Afterwards the clothes were hung out to dry in the yard. To avoid conflicts there was a notice on the wall that listed the day and the time that the washing could be done for each family in the building. We didn't change our clothes every day and we slept in our underwear. I had two dresses for every day and one for Shabbos. One of my sisters had a bladder condition and she always took her sisters' knickers. My mother was always washing knickers in the kitchen sink for us to wear.

We had no toys but I played skipping with my friends and other games such as hinkesten, which was hopscotch, skjul, which was hide and seek, and also sa-fat – a kind of tag.

When the Germans occupied Denmark we were afraid, but for the first three years they did not touch us. When they did start to round up the Jews, they went to every Jewish home and took them in big vans to Germany. Men did not sleep in the house because of the rumours that the Germans would take the men and not the women.

On Rosh Hashanah in 1943 the Rabbi told the congregation of Copenhagen that we had to go into hiding immediately. On the second day of Rosh Hashanah we took the train to the coast where we had been told that a certain priest would hide us. When my mother went to the priest he had changed his mind. It was cold and very stormy and he told us to go to a shed by the sea. We found it and took shelter there. There was no toilet and we had to use a corner of the shed. Suddenly the window fell in. We could not leave the window out because of the storm. My mother searched her pocket and found there a

A typical Danish boat that took refugees to Sweden

very large nail. We banged the window back. I never discovered why she was carrying a nail, but everyone knew it was a nes, a miracle, from Hashem. We had no food and in the morning we went back on the train to our apartment in Copenhagen.

That morning I phoned the office where I worked. They asked me where I was and arranged for the family to come to the office by the back door. When we went to the office, they brought us something to eat. I phoned a friend and he told us to come to Gilleleje, a town with a church where a lot of Jews were hiding. We decided not to go there and later learned that the Germans eventually found and took all the Jews who were hiding there.

My Jewish boss phoned the office and instructed one of the men to help us. He took us to his home in the late afternoon where we went to rest with our clothes on. The lady of the house said she would make us a cup of camomile tea, but before she had made it we were asleep in their beds.

In the middle of the night they woke us up and the man accompanied us on a train to the coast south of Copenhagen. We were taken to a house where there were four or five goyim who got out of their warm beds to let us sleep there. I felt ashamed to sleep in someone else's warm bed. Eventually these goyim woke us up and took us to the water where a boat was waiting for us with other Jews on board. The goyim paid the boatman and he took us to Sweden.

In Sweden we were taken to a school where I fell asleep from exhaustion. Jewish families took us in and I obtained work as a housemaid with a non-Jewish family. My mother went into a refugee camp for Jewish people cared for by the Swedes. I heard there was Jewish camp where I could get work in the office.

I feel that life only started for me when I got married. I was always in love with my husband, even as a young girl when I went to school with his two sisters. The doctor in the office where I had gone to work was this man that I had admired as a schoolgirl. In November 1944 we married and my life finally began.

✦ ✦ ✦

Editors' Note:

Unlike most European countries, Denmark protected its Jewish population. At a time of challenge the Danes succeeded in transporting the vast majority of its Jewish residents to Sweden, which was a neutral power during the Second World War. Unlike the rest of Europe, when the Danish Jews returned after the War, they were welcomed home and found that their homes and belongings had been cared for by their neighbours.

Hanna Yeret
born in 1923

'It was the bread that saved them'

T he night of Kristalnacht was on the 10th November 1938. I was fourteen years old. My father owned a bakery and a pastry shop. We lived in the building that housed the pastry shop at number 9, Northstrasse in Leipzig, Germany; the bakery was in another street nearby.

At 4 a.m. a terrible noise woke me and I looked out of our second floor window. Because we had a corner house I could see my father's bakery. I saw that all our cakes were all over the street. There was a grocery across from the shop that had big glass containers, which held rice, sugar, oil, and herrings. Everything was tossed out on the street amidst lots of broken glass. I remember the smell of the herrings.

My father was at work in the bakery, at this early morning hour, when my mother telephoned him. On this day, all over Germany, there were hooligans on the street. Young boys, dressed in yellow shirts, roaming the streets, especially around the synagogues. Our Beit Knesset was on a nearby street at number 4, Keilstrasse.

At 6:00 a.m. my father came home, accompanied by two young Nazis. One of them worked for my father delivering bread, and gave him away to the S.S., for which he received a reward. The young Nazi told my mother and my grandfather, who lived with us, that they had to go with him. My mother asked him 'where are you taking us?' He responded, 'where all the Jews are going.' My young sister, who was only four years old, was crying.

She had pigtails. One of the boys took her by her pigtails and held her up off the floor, and said 'I will hold you like this until you stop crying.'

As they took our parents and grandfather, I was shivering with fright. When daylight broke, we looked out of the window and saw the Germans throwing Sifrei Torah, Seforim, and tallesim on the street and setting them on fire. My eleven-year-old brother told me that when you see a Sefer Torah burning you have to do kriah; so we tore our clothes. This was the education we had in those days.

Then the doorbell rang and there was banging on the door. It was the Hitler youth. 'Your parents! Your parents!' they shouted and we told them that they had already been taken away. 'You are lying', they shouted and stormed into the house, opening anything that could be opened, sideboard, wardrobes, cupboards, throwing the contents all over the floor. They smashed the mirrors screaming 'we are looking for your parents.' They eventually left.

At about 2 p.m. we received a telephone call from my mother. They were at the Roumanian consulate, a neutral place, and the three of them were all right.

We learned that they were taken to the River Parthe, which is the small river that runs through Leipzig and almost dries up in the summer. Now, in November, the water level was still low. The Germans brought all the people to this river and told them to stand in the riverbed in order that they would not run away. All the Jews were there, young and old, men and women. Big lorries came to take them away to the Dachau Concentration Camp. As my mother was climbing into the lorry a young Nazi spotted her and said, 'Mrs Scheinowitz, you are also here? Go behind me, with your husband and father. To the left is a big street, try to find a place to hide. The railway station is best.' The railway station catered for international traffic and lots of people would be there. The Nazis would not go there because they didn't want people to know what they were doing.

This young Nazi worked as an errand boy in the bakery delivering bread and rolls, and was from a poor family. When he went home at night my mother always gave him a sack of leftover bread and cakes. My mother said it was the bread that saved them.

My parents and grandfather went towards the railway station. In the station they met Roumanian Jews, who were good friends of my father and who were running to the Roumanian Consulate, which was neutral territory. In the evening the Consul told the Roumanians that they could go home. Roumanian Nationals were safe because Roumania had made an agreement with the Germans. The Consul told my parents, 'you come home with me.' In his home were a dozen and a half other Jews.

My mother came home because the news was that women were not being taken to the Concentration Camps because there was no room.

We had an Aunt who lived on the same street, whose husband was Polish. If you were not German you were not taken to the Camps, so my mother decided that it was safer to live with our Aunt. She told the five children to carry what possessions they could and we went to our Aunt.

We made contact with an Uncle who lived in Amsterdam who said he would find someone to smuggle my father and grandfather over the border. The greatest danger was for them not for us.

The Jews knew that the situation was dangerous for them and deteriorating rapidly, so they converted their possessions into precious stones. We couldn't go to Israel because during the time of the British mandate we could not afford a Certificate for Capitalists, which cost 1,000 pounds sterling, for each person including the children. The British were not interested in saving lives or helping the Jewish people, only in making money. We could not go to America because there was an established quota system that was closed at the time. It was not possible to get to Israel until 1948, when the State of Israel was founded.

Meanwhile my father and grandfather stayed for two weeks with the Consul, until someone came to help them get to Amsterdam. A few weeks later my mother took the two younger children to Amsterdam. I stayed with my 9-year-old sister and 11-year-old brother at my Aunt's house, with her two small children. The five children slept crowded into two beds. It was winter and snowing. At nighttime we took a sleigh to rescue possessions from our house. Children playing with a sleigh would not attract suspicion. My Aunt told us what to bring: Seforim, bed linen, clothing, and silverware.

We stayed with my Aunt for three months and then were put on the kinder transport to Amsterdam.

I learned to knit in a shop where yarn was sold and knitted a rust coloured cable sweater. I chose the colour and worked on it until it was finished. Because it was something that I had made, I treasured it. When I tried to find it, it was gone. I think that it was stolen. I learnt from this that it is very easy to part with worldly accumulations because they can be replaced.

When we saw the Jewish people being taken away they only took with them their tallis and tefillin. I learned as a girl of fourteen that no one could take away our Judaism. We are the eternal wandering Jew and no one can take it away from us.

Sorelle Parker
born in 1923

'A blood libel in America'

M y mother wanted to name me Shirley and my father wanted the more traditional Sarah. As a compromise they took the Hebrew diminutive of Sarah and then anglicised it and I became Sorelle.

World War Two came as a big shock because we didn't realise we were on the brink of war. The Japanese Ambassador and President Roosevelt were negotiating peace to avert hostilities in Washington D.C. We heard rumours regarding the holocaust but could not grasp such horror. At that time, shortly before America got pulled into the war, there was no proof and we couldn't believe the stories.

I had one brother who served in the Armed Forces in New Guinea and the Philippines. His battalion was trained to be the first in the invasion. Father said at this time that it was pikuach nefesh to eat treifeh, however, as hard as my brother tried, he could not eat the non-kosher food. As a result of poor nutrition he developed pneumonia and was in hospital when his whole unit was sent to fight in the first wave of the war in the Philippines. They were all wiped out and he was the only soldier in his unit to survive.

In 1941 a ship of Jewish refugees from Europe, the St Louis, entered into Cuban territorial waters. They had paid full price for the trip but Cuba turned them away. When the ship was rerouted to the United States, they also turned them away. A very anti-Semitic congressman convinced the Unions that our boys currently serving in the Armed Forces would be forced to sell apples on the street corners when they came back just as the soldiers did after World War One, if we allowed foreign refugees to come into the country. This was persuasive to Roosevelt, President of a country emerging from the Great Depression.

I remember attending a mass meeting organised by a friend of Roosevelt to try to persuade him to take refugees in. Roosevelt was not the paragon of virtue people believed he was. When he met Churchill and Stalin in Yalta, Roosevelt said 'we will give you New York with all its Jews and we will take care of everyone else.'

We sent telegrams to Winston Churchill, but the English made a commitment they didn't keep. They reneged on the White Paper, which permitted the Jews to go to Palestine. Roosevelt had fireside chats on the radio with the American people as the war progressed. We heard more about the holocaust, but we felt it couldn't be true; it was too difficult to accept.

My husband's family was from Isaslova in the Ukraine, from where his father had left to come to America in 1912. It was not until 1921 that he was able to bring over his mother and siblings. World War One had begun, trapping everyone there until after the war. The rest of his mother's family was completely wiped out. In the early part of the War the family had hired a local villager to take them to a safer village because they knew the Germans were coming. He took their money and when they had travelled a safe distance from Isaslova he forced them out of the wagon and killed them all. He did this to curry favour with the Germans.

I have a friend who came over from Lithuania with her mother, father and the eldest child, Joey. In the 1920's and 1930's marauders liked to kill Jewish boys and people lived in constant fear of pogroms. Joey's parents used to hide him in the oven to save his life. Until he was Bar Mitzvah and came over to America, he had spent most of his life in the oven. As a result his growth was stunted.

Uncle Berel, my father's brother in law, was the Rabbi in Massena, New York, near the Canadian border. Nearby was a town full of Poles near the St Lawrence River. Between Rosh Hashanah and Yom Kippur in the year 1926 a little girl disappeared from this town. The Priest roused the local people by saying that the Jews must have taken her to get her blood for Yom Kippur. Uncle Berel was arrested and thrown into jail because he was the Rabbi. The Poles, led by the Priest, wanted to lynch him but the local Sheriff protected him and said he had to be tried by a court of law.

He was in jail for three days, including Yom Kippur, when they found the little girl in the nearby forest. She survived on berries and was very frightened. The Priest then claimed that the Rabbi had left her there in the forest. However, she was lucid enough to say that she had been lost and Uncle Berel was freed.

This incident might have been the closest thing to a blood libel on American soil.

Shlomo Aaron ben Ya'akov
born in 1900
Told by his granddaughter

A broken leg for Shabbos

My grandfather was born in Warsaw into an orthodox, but aristocratic family, in 1900. When he was six years old, because of dire poverty in Poland, his family moved from Warsaw, to Mannheim, Germany where he remained until 1930. Mannheim was disputed territory, with France and Germany each fighting for control of the region. At the time of the Second World War, Mannheim was under German control with many French citizens residing there.

In Mannheim my grandfather married my grandmother who was a French citizen and they settled in Strasbourg, France, soon after their wedding. My grandfather made his living there as an accountant in a bank.

Even before war broke out, grandfather received his call up papers for army duty, issued by the French police. Because he held Polish citizenship he was surprised to be summoned, but seeing no alternative, he went to the conscription office to sign on. During his physical examination, the French army doctor informed him to his shock and amazement that he was suffering with heart palpitations and was unsuitable for army service. This was the last he ever heard of this timely, but fleeting, sickness.

When war broke out and the Germans occupied France, he and his family fled to Vichy. He begged his family in Mannheim to come to France, but to no avail. His mother and two brothers were all caught by the Nazis and perished. Although Vichy was still safe at the time and his French wife was not in danger because she spoke excellent German and held a prestigious government position, because of his Polish citizenship he was in grave danger. They went into hiding in a small village called Chantelle, about thirty kilometres from Vichy. Grandfather considered himself lucky to find a job tending cows, on a farm which belonged to a non-Jew. The farmer did not suspect that grandfather and his family were Jewish.

While war raged, the family felt relatively safe in the village looking after the cows, milking them, giving them feed, cleaning the barns and generally taking care of the maintenance of the farm. For some time, Shabbos was grandfather's day off, but then there came a time when the owner of the farm wanted him to work on Shabbos also. When grandfather asked him not to make any changes in their successful schedule, the farmer warned him that if he refused to work on that day as well he would report him to the Police.

His religious upbringing made it unthinkable to work on Shabbos. He thought about the matter for some time and decided upon a drastic solution. He climbed onto the roof of one of the barns, and jumped off, hoping to inflict some damage on himself; which would prevent him breaking Shabbos. He was more successful than he hoped because instead of breaking Shabbos, he broke one of his legs seriously. Because he was reluctant to draw more attention to himself by seeking medical help, grandfather remained handicapped for the rest of his life.

Grandfather now informed the farm owner, in all honesty, that he was unable to do the work he previously did. When he recovered sufficiently, he asked the owner if he could watch the cows in the fields during the day. This was the usual procedure in those days.

The farm owner agreed and grandfather had the perfect job. He went out to the fields in the morning and came back in the evening, and had no problem carrying out his duties on Shabbos. Since he was in the fields, he was able to sit down and learn Torah, Pirkei Avos and say Tehillim without fear of being caught by the Germans and out of view of prying eyes.

There were times when the Police swept through the village looking for refugees and illegal immigrants. There was an Orphan's Home not far away from Chantelle, which housed a lot of Jewish children. The Nazis would always go to this home first and the Home would send a messenger to Chantelle to warn the Jewish refugees. They came twice to look for grandfather and both times grandmother knew in advance. She ransacked her own home turning over mattresses and emptying closets. When the Nazis arrived she explained that she was also looking for him, that he was drunk and he hit her and disappeared. She said 'when you find him, send him to me.' They apparently believed her and left her alone.

Meanwhile, grandfather was hiding in a small hut constructed in the fields. In this way, grandfather and his wife and children survived the horrors of the war. After the war, grandfather was unable to follow his previous occupation and my grandmother became a furniture representative in Strasbourg.

My grandfather lost his entire family in the war, and grandmother lost almost all her family. Bereft of relatives, grandfather and grandmother were, nevertheless, able to build a family through their four children and their descendants currently number around 350 souls across France, England and Israel.

Grandfather walked with a limp until the end of his life and he had to wear a specially built shoe to balance his injured leg. The family believes that it is in the zechus, merit, of his mesiros nefesh to handicap himself for life in order to keep Shabbos, together with his decision not to speak a word of lashon hara, that each and every one of his descendants today is Shomer Shabbos.

Nini Neufeld
born in 1926

'I never wore black boots again'

I was born, along with my twin brother, in Eisenstadt,
Austria, as the last of nine children. My parents came
from Hungary in the early 1900's. My father had a shop
where he made and sold orthopaedic shoes. I was
twelve years old in March 1938 when Hitler came and
occupied Eisenstadt. At that time I didn't know much
about Hitler.

When I got up that morning and looked out of the
window I saw white snow. In the white snow stood a row
of black boots. I saw only black boots. They were
standing there, a whole row of black boots. I never wore
black boots again. My children wear boots. They want to
buy me boots. I would rather walk barefoot in the snow
than wear black boots. I asked my mother, 'what is it all
about?' My father said 'it must be the Nazis'. They broke
down our door and came in, and then they kicked us out.
Some of my sisters were in the house, together with my
grandfather who was 87 years old.

A Nazi escorted us to a dilapidated shack. We were
allowed to take only the barest essentials. My father asked
'can I take shoes out of the store for the children?' 'What
do you mean your store? Nothing is yours,' came the
reply. A few days later I sneaked back, with my father.
The door was open but there was nothing left except the
furniture. Later on we discovered that a neighbour had
rescued photos of my parents and grandparents, which
they took home with them. They eventually sent them to
Denmark.

We went the next day to school as usual but the Professor said, 'all Jews out.' We left, and trudged back to the shack. We didn't return to school. A month later they destroyed the shul. Since the windows of the shack faced the shul we could see the destruction. I heard them destroying the chandeliers. I remember feeling very frightened. This was the shul where father would gather his guests for Shabbos and bring them home on Friday night. We understood Kavod. We were not allowed to sit down at the table until grandfather sat down first.

One day, June or July, the Nazis came and loaded us onto buses. Before we were deported my parents risked their lives and took grandfather to Vienna to an old age home. They instructed the owner to 'put grandfather to sleep if the Germans come so that he would not be killed by them.' We learned a short time later that is what happened.

They told this group of Jews from seven communities that we were being taken to Greece. When we reached Yugoslavia we were thrown off the buses because Greece refused us entry into the country. We sat on the kerb in Yugoslavia over night, with no food and no drink. The next day we were taken back to Eisenstadt. I was still with my brothers and sisters and parents, except for two sisters who were married and living in Czech. One sister's husband was shot in front of her, but both of these sisters survived the war.

We went back into the shack with only the clothes that we wore. After a week or so we were again loaded onto buses. They took us to Stettin in Germany, where we were dropped in the middle of the street. It was June 1938.

In Stettin there was a German Jewish underground. Two men saw us standing there and one approached us saying, 'be very quiet and follow me.' We didn't know who they were but we felt that we had nothing to lose, and followed them. I can trace the steps in my mind, even now. There was an open door with food on the table. A lot of people were sitting round the table and eating. My brothers and sisters and I sat down, but not my mother or father. My father said 'I have to see if this food is kosher.' He went to the kitchens and came back and said 'no, we cannot eat it. It's not kosher.' However he allowed us to eat the bread. We were not at all angry that father said it was not kosher; that was enough for us. We didn't ask questions.

We stayed there overnight and slept on the floor in one of the rooms. There must have been 30 people in the room. In the morning they said we could not stay there because the Germans might discover that there were Jews hiding there.

They took us in cars to the port where they arranged for us to board a ship bound for Helsinki, Finland. We were covered with blankets and hidden on deck in case the Germans would inspect the ship. When we arrived in Finland the Fins would not allow us to disembark and we were sent back to Stettin. In the middle of the week the underground came to us again with false papers that they had made, together with train tickets to go to Sweden. This time, however, they had to separate us because there were too many people with the same name.

As we were on the train heading for Sweden, the German conductor read the terrible fear that was on our faces. 'Don't go to Sweden,' he whispered, 'they won't let you in. Get off in Copenhagen.' I was travelling with my mother and father and twin brother. The Germans caught my other brothers and sisters on the train in Germany. They never arrived in Denmark. Some survived the war, some didn't. We got off at Copenhagen on Shabbos morning. My father was devastated to desecrate Shabbos. When we arrived he asked, 'where is the Synagogue?'

Someone took us to an old age home, which had a shul on the premises. When the porter heard our story he said 'someone has died, you can have her room.' My mother was sick. The porter called a doctor and took my mother to hospital where she remained for ten weeks. At the Shul that first Shabbos we met a family by the name of Kohn who invited us for the seudah. My brother and I stayed with the family for ten months, while my parents lived in a building nearby. Eventually we were able to rent an apartment and live together.

My father was not allowed to work because he was an immigrant. In spite of the enforcement I worked illegally as a dressmaker in a store. The Danish man knew that I was not allowed to work but he gave me a job anyway. On Friday afternoons he would say 'you have to go home, it will be Shabbos soon.' The Danish King was a truly righteous gentile who saved the Jews from total annihilation. The Nazis wanted to arrest Jews in Denmark and force us to wear yellow stars on our arms. King Christian 10th said 'if the Jews have to wear a star, I will be the first one, because they are all my people. They are Danes.'

On the evening of Rosh Hashanah in 1943, the four of us were on the way to Shul. Some members of the non-Jewish Danish underground, whom we didn't know, stopped us on the way. They were there to save the Jews from disaster. They said 'don't go to the synagogue because the Nazis are going to empty the shul. We will take you out of Copenhagen. You can't stay here anymore. The Germans will arrest you all.' My father and Mother looked very tired, but father said 'we have nothing to lose; the only other choice is certain death.'

They gave us a plan. If the Germans should stop us we would say that father is a doctor, I am a nurse and Mother is very sick. They put my brother in the trunk of the car because they couldn't find an adequate place for him in the story. They drove us to upstate Copenhagen and we were not stopped. They took us to a goyishe family. I don't know their names because they were all nameless. The family took us in. They said they would take us to Sweden on the next boat. We stayed there from Rosh Hashanah to Yom Kippur.

The man of the house worked for the Danish underground to save the Jews. They notified him that on that particular night the Nazis would check his house too. Information such as this gets passed along the underground from one man to the other.

Shortly after we arrived he said 'all of you go under that bed. The Nazis are at the door.' The Nazis came into the room with their dogs. The dogs sniffed around the bed but did not bark. The Nazis did not lift the bedspread. They left when they thought there were no Jews to be found. Hashem did not let the dogs bark and did not let them lift the bedspread. I had absolutely no feelings, nor did my parents, because we said whatever will happen, will happen. We were like robots.

After this incident this family said that they could save my brother and me because they said they could call us relatives, but not my parents. We said,' no, what will happen to them, will happen to us.'

We went together on a boat to Sweden. The motor broke down in the middle of the ocean. German boats surrounded us. They threw their lights on our boat but they didn't come near.

Hashem was very good to me. He tested me many times, but I never stopped believing in him and loving him to this day because of the upbringing of my parents. When my mother got the news that my brother had died, my mother said, 'G-d gives and G-d takes away.'

Rochel Klueger
born in 1937

A wedding band
or a piece of bread

*Me on the day the government
recognised my marriage*

My mother, one of seven children, was born in 1902 in Moldovitza, part of the Austro-Hungaria, which until 1918 was under Kaiser Franz Joseph. During the First World War, like so many other refugees, my mother moved away from her birth town and lived and worked in Braunau am Inn. This village is situated on the river Inn, and is the birthplace of Adolph Hitler who was born in 1889. My mother learned bookkeeping in Braunau and worked as a bookkeeper in the school attached to the convent. After the war my mother returned to Moldovitza, which was now in Romania, where I was born in 1937. My birthplace is Gura-Humorului, which means – the mouth of the river. My father was a metal worker.

When the Second World War started in 1939, the Romanians allied with the Germans. The Romanians made a ghetto inside the village and forced all the men to wear a yellow star to differentiate between the Jews and the non-Jews. The Burgomeister and the first Secretary were not anti-Semitic and they were friends of my father. They did not agree to do a lot of the things the Nazis asked them to do.

My parents

The Germans asked them to put all the men in the Synagogue, which they did on several occasions, for two days at a time. However they did not do it every time they were asked, nor did they burn the synagogue with the men inside, in spite of warning the people that this would happen. They also did not confiscate the possessions of the people. After the war, during which the Burgomaster died, they made the first Secretary a judge after my father highly recommended him.

My first memory was of my fourth birthday. I had a nice party and was given a big red ball with white spots. Ten days after my fourth birthday, on the 1st October 1941, we heard the drums beating. Since there were no telephones, this was the sign that the villagers should meet in the market square. Everyone came, but the beating drums were only for the Jews. We were told that at 4p.m. the same day we had to be at the train station. My parents started to pack but they knew something bad was going to happen.

My mother would not let me take the red ball. My father said he only wanted to take a rucksack, because the time would come when he would have to carry us both.

When I was born my father built, with his own hands, the house in which we lived. At 4p.m. on the 1st October, we left it. My father was a wise man. He decided not to lock the door because he knew that the Romanians would come very fast and break down the door, which would be a pity for the door.

We went to the train and the Romanians put us in cattle wagons, without water, food or toilet facilities. I remember, even as a child of four, the first people dying. My friend's father was sick when they put him in the wagon and he died on the first day. We were eight to ten days in the wagons. They occasionally stopped at small villages and we were able to get water, but they did not provide food. The only food there was to eat was what the people had brought with them.

One day we arrived at the river Dnestr that was in the Ukraine. The nearest town on that side of the river was Ataki. The town on the other side was Mogiliov. However the Germans had bombed the bridges. In October in the Ukraine both the weather and the water are cold. They put us into boats. The Ukrainians are very anti-Semitic and tried to kill us by overturning the boats.

My father threw away his rucksack, put me on his back, my mother under his arm and swam to the other side. He was a very strong man. The people who could swim against the strong current and in the cold water survived; the others the water pulled down.

A lot of the Jews in this town had escaped when the war began, and had abandoned their houses, which were partially destroyed in the bombing. The Ukrainians had stolen all the contents of the houses, which now stood empty.

The Ukrainians waited on the other side of the river for the people who survived the crossing, and housed them in these houses. We slept on planks of wood. It was the beginning of the Ukrainian winter and the glass in the windows, which had been shattered in the bombing, offered little protection against the winter cold. The Ukrainians pushed twelve to fourteen people into each room. Eventually my father repaired the windows.

After the exposure in the freezing river everyone in the room became sick with pneumonia. We covered ourselves with my mother's black coat, which we had dried on a little fire. These houses were in the town, and we begged or stole food in order to survive. Anyone who obtained food shared it with everyone else. The Ukrainians, who were repairing German planes, had put us into a working camp.

After a couple of days the Ukrainians came round to establish who could work and who could not. If they gave you work in the factory repairing the planes you got food, if you didn't work, you didn't get food. Those who got food shared it with the people who didn't. Very soon the people who could not work were sent to other camps, from which they never returned. Families were not split up, so my mother and I remained in the working camp.

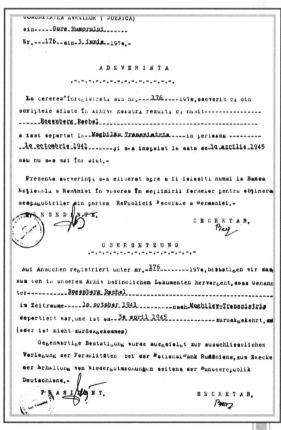

*A certificate to show
I was in the camps*

The three of us were very sick, but my father was the first to get better. The Ukrainians wanted him to work in the factory because he was both strong and a metal worker.

Then one of my cousins came to the camp and brought with him lice, which carried typhus, and we all caught it. At the same time a doctor came to the camp and was able to bring us water and care for us. Although he didn't catch typhus at this time, eventually he also became sick and died. The doctor's son is my friend to this day. We were sick for two or three weeks. My cousin died after one week. My father had shared his bed with him, but everyone was too sick to take him out of the house. We had no medication, those who were strong survived. The typhus left my father deaf and paralysed on the left side. He knew that if he could not work his family would die, so he went to work. During these few weeks the Doctor procured food for us.

After the people had recovered the Ukrainians wanted to know everyone's profession so they could allocate work. My father took charge and told them that this person was this, and that person was that, in order that they would be given work. In the factory my father taught them what to do.

My father never ate his food in the factory, but brought it home to share with others in the house. He made a little metal box with which to carry home the food.

One day the S.S. came to the camp to take away and shoot the people who did not work. All the people in the houses were taken to be shot. My mother spent her day singing. She had a voice like an opera singer and was very fond of singing German songs. The S.S officers were entranced with my mother's voice and went into the house to ask her to continue singing. They did not take anyone from this house. That day when the people returned from the factory they buried their dead.

On one occasion the Nazis sent orders for our family to be deported to a death camp. The Ukrainian secretary to the Nazis saw my father in town and asked him why he looked so sad. He told her we would be deported to a death camp and would not come back. She went to her boss, the Nazi in charge of deportations, and told him she had a cousin in the camp who had received orders. Could he possibly change them? She gave our name as Greenberg, even though it was actually Rosenberg. We received papers to stay under the name of Greenberg. My father quickly tore and burned the old papers of Rosenberg, who were scheduled for deportation to the death camp.

My father would speak to people in the street and once he came across a woman who was starving. She was a kindergarten teacher and had all her books with her. My father came home and said to my mother 'we have to save this woman. She won't take from me but we can ask her to teach Rochel.' My father was now sharing his food from the factory with four people. On another occasion, my father met an engineer who told him that his wife had run away and his son was so weak from starvation that he could not walk. My father shared his own food with the child until he could walk again.

Someone in the factory gave my father a safe to repair. In the safe was a ring. He sold it to the Ukrainians in the town and bought half a kilogram of meat. My mother cooked it and divided it amongst all those people with whom we shared our food. In order to supplement the meagre rations from the factory, my mother would go to the garbage containers in town and collect potato peelings, with which she would make soup. She would also go to the market place and rescue food that the stallholders had thrown on the floor.

My mother sold the gold from her teeth and bought clothes with the money. She exchanged her wedding band for a piece of bread. The weather was so cold, at least minus 25 degrees, and colder, that the earth cracked. The wind was so strong that you felt that you were undressed.

When the Russians came and liberated us in 1945 they sent the children to school. It was so cold that I wore all of my clothes and on top of these I put on the pyjamas that my mother had made for me. My father found some plastic that the Germans had used to cover the tanks so that they wouldn't freeze, and from this he made a pair of long boots for me. I was the most elegantly dressed child in the whole school.

When the Russians offered us the possibility of going home, my mother chose to do so, because she wanted to find her brothers. We hitch hiked on wagons to a town called Saret on the border of Romania. We were housed in a large, empty casino. It was there that my mother met her youngest brother. My father said he would go first to our village to see if there was anything left of our home. He went alone and on foot. The return journey took him almost three weeks. Our house was there, but empty, everything had been stolen. On the 1st April 1945 we returned to our house. My father made beds and a table from scraps of wood that he found. He continued his trade as a metal worker, and I went to school.

We had lived in this work camp for four years during the War. I was now only eight years old and had been exposed to more cruelty, illness and death than most people see in a lifetime.

Tuvia Nadel
born in 1923

'Mussar teaches that simcha should not be uncontrolled happiness'

B oth my parents came from Lithuania where my father was born in Skaudville. He immigrated to America straight after World War One.

In the 1920's, America had a lot of small towns, some of which had a Rabbi of a small community who single handed kept Yiddishkeit alive. The Rabbi was the shochet, the mohel, the teacher, and the chazzan. He did every-thing.

Jewish people went into certain businesses, such as the scrap metal business. There were two reasons for this, it didn't need capital and people were able to keep Shabbos. Ninety percent of people in the scrap metal business were frum Jews. They rented a horse and a wagon and collected paper, rags and scrap metal. Today their children are multi millionaires from the scrap metal businesses started by their immigrant grandparents in those small towns across America.

In the 1930's I saw yiush, despair and hopelessness. Parents were not putting in a big effort to give their children Torah knowledge because they did not believe that Torah learning would lead to success. For these parents it was enough if their sons married a Jewish girl. It did not enter their minds that their children would marry goyim.

In 1942 I was sent to Yeshiva in Chicago. Older Bochurim would perform the High Holyday services in small towns all over the United States in places such as Texas, Michigan and Alabama. That year I went to Hamilton, Ohio to assist with the services. My job was to daven Shacharis and to blow the shofar. As my skills improved during the services I davened Mussaf as well.

The next Rosh Hashanah, in 1943, I went to Dakota where I was hired to daven Mussaf. A woman approached me after the services and said 'Rabbi, your prayer shawl is pretty, why do you have those strings on the corners?' I had never heard such a question before. The woman thought that they were fringes for beauty.

The next year, in 1944, I went to a town in Georgia where I was paid the sum of 500 dollars to daven the entire Rosh Hashanah service. I was a young boy of twenty-one. I did everything myself including calling everyone up to the Torah and the Haphtarah. On Yom Kippur in addition to reading from the Sefer Torah I davened Shacharis, Mussaf, Mincha, Neilah and Ma'ariv. I was also asked to give a sermon and although I am not an accomplished speaker, it didn't bother me one bit.

In all these places I made an interesting observation. No matter where I went I was introduced to everybody's daughter. In the 1930's and 1940's everyone kept kosher and parents didn't want their daughters to intermarry.

I started to become more serious about my learning and went to Yeshiva in Baltimore. The first year I was there the biggest Conservative synagogue in Baltimore was willing to pay five hundred dollars for a chazzan for the Yom Kippur Mussaf service only. Five hundred dollars! They approached me and I told them that I would do it only if the Rosh Yeshiva allowed it. I wasn't asked again.

During the winter months we used to spend Friday mornings playing ball. One day a man asked me 'what are those strings that the boys are wearing when they play ball?' I explained what they were. Then he asked, 'are those boys from the school that refused to send a cantor to our synagogue?' I told him that I was the man whom they had approached.

That year was 1944 and there were fifty boys in Baltimore. Today they have five hundred bocherim and a Kollel. I was close to Rabbi Dovid Kronglass. He was regarded as the beneficiary of the Ba'al Mussar mantel from Reb Yechezkel Levenstein. Rabbi Kronglass had come to Baltimore from Shanghai and he was in his middle forties and unmarried. One of the reasons was that frum women wouldn't marry men who sat and learnt because they wanted a husband who could support them.

He eventually got engaged and I attended his wedding in New York. It was a frum wedding with separate dancing and done in the Mir Yeshiva way with one man conducting the Hakofos. I never experienced dancing like this before. Mussar teaches that simcha should not be wild, uncontrolled happiness. Simcha was controlled and Mussar guided their lives. This was in the tradition of Reb Yerucham Levovitz. Dancing at a wedding was controlled because of refinement of character. One man directed the men and they followed his direction.

Rabbi Kronglass was a strong, proud, advocate of high level learning, despite the streets of America. The biggest issue for a yeshiva bochur was to understand the difference between a goy and a yid. Yiddishe Bochurim were lured into sports just like the American goy. Now that the bochur played sports, he had to study all the statistics of sports.

One of the Rebbes, Reb Mendel Kaplan taught himself English so that he could relate better to the boys in the class. He came into class one day and read a newspaper article to the boys announcing the wedding between two well-known and wealthy families. The wedding was scheduled, but the day before the wedding it was called it off. Nevertheless, they had the party anyway. Reb Mendel made his point, where is the joy coming from? In the midst of tragedy the party goes on?

Reb Dovid Kronglass would say 'I know you have to play ball, but do you have to sink into the swamp?' That was the nekudah, point, which was holding back the potential of Jewish American boys. Goyishkeit had sunk into the life of the children.

I know ten boys who are now Roshei Yeshivas. There was a much higher understanding amongst the Jewish adults of the futility of joining the goyim. It was unheard of that a Jewish boy should marry a non-Jewish girl.

Reb Mendel had constant strife with the President of the school. The President would approach him and say 'I hear that you are telling boys not to go to school.' 'It's not true,' Reb Mendel would say. 'You should tell them to go to College,' the President added. Reb Mendel said 'pooh!' in such a way that told the President that he had the wrong guy. The President's own son was turned over by Reb Mendel and later he became a Rosh Kollel in Los Angeles. Years later I met the President and he said to me, 'did you hear about my son?' He knew I never took his side in the arguments he had with Reb Mendel. The President took the credit for the education of his son.

When Reb Mendel was a Rebbe in Philadelphia he had a car. When he visited for Shabbos he was the type of man who picked up hitchhikers. After he had gone part of the way he gave the hitchhiker ten dollars and told him to go and buy something to eat while he was filling up at the petrol station. His son told me that one day he picked someone up. When they reached New York the hitchhiker said to Reb Mendel, 'Rabbi, usually when people pick me up I beat them up and take their wallet. I couldn't do that to you.'

Reb Mendel went to the weddings of his many students, even if the wedding was out of town. The families were not necessarily frum; the grandfather wasn't frum, but Reb Mendel would look for a grandson to be b'simcha with him. He went out of his way to go into the circle of dancers with him, just to make him happy. He was a giant of mussar and head and shoulders above other people.

He was extremely popular with the boys. Right after Ma'ariv the boys would come over to talk to him. The Rosh Yeshiva was not as popular, so Reb Mendel made a special point to go out of shul before Aleinu so that it wouldn't embarrass the Rosh Yeshiva.

When circumstances decreed that the Yeshiva had to move, we had no permanent place to daven. I asked Reb Mendel 'where are we going to daven this year?' 'What does it matter?' he asked, 'are you thinking of Olam Hazeh? You should be thinking of how you are going to daven better, not where.'

When I was twenty four he told me 'don't dance this Simchas Torah.' He was saying that if you don't dance leShem Shamayim, for the sake of heaven, you are just dancing to have a good time. I didn't dance that year. What ever he said was immersed in truth and mussar, way above most people.

Reb Mendel made wine from supplies he brought with him from Europe. At one time he made a business out of it and struggled to make money. Another person made cheap kosher wine called 'Magen Dovid.' The African Americans bought this and he did quite well. This person told Reb Kaplan 'you don't want to make money enough.

You have to get immersed in the whole thing.' But this Reb Mendel refused to do.

I visited his home one day during the winter. It was zero degree weather and he needed to go to the shoe store to buy shoes for his little boy. Two black Americans stopped him and pulled out a knife. He threw his little boy into the snow then took the two black Americans and knocked their heads together. Besides being highly respected by the boys, he was very strong with a lot of guts.

Pinchas Ofner
born in 1932

'A world where you could have as much bread as you wanted'

Although I was born in Krakow, we settled in Wabowice, which was a town of three to four thousand religious Jews. The previous Pope, John Paul the second, was born in this town. He had a lot of Jewish friends and was an amateur actor.

At noon on a Friday, we heard the first bombings, which marked the beginning of the Second World War. When the Germans expelled the eastern Jews they came to Szlezia in Poland and told horrible stories. Szlezia was a frum Jewish town near Wabowice and we didn't realise then that the horrible stories had not yet begun. My father, who wore a streimel, had payot and didn't touch his beard, decided that he didn't want to see Germans.

The Rav of our town had given a psak that we were allowed to get everything ready to prepare to leave. My mother's sister sewed bags to use to carry our baggage. No one thought we were escaping forever. On motzei Shabbos we buried our silver candlesticks and all our other valuables, in a container in the basement. When my father returned, many years later, the container was empty.

On motzei Shabbos there were no trucks available, but my father was able to hire a goy, with a horse and carriage, to take us to the next city. My parents, grandparents and one year old sister and me all piled into the carriage to escape from our village. Everyone thought that the strong Polish army would beat the

Germans. Other Jews were coming out of their homes screaming that we were trying to save our shmatters and not trying to save the children. They threw our bags off the carriage and pushed their children on. The older people like my parents and grandparents, walked beside the carriage, all night. Some of the baggage thrown off the carriage contained my father's money.

In the morning we came to Misclenice. All the Jews were flooding into this town, but my father wanted to continue. The Goy asked him how far he wanted to go and my father answered 'until the next town.' After two days we joined the retreating Polish army. The Germans were bombing the area with their messerschmidts. When the bombs were falling, my Aunt and sister lay down in the path. Right next to them a Polish officer and his horse were killed. Although we were running day and night we could see the nissim, miracles, all around us.

A week later we arrived in Kolbieszov on a Friday evening. I remember seeing lights everywhere as the women lit the Shabbos candles. The Germans were not far from the city but my father did not want to run on Shabbos. Kolbieszov was a town of very frum Jews. Someone leaving offered to take my baby sister. Then my father decided that we, too, should flee. That night, leil Shabbos, the Germans entered the city and started killing the Jews. This was the first act of German violence against the Jews in the war.

The Polish army had potatoes and bread, but we had nothing to eat. It was raining so my mother took the water that had gathered in the mud and boiled it. This is what we drank, even my baby sister. That Shabbos we started saying selichos. The horse pulling the carriage did not have the strength to carry all of us any longer, so my father bought a horse from a Polish Officer. We were exhausted from running, and I can remember only fragments of our escape. On one occasion we were in a shelter and a bomb was dropped which collapsed the door to the shelter. People were screaming and somehow we got out although I don't remember how.

A few days later we arrived at the River Bug which was the Molotov and Ribentrov border, dividing Poland and Russia. It was Rosh Hashanah. My father got wet saying tashlich in the river. He believed that this was the end of the war for us. We took a barge to carry the carriage to the other side of the river. There we met very elegantly dressed Polish officers. My father said to them 'the war is over.' The officers said 'no, the war has just begun.'

After this it was much easier because we were not under attack. We were in a Jewish town for Yom Kippur. The goy finally left us. We had family in Lemberg so we hired a different carriage and went there. We had been running for six weeks.

We stayed in Lemberg for nine months where my father merchandised cloth. Then, in August, the Russians

A cattle truck at Yad Vashem

decided to take all the Jews to Siberia. We travelled for six weeks in a cattle wagon on the train to the northernmost point of the Urals where the rail tracks ended. Since it was summer, the sun didn't set. We crossed a river on a raft and came to a forest. Here, whoever was able to work was taken by the Police in order to work. The children went to classes. Only when it got cold, when the temperature fell 40 degrees below zero, were the classes suspended. My grandmother passed away from hunger.

In 1942 when the war broke out between the Russians and the Germans, the Polish army started to take Jews into the army. If a Jew went into the army the family was taken to Teheran in Iran. A lot of Jews went into the army. My father heard from somewhere that the place to go to sign up was Tashkent. We were in the Urals when I asked my father how he knew to go to Tashkent, the capital of Uzbekistan. He said he didn't know. There were no radios or telephones where we were and to this day it remains a mystery to me how my father received this information.

We travelled to Revda by train with Tashkent as our final destination. Food was always a problem. At every station my mother and Aunt would get off the train to try to find food. When we arrived at a big town, the capital of the Urals, we were told that the train would stay here for a day. I stayed on the train with my father and sister while my mother and Aunt went off, as usual, to find food. After half an hour the train started again, without my mother and Aunt on board.

My mother found a train carrying injured Russian soldiers; the train was taking them from the front to Tashkent. My mother and Aunt were not allowed to board the train, so they hung onto the rails on the outside of the train. There were 300 or 400 kilometres between the stations. They hung on to the train for almost a day before the Russian army realised that they were stubborn, that they refused to give in and they were allowed on the train. It was eight days before we saw mother again.

It was cold in Tashkent. The children were sleeping in the station. The older people were sleeping outside in the public gardens. The children started dying from a disease. My mother's friend, who was travelling with us, lost her three children in this way.

Then the Polish army decided not to take any more Jews. With their families settled in Teheran, the Jewish soldiers were deserting from the army.

We went to Leninabad, which was near Tajikistan on the border with Afghanistan. We stayed there for four years. There was only one possibility of working and that was in the factory. My father, together with my uncle, opened a kiosk selling sweets and candy. Officially it belonged to the factory, but in fact it belonged to my father and Uncle. Officially nothing was privately owned, everything belonged to the government. In Russia, at that time, if you sold any food everyone was willing to pay for it.

During the summer, children over the age of twelve worked on government farms. We were taken to a silkworm factory where our job was to take the silk from the cocoons. We sorted the butterflies on platforms when the butterflies were born. When it is pregnant a butterfly has 700-800 eggs. We threw away the male butterflies and put the females into paper bags with holes. The peasants then placed them on the trees.

Everyone who worked there took the paper. Usually we never saw paper. If you went to the doctor and he needed to write out a prescription, you took your own paper for him to write on. If you wanted to smoke, you bought the tobacco and rolled your own cigarette with

The rail tracks at Auschvitz

newspaper. Everyone was stealing in every factory. It was normal to steal. Wherever you lived in Russia you couldn't live if you didn't steal. We were in Russia until the end of the war.

At the beginning of 1946 we took the train back to Poland. The size of the track in Russia did not match the size of the track in Poland. The line that connected Russia with Poland ended in Auschwitz. My father went to see the concentration camp at Auschwitz. I was Bar Mitzvah but I didn't know what Auschwitz was. Everything remained the same as it was at the end of the war. All the files and buildings were open. We saw thousands of photographs in huge piles. I remember my Aunt screaming. On the top of one of the piles were photos of her brothers and sister, evidence that they were not alive. The Germans did everything in an efficient way so naturally every murdered Jew had a photo and an I.D. card.

My father travelled from Auschwitz to Krakow to see what Jewish life was left there. Before the war whole neighbourhoods of Krakow were completely Jewish. It had been a thriving Jewish metropolis. He found some

Jews and returned to us saying, 'life is normal again. You can have as much bread and rolls as you like.' My ten-year-old sister and I thought our father was lying. We couldn't imagine a world where you could have as much bread as you wanted.

In 1946-47 the Jewish organisations, financed by the Joint, walked round Krakow looking for the Jewish tombstones embedded in the sidewalks, streets or walls

The Rema cemetery

of the city. They used frum children who had more feeling for this task. We found pavements made from tombstones. In the Rema cemetery, they built a wall with the tombstones. We also searched for them in Warsaw, where we gathered up the bones in the area of the Warsaw ghetto.

Mendel Yeret
born in 1921

By any name – a Jew

I n 1942 I fled to France from Holland via Belgium. Young people were taken to work camps in Holland, where eventually they were sent to Germany. With a minimum of possessions I travelled to Belgium on the train, together with a cousin and her husband. A young person travelling by himself would raise suspicions. Since the Germans already occupied Northern France, I continued to Vichy in the South of France where the Germans had not yet arrived.

I went as a Yeshiva Bochur to Lyon. I knew people from Heide Yeshiva near Antwerp and met them again. A few bocherim started a Yeshiva, which learned in the Beth Knesset in Lyons. The Jewish refugee committee in Lyons supplied us with food. I was invited to sleep with a family I knew from Antwerp. I learned with the Yeshiva for a few months. When the Germans came to the South of France I didn't stay because the ground became too hot. I went to St Etienne, not far from Lyons and stayed with a Jewish family and taught Jewish lessons to the three children.

The French underground arrived and advised the refugees to work with the peasants in the fields. There I pretended to be a goy. The Dutch Government of the Netherlands had a consulate in Lyons and provided me with Protestant identification papers. I was not a Dutch citizen and had not yet arranged my naturalisation papers. Although I was born in Germany, my parents were Polish. My father had a Polish passport; therefore I was officially a Pole. I told the consul who was Jewish that I needed another name. He gave me a Dutch identity card with a false religion and a false name. You could also buy, for a few francs, a French identity card at shops in France that sold cigars. I also got one of these by telling the clerk that I had left my papers in Holland.

In 1943 I tried to go to Switzerland. I smuggled myself through the border but the Swiss police picked me up. The Swiss were taking in families, but not single men, since the Germans now occupied the South of France. The Swiss Police escorted me back over the border. The French Government ran a work camp for Dutch and Belgian citizens. There I stayed for a year and lived as a Dutch goy. I couldn't daven and I asked not to be served cooked food. When the goyim asked me why I didn't eat the food I told them I had a problem with my stomach.

My parents had been sent to Auschwitz never to return. I was alone in the world.

The French people were not in danger, only the refugees. The Gestapo came to the camp and sent the Jews to Auschwitz; the goyim were sent to Buchenwald. Since I was masquerading as a goy I was sent to Buchenwald. Once there, I was asked what I did. When I said that I was a student they gave me a job in the bookkeeping department in the office of the SS. I had a better life than others because I had authority to go into the kitchens and get food.

There were a lot of Polish goyim and I learnt to speak the language. The goyim didn't wash and didn't care for themselves and were generally demoralised. Having nothing to live for, they died very soon. I had no lice and I washed myself every morning with cold water and kept myself clean. This kept me alive.

Since I had free entrance to the kitchens, if I had extra food I gave it to the Jews. I deliberately saved food to give it to them. Once I overheard two people saying that I am the only Dutch person in the camp who is not an anti-Semite. The Polish goyim were suspicious and asked me why I gave food to the Jews and not to the Polish goyim. I told them that in Holland we make no difference between Jews and non-Jews.

In 1944 they started to close Auschwitz because the Russians were near the German border. Buchenwald was close to the East German border. Jews were brought to the camp. I asked a Jew for the date and he took a calendar from his pocket. I saw that two months later it would be Yom Kippur and on that day I fasted. I did not tell them I was Jewish.

In 1945 when we were freed the first Officer I met was a Jew. He looked at my papers, which stated that I was a goy. Since I looked Jewish, he asked me if I spoke Yiddish. 'Yes,' I said. 'If you speak Yiddish you can't be Dutch because the Dutch don't speak Yiddish.' I agreed, 'you are right, I am not Dutch.' 'Your name can't be Dahane'. 'You are right' I said, 'this is not my right name. I want first to go to Holland, but I must go to Holland on false papers.' He let me do this.

I went to The Hague to change my name to my true one and to go to a lawyer. My lawyer asked me if I had any witnesses to my identity. I took a Jewish friend who had stayed alive in Switzerland and he said to the lawyer in Yiddish 'I was at his bris.' I had to translate this short statement to the goyishe lawyer, who then accepted my real name.

Back in Holland I went to my parent's house. Neighbours had moved in and were now living there. In the garden they had buried jewellery, candlesticks, cutlery and a menorah. They had buried them because they were Jewish articles, and they didn't want to throw them out.

They returned them to me. To this day my wife wears the jewellery that belonged to my family.

I regret that I lived as a goy for three years with no Yom Tov, but today there are four living generations of children, grandchildren and great grand children living a full Jewish life. This is my compensation.

In The Hague I learnt and taught for 30 years and now that I live in Israel I learn in Kollel and give shiurim to my community on Shabbos afternoons.

The facts are hard. I lost my family, my possessions and even my name, but today, I am alive.

Joan Sklan
born in 1928

'We're going to hang out our washing on the Siegfried Line'

I was ten years old and living in London when I realised talk of a forthcoming war was general conversation amongst family and friends. Even as young children we sensed the change in our every day lives. Suddenly names like Hitler, Mussolini and Stalin entered our vocabulary. Before very long we were to realise the reason why. I also added a new word to my vocabulary, a word I had never heard before – inevitable. They spoke of a Second World War that was – inevitable. It was inevitable that we would shortly be at war with Germany. This would be inevitable because Hitler was persecuting Jews and invading the Low Countries without too much opposition. It was necessary to declare war and defend our country. The inevitable war began on 3rd September 1939.

We gathered around the wireless as the Prime Minister, Neville Chamberlain, imparted the frightening news. From that moment we went everywhere with a cardboard box over our shoulder. These square boxes contained our gas masks, horrible smelly rubber masks, which made me feel terribly sick. We had to practice putting them on as quickly as possible should the enemy use gas in air raids.

We lived on the fourth floor in a block of council flats. We were the only Jewish family amongst the kind, genteel families that lived there. Our flat backed onto a delightful park where we would walk on fine days after Shabbos morning services. My sister and I shared a bedroom overlooking the rolling acres of bright green grass and tall shady trees. It was such a welcoming sight when we opened our curtains in the morning.

The view changed rapidly. Trees were chopped down and many men and women in army uniform could be seen busily clearing shrubs and flowers. These now bare spaces would house barrage balloons. From our window we would watch yards of shiny silver silk lying flat on the ground being inflated and rise up, tethered, into the sky. The purpose of this was to prevent enemy planes infiltrating the Capital city of London.

The residents of the flats now hastily prepared an air raid shelter. It was a large concrete type of shed, which had stored unwanted items, which the residents no longer required, and which also housed coal for the coal fires in the winter. It was emptied out. Everyone knew that there was not the slightest chance of survival should a bomb hit this shelter directly. Empty, smelly, canvas bags and enormous mountains of sand were promptly delivered. Men, women and children would congregate in the yard to fill the bags. We used shovels, spades bought at the seaside, tin trays and soup ladles, anything that would transfer the sand into the bag. As these were filled they were stacked close together and built as high as possible around the brickwork of the shelter.

Soon the blitz, as it became known, began in earnest. We dreaded hearing the blood curdling wail of the air raid siren. We left everything and rushed to the shelter carrying our pillows, blankets and previously made flasks of hot tea. We could hear the easily identifiable sound of enemy planes approaching. We hoped the strong wires attached to the barrage balloons would be a deterrent and prevent the bombers from reaching their targets. The night sky became an intricate pattern of bright beams from the searchlights and the ack-ack guns, which were now situated in our once pretty park.

Sometimes we would spend the entire night in the shelter, emerging only when the all-clear siren sounded in the early hours of the morning. Sleepily we would climb the four flights of stone stairs and gratefully climb into our cold beds, still clothed in our siren suits, which we could don easily and rapidly. One closed a long zip from crotch to neck where a hood was attached to keep our head warm. Often, just as we snuggled down, the siren would sound again and once more we would repack our belongings used the night before, pay a hasty visit to the toilet and make our way down the stairs again to the shelter.

Schools began operating strange hours. Pupils attended either morning or afternoon sessions, according to the order of our surnames. Sirens warning us to take cover frequently interrupted school hours. Our teachers herded us into underground cellars where we waited for the All Clear.

As the air raids became worse, we realised that the surface shelters were totally unsafe. It was agreed that we would now walk to the nearest underground tube station. This was known as Manor House, London N.16 some two to three miles away. Wearily we would walk the long distance, each of us carrying essential items needed for the long night ahead. If we arrived early enough we would find vacant wooden benches against the tiled walls, where we could rest our backs. These afforded a little more comfort than the middle rows, which were without any support. Underground trains would arrive and leave throughout the night, loading and unloading passengers who trampled over our legs, our feet and our belongings. In the morning, when we emerged into the daylight, fires would still be burning and there would be empty spaces where buildings had once stood. Police, ambulance and firemen could be seen desperately digging in the rubble and calling loudly, 'is there anyone there?'

I had, meanwhile, sat the Junior County scholarship and had been awarded a place at the Skinners school for girls in Stamford Hill. My uniform was a black and red striped blazer with a black velour hat and matching striped headband. Our education was constantly interrupted. We spent most of the time in the huge underground basement. Down there we were unable to continue our lessons and many of the girls, particularly the younger ones, were very nervous. They would become hysterical when we heard bombs drop nearby.

Our music teacher, Miss Barton, a motherly lady, tried hard to distract attention from the noise that we could hear, even though we were underground. She would ask for volunteers to sing, recite poems or tell stories. I loved to sing and, urged on by my friends, would offer my repertoire readily. We had been practising old sea shanties in order to perform at the end of term concert. Miss Barton invited me to lead the girls in singing as she accompanied us on the old upright piano that resided in the basement. I stepped onto the make do platform and sang my heart out to modern tunes of the day. I knew by heart 'The White Cliffs of Dover' and 'We're going to hang out our washing on the Siegfried line' and all the girls and many of the teachers would join in and sing loud enough to make the rafters ring.

Now we were preparing to leave London and move to a safer haven. We were evacuated to Buxton, a town in Derbyshire. Food was hastily cooked and wrapped, ready to consume when we reached our new home. Our clothes were packed into suitcases and two huge wicker hampers were filled with linen, cutlery, china and saucepans. We left our London home on an early morning train and thus began a whole new way of life.

After travelling for many hours on buses and trains, we arrived in Buxton tired and irritable. Our luggage was then piled high onto two carts, which was the alternative to a taxi, which was unaffordable. Mother, father, sister and myself trudged behind the elderly men pushing the barrows. Eventually we arrived at the tiny house my parents had rented. We viewed with delight the hills and dales of our Derbyshire surroundings. How different to the devastation of the bombed city we had left behind.

When the winter arrived and the snowfalls became frighteningly heavy, Buxton often became isolated when the snowploughs were unable to reach us. How incredible to see about four or five feet of snow fall into the hallway, when we opened our front door. We would climb onto our home made toboggans constructed from pieces of slatted wood hammered onto four wheels, or we'd sit on tin trays, screaming with the sheer joy of climbing up and sliding down those glorious hills, covered in many feet of snow.

The Jewish population in Buxton continued to swell and the Council gave permission to allow the increasing community to attend services in disused buildings. An enterprising young couple opened up a Jewish shop and we were able to buy kosher food, the meat being supplied by kosher butchers in Manchester.

Food coupons were issued to everyone in buff coloured Ration books. Some foods were in very short supply, but there were many local farms in the Dales where one could buy live chickens and sometimes an egg or two. The farmer would deliver the live chickens to the door. My sister and I would place them, with difficulty, into large brown carrier bags and walk with them to the bus stop. The bus would only operate twice a day, due to the shortage of petrol. We would take them to the back yard of the local fishmonger, who allowed Rabbi Lopian to schecht them. We then returned home with the newly killed chickens.

The wireless kept us in touch with the worldwide situation. We listened regularly to an Englishman, a traitor, who broadcast daily from Germany. He was known as Lord Haw-Haw because of his frightfully English Oxford accent. He told exaggerated lies: stories of numerous battles between the German forces and our own, we were always the losers. He told tales of battleships sunk wholesale and of the many lives lost each day in the conflict. We sat listening most evenings; the women and girls would usually be knitting warm hats, gloves and socks that would be sent to the soldiers overseas. To save us buying wool with our precious coupons, we would spend many hours unravelling our old woollen jumpers; eating chestnuts roasted on an old metal shovel plunged into the burning coal fire.

When my sister was eighteen she became betrothed to a young man from Manchester. He worked at the local hospital in a job that exempted him from being called up. This was the first Jewish wedding in Buxton and took place under the chupah erected in the Mayor's parlour. Kind relatives and friend donated their precious clothing coupons to the bride to enable her to buy a minimal trousseau of a wedding gown and white shoes. I wore a pink taffeta dress my sister had worn at a wedding several years before, and the local dressmaker fashioned a headdress from a long length of pink ribbon rescued from an old hat. This sat on my newly permed hair like a large dinner plate.

I left school and took a course of fashion design. I secured a job during the College vacation at Madame Lola's gown shop. Madame Lola was a veritable dragon of large proportions. I received a weekly wage of seven shillings and sixpence, out of which I had to buy four, sixpenny savings stamps. Shortly after I started work Madame Lola left a customer she was serving and sailed towards me like a galleon in full sail. She had a dress draped over her ample arm. 'Joan,' she commanded, 'please go downstairs and bring this dress in a larger size.' 'But Madame,' I began to reply, 'shut up, 'she hissed, 'I know there is no downstairs, go behind the counter at the back of the shop and lower yourself gradually downwards as though you're negotiating a staircase. Hurry up and go, girl, and do this in reverse as though you are coming up again. We don't have this dress in another size so just bring the same one back with you and I will fit it on the customer.' I followed her instructions and Madame Lola sold the dress to the customer who left the shop happily with her new purchase.

I spent many happy years in Buxton and felt very sad when the time came to leave. We returned to London after the war ended in 1945. We were deeply moved and shocked to see the devastation the war had brought in the city.

Simon Braun
born in 1918

'This woman has six fingers!'

T he year 1930 brought a lot of disaster and troubles upon the earth, including Hungary where I lived. The collapse of the New York Stock Exchange reached all parts of the world. When the rich lost their riches, some of them leapt to their death from the tops of high buildings, and some simply suffered under the deteriorating circumstances. The bourgeoisie tried to push on with their small businesses, and they often fired many of their employees without compensation. The poor only got poorer and hungrier. There was no possibility of finding work because there simply wasn't any. There were no social services and no outside help. They had only their pride left. Here and there kitchens were set up for the poor where they could get a hot plate of soup for the day, but this also lessened day by day and not everybody was willing to stand in long lines to get their beggar's portion.

Some people were resourceful and tried a trick. They fell 'unconscious' in front of a food store, and waited for somebody to come out with half a cup of milk and a slice of bread. After eating they got up and moved on the next food store to repeat the performance.

We did not escape this dire poverty. My father, who had been a well to do merchant, lost everything he had and was left absolutely penniless. He still had his pride, however, and we kept our pride as well. Nobody was allowed to know whether we had eaten breakfast or lunch, and we had to walk in shoes with holes in their soles, which nobody could see.

My sister, Rozsika, was the only one in the family who worked. As a secretary in an office, she earned 80 Pengo a month, a sum that was sufficient for the rent of the flat where we lived. She was the one who kept us alive. From where she got the money is a secret she took with her to the grave. One thing is certain, however, she earned her money decently, and she gave all of it to keep alive our father and our mother, herself and her brothers, aged eleven, thirteen and fifteen. Our father suffered terribly through this, and his good mood and jovial personality disappeared altogether. This was our life.

One day Father came home late and without speaking to anyone, and without eating his meagre portion, he went into his room to lie down. After a few days of this strange behaviour we put two and two together and understood that he had a debilitating toothache. To pull a tooth out with an injection for pain cost 10 Pengo, a sum of money that he couldn't spend simply for the luxury of an injection. One day he came home earlier than usual, with a flushed face, bloody lips and a smile. He had pulled out his own tooth without an injection. As children we couldn't imagine the pain that he went through. Our sister Rozsika took the bloody tooth from his hands, wrapped it in cotton wool, and put it into a small box.

In 1944 Hungarian Jewry was deported, and so were my two sisters. After a long journey on foot without food and water, and another journey by train, they arrived at last at Auschwitz where the gas chambers awaited them. When the dead bodies were removed from the gas chambers, they were checked for valuables that might have been put in hidden places. One of the Jewish women who did this terrible task, suddenly cried out, 'this poor woman has six fingers!' When they looked closely, they recognized my sister, who held a tooth in her clutched hands. Try as they might they couldn't remove it from her grasp, and the body of my sister was burned in the crematorium with the tooth of my father.

Bernard Kraus
born in 1914

Stick telephones,
hobos and crystal sets

I grew up in Elizabeth New Jersey, one of six children in the family, and lived not far from Newark airport. Every time a plane flew overhead it was an event and everyone would stop whatever they were doing and watch. Newark airfield opened up in the late 1920's, with just one hangar. Because we didn't have a car in those days, a friend with a car would drive us to the airport. In those days the pilots were really flight pioneers and were known as barnstormer pilots and dare devils. They initiated commercial and recreational flying. There was no such thing as licences to fly. The planes were small with only two seats, one in the front for the pilot and one at the back for the passenger. Initially, all the flights were commercial and before a passenger service began, mail was flown from one city to another.

My mother was a housewife. In order to do the washing she had to put the boiler on the stove to boil the water and then use the washboard and hand wringer. In the wintertime the wet clothes froze stiff on the line. There was no central heating, only a coal-fired stove in the kitchen, which was used for cooking, baking and heating. In the winter the windows of the bedroom would frost over and we ran downstairs into the warm kitchen to get dressed.

My father was a carpenter for a construction company and during the depression was out of work for a time. My sisters, who were stenographers, supported the family. Unemployed people stood on street corners selling items and produce such as apples. Volunteer organisations, like the Red Cross and Salvation Army, ran bread lines and soup kitchens. The times were extremely difficult. When the market went down in 1929, a lot of people were buying on margin. If a stock cost one hundred dollars, they put down twenty dollars and waited for the market to go up, counting on the profit to pay off the rest. At the start of the depression the market went down and the brokers called for their money. Some stock market investors couldn't take it and committed suicide by throwing themselves out of the windows.

The banks didn't foreclose on mortgages because there was no point in foreclosing. We didn't pay our mortgage for eighteen months. When times were bad, I waited for my elder brother to go to work, then I borrowed his sweater or his coat to go to school, and put it back before he came home.

In the 1920's and 1930's hobos travelled from town to town, living in ramshackle shacks made out of tin. They rode the freight trains, 'riding the rods', as they called it, to go from one town to the next, making their living by asking for handouts. Tinkers came round to fix things, such as teakettles or umbrellas. There were also gypsies, who worked mainly as fortune-tellers. They set up a stall on the street where people went to have their fortunes told. Peddlers came round with a horse and cart and hollered 'nice ripe yellow bananas, a dozen and a half for a quarter.' The ragman did a circuit with his horse and wagon buying rags, which he then took to a rag dealer. The knife sharpener went with his truck and knife-sharpening machine, to sharpen knives on the spot. An Italian came on foot, door-to-door, selling garlic, carrying a special bag over his shoulder. It was divided into two, with one bag at the front and one bag at the back. Milk, bread and meat were delivered to the door and in wintertime when it snowed, the milk delivery arrived by horse and sleigh. They all had a regular route at a regular time and Mother would know when to be at home when she needed to place orders or wait for deliveries.

We had an icebox, and every day, the iceman, usually an Italian, came to put ice inside. He carried four hundred lbs blocks of ice on a piece of burlap, which sat on his shoulder. He had a pick, and knew exactly how big to cut the ice. In between deliveries I went to the icehouse to collect ice and carried it home with a pair of tongs. There was a pan underneath the icebox, which had to be emptied from time to time. My father drilled a hole in the floor of the pantry, attached a hose to the icebox and threaded it through the hole into the basement where it emptied into a drain. This avoided the problem of emptying the pan day and night.

The local surgeon owned one of the first cars in Elizabeth, which was chauffeur- driven because he didn't want to do anything to damage his hands. At that time the model 'T' Ford was the most popular car. There were also cars known as 'touring cars', which were open on the top and sides to the elements. To protect passengers in bad weather one hooked canvas onto the body of the car. There were no automatic windscreen wipers on the windshield. The single wiper was operated by hand on the driver's side, so the driver could either have his hands on the steering wheel or he could operate the wiper, but not both. There were no directional signals at all; you had to use your arm to indicate the direction you wanted to go. In order to drive at night, lights were necessary. We used a lantern with a cartridge inside containing carbon, which

STICK TELEPHONES, HOBOS AND CRYSTAL SETS

we lit with a match. Although there were a hundred different types of cars, I remember that one of the first cars was the Stanley Steamer, which ran on steam.

I never went on holiday, but from time to time a neighbour would pile the kids into a truck and my mother would give me a shoebox containing a sandwich and a piece of fruit, and we would go to the seaside about forty miles away. At the beach there were separate facilities for men and women to change into bathing suits.

For fun, in the early 1920's, the children made homemade radios. Marconi had a radio station in Roselle Park, New Jersey. To receive the frequency the kids made crystal sets. They took a crystal and a whisker, a little hair or a little wire and were able to hear the station broadcasts.

The 1920's telephone was a stick telephone. One took the handset off the stick and the operator came on to say 'number please.' She called the number, not by dialling, but by putting pegs and wires into her switchboard. Some subscribers had four way or five way party lines, which meant you shared the telephone line with other subscribers. If you wanted to make a call and you picked up the handset, you heard the other party's conversation. If you wanted to make an emergency call there might be an argument. My mother liked to tell the operator the number she wanted. Eventually, when we were able to dial the number ourselves from a more modern telephone system, it became a problem for my mother to make a telephone call.

From 1942-1945 I was in the American Air force, stationed at Whatton in The Wash. [Norfolk, England]. We went over to England on the ocean liner, the Queen Mary. The British Government requisitioned the liner and leased it to the American government, who paid seventy-five dollars for each of the fifteen thousand soldiers carried on the liner. The Queen Mary was not finished at the time of requisition. Although it was seaworthy, it had not been put into service as a passenger cruise ocean liner.

When we embarked on the boat, we didn't know our destination. Only after meeting some British soldiers who knew they were going home, did we understand that we were going to England.

There were six messes [sittings] for breakfast. I was in mess number six, so although I got up early I could not have breakfast until 10 a.m. As you went into the dining room you were handed an orange. There was no lunch served. If you wanted to eat at midday you bought a snack from the canteen. The next meal served was in the evening.

The liner was crowded, and if you stood at the rails to look at the ocean and left your place it was immediately taken by another soldier. Some of the soldiers spent part of the day lying on their bunk because there were very few places to sit. There were nine soldiers in my crew and we shared stateroom 273 on the B deck with another crew of nine. There were nine bunks in the room. One night we slept on the bunks, and the next night we had to find somewhere else to sleep, usually in the hallways or in the ballroom.

We docked at Greenock in Scotland, and then travelled by train to Whatton in Norfolk. Whenever the train stopped at a local station the local townspeople, seeing an American army train, came out to greet us and to give us food, meat pies, and cakes.

I was an armourer in the Air force. We handled the armaments on the planes especially the machine guns and the bombs. My job was to take care of the gun camera, and load the bombs onto the planes. The pilot had a joystick to fly the plane upon which was a gun trigger connected to a movie camera located on the wing. When the pilot saw an enemy plane and engaged him in battle, the movie camera took a film of what was happening with the other plane during the sortie. Since the pilot was alone in the plane, the camera was important for verification of all flights and actions. In the European theatre of operations it was essential to know who the Ace pilots were, and to observe different manoeuvres; what worked and what didn't work. Also on film were the strafing missions, which blew up boats and trains. Everything was evaluated by experts who studied the films and pinpointed the effectiveness of the mission. The pilots would review the films and describe to the other pilots what he did on his mission. It was educational. In my battalion there were three squadrons of planes and fifteen thousand soldiers. In my outfit there were two hundred and fifty to three hundred soldiers and only twenty of them were Jewish.

I was at the first Pesach Seder of Liberation in Mons, Belgium, at the beginning of April. It was an army Seder and we were in Belgium to give support to our planes during the Battle of the Bulge. A protestant Chaplain organized the Friday night services and sang along with us.

When I came back to work after the war everyone was asked to produce his or her birth certificate. I went down to City Hall, but there was no record of my birth because I was born at home. I had to get an affidavit from my father and the school records, because the doctor who delivered me did not register my birth. However, in spite of this I was able to rebuild my life.

Max Todes
born in 1892
Told by his daughter

'Father slept on the counter'

My father was born in Yaneskel, Lithuania. When he was eighteen, he joined his brother Morris in South Africa, who had emigrated earlier because of the financial and political situation in Lithuania, which afforded no hope of making a living.

The blacks lived in different parts of South Africa and in the surrounding countries of Rhodesia or Portuguese East Africa, now known as Mozambique. The mines were located in Witerwatersrand in the Rand regions with Johannesburg situated in the centre of the Rand area. The owners of the mines allowed businesses to establish themselves on mining land.

At that time a lot of people went to South Africa to make money out of the gold mines. Many Jews set up businesses close to the mines that catered to the black labourers. They opened clothing and food shops. The blacks loved spending money and loved clothing and were only too happy to spend their wages on clothing for the family back home when their labouring contracts were up.

My father started working in a man's outfitting store, situated near these mines. For the first few months after he arrived in South Africa he had nowhere to sleep and no money to pay rent, so he slept on the counter of the shop, rolling up his mattress in the morning and storing it under the counter. This was common practice for Lithuanian Jewish refugees emigrating to South Africa at this time.

When he was twenty-seven, he married and went into the outfitting business together with his brother, setting up shop near the mines, where they prospered. In 1930 my father bought a hundred shares of Land securities, issued in London, from which I still receive dividends.

During the Second World War tremendous numbers of South African troops were stationed at El Alamein in North Africa. South Africa was part of the Dominion of the British Empire, therefore when Britain declared war, South Africa declared war despite the fact that many South Africans were against fighting the Germans because they regarded the Nazis as ideological allies.

In South Africa we did not suffer rationing or know the discomforts and horrors of war as the people in Europe did. Our war efforts were limited to knitting balaclavas and socks for the soldiers. The women joined the Wrens, the womens section of British Military, and otherwise just sat and waited for the soldiers to come home. We were aware of what was going on in the concentration camps of Europe.

While I was growing up, living in South Africa was a good and easy life as long as your skin was white.

At the time that Nelson Mandela, the head of the ANC, the African National Congress, was incarcerated in 1956, my husband and I ran a bookshop. We obtained books from England that were banned by the South African government, for being subversive, left wing or communist, and sold them in our shop. The buyers of these forbidden books were members of the South African Congress and the Indian Youth movement. These were banned organisations because the South African government was determined, by any means necessary to squash any attempt at self determination by black or coloured groups to gain control of the country.

Simcha Mandelbaum
born around 1870
Told by his grandson

Mandelbaum's Gate

M y grandfather, Simcha Mandelbaum, was born in
White Russia in the area of Pinsk. His father, Rabbi
Baruch Mandelbaum, was a Dayan and a Rabbi in White
Russia and as a Karliner Chassid he was very connected to
the chatzer, court of Karlin. Rabbi Baruch came to Eretz
Yisroel well after his son Simcha had become well
established here.

Simcha married the daughter of Rebbe Nachum Epstein,
the Kobiner Rebbe, a great Zionist. He was the Dayan of
Avraham Yitzhok Kook. One of his daughters eventually
married Rav Raphael Kook, the nephew of Rav Avraham
Yitzhok.

Simcha, together with Rav Shtamper and Rav Solomon,
founded the settlement of Petach Tikvah. Even today,
streets in the town are named for these men. Before this,
however, he settled in the Old City of Jerusalem., where
he was a textile merchant. Besides having a shop where he
sold his goods, mostly socks, he also sold wholesale to
other shops.

My grandfather Simcha purchased land from an Arab,
which eventually became known as the Mandelbaum
Gate. It was situated at the corner of Rehov Shmuel
Hanavi, which was the border between Israel and Jordan.
It was his dream to protect Jerusalem by establishing a
fortress between the Arab area and the Jewish area.

People were shocked and asked him why he invested
such a fortune of money in this land, when parcels of land

could be purchased in safer, more stable areas such as Rehavia. He told them that this point is strategic and will establish a shelter for Jerusalem right here at the border. It was an empty area between the Jews and the Arabs, before the War of Independence in 1948, and prior to the establishment of the State of Israel.

Construction started in 1925 and was finished in 1929. Simcha passed away around the age of sixty in 1930, and only lived in the building for two years at the most. However he merited seeing the realisation of his greatest dream before his death. Originally Mandelbaum House was built as living quarters for the extended family. My father Baruch Mandelbaum, Uncle Yechiel the founder of Bank Yisroel, my uncle Raphael Kook with his wife who was Simcha's daughter, and Simcha and his wife, all lived together with their families in apartments at Mandelbaum House. After my grandfather Simcha died, his wife lived with her daughter and her family in Simcha's apartment.

I lived there as a young boy until I was eleven years old and it became too difficult to stay there because of the shooting. Before the unease began, life was not particularly difficult. I walked to school every day, which was twenty minutes from the house. I remember the Police station at Meah Shearim, which I'm not sure exists any more. I remember more about the political situation at that time. A man named Liebovitch, who as a policeman in the British army and who was also a member of the Haganah, lived in the building along with us. It was rumoured that the Haganah used the building to hide weapons. I remember the underground groups of Etzel, headed by Menachem Begin and Lechi, who fought against the British soldiers.

The British wanted to make it impossible to live there, so they divided Jerusalem into two areas, one Arab and one Jewish. They also established a curfew. Of course, Mandelbaum House was on the Arab side and we were

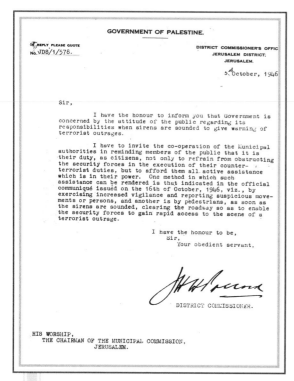

GOVERNMENT OF PALESTINE.

IN REPLY PLEASE QUOTE
No. JDS/1/578.

DISTRICT COMMISSIONER'S OFFIC
JERUSALEM DISTRICT,
JERUSALEM.

5. October, 1946

Sir,

I have the honour to inform you that Government is concerned by the attitude of the public regarding its responsibilities when sirens are sounded to give warning of terrorist outrages.

I have to invite the co-operation of the Municipal authorities in reminding members of the public that it is their duty, as citizens, not only to refrain from obstructing the security forces in the execution of their counter-terrorist duties, but to afford them all active assistance which is in their power. One method in which such assistance can be rendered is that indicated in the official communiqué issued on the 16th of October, 1946, viz., by exercising increased vigilance and reporting suspicious movements or persons, and another is by pedestrians, as soon as the sirens are sounded, clearing the roadway so as to enable the security forces to gain rapid access to the scene of a terrorist outrage.

I have the honour to be,
Sir,
Your obedient servant,

DISTRICT COMMISSIONER.

HIS WORSHIP,
THE CHAIRMAN OF THE MUNICIPAL COMMISSION,
JERUSALEM.

subjected to that curfew, despite the fact that we depended on the Jewish side.

When the War of Independence started in 1948, we left the building and sought sanctuary in other, safer parts of the City, and we turned Mandelbaum House over to the Haganah. All day they shot from there across the border. It was an extremely useful strategic point from which they conducted their operations.

The Underground soldiers had a poor array of weaponry; tommy guns and sten guns whose range is only moderately effective for up to sixty metres. It was a miracle that they could defend Jerusalem with the pitiful amount of weapons that they had, because the Arabs were much better supplied. The Haganah made Molotov cocktails as well, and threw them at the Arabs. With their bodies they stopped the advance of Arab soldiers and their vehicles into the heart of Jerusalem. The Arabs counter attacked and eventually the building was destroyed. The house does not exist anymore. The Arabs left a bomb, which exploded the whole structure. The Arabs knew that many great battles were won because of the strategic importance of this building.

The building may be gone but its fame lives on in the memories of Jerusalemites.

Esther Liebes
born in 1924

'In cattle wagons deep into Siberia'

I was born in Gorlice, Poland. It was an oil rich town in which the Jews had a stake, and many of them became wealthy because of this. Later we moved to Krakow where my father was the Rabbi and the head of Tahkemoni Hebrew School in Krakow.

In September 1939, when the Germans invaded Poland, I was fifteen years of age and was staying in my grandparent's house in Gorlice with my Uncle and Aunt. My Grandmother had had an infection in her ear. Because there were no antibiotics and at that time they couldn't operate, my grandmother died. My mother sat Shiva in Krakow.

The Germans moved into Czech and then into Gorlice, which was near the Czech border. On the radio we heard that the Germans were on the threshold of Poland. The Rav told the community on Shabbos that they could leave Gorlice that day. My family did not want to desecrate Shabbos so we remained and immediately after we lit the havdalah candle on motzei Shabbos, we left. I was with my Aunt and Uncle, three cousins and my three younger brothers, aged six, twelve and thirteen. We proceeded to the train station and took the last train that left for the south of Poland where my father's parents lived. As my mother and father were in Krakow and my sister was with them looking after my mother, they decided that we should meet with them at my father's parents' home.

When the train arrived at Sambor, the Polish Police stopped the train and told the passengers to get off. My

Uncle was a businessman and had connections in the town but it was very late at night. He looked around for someone to take us in, but it was futile. No one would take us. The driver of the horse and buggy, a goy, offered to take us to his stable and said that we could sleep on his straw. We paid him of course.

In the morning, my Uncle said he was staying in the town but that my brothers and I should try to get to the town of my father's parents. We took our possessions and trudged out of the stables with my Uncle. There were many refugees in the town and he heard of an autobus going in the direction of my father's parents' village.

We boarded the bus with no food at all, just our little packages. The autobus stopped a few times when the air raid siren sounded. We got off the autobus to hide underneath it so that we would not be seen by the planes overhead and we would be protected. Eventually the bus stopped completely and couldn't go further. The driver said that the town was about ten kilometres away and we should start walking.

We were in the middle of nowhere, walking through fields of grass, in a completely flat plain. We walked for an hour, perhaps an hour and a half until we were completely exhausted. The children couldn't carry the bundles anymore. Suddenly we saw a horse and farm wagon, with a driver and passenger. The driver approached us in the wagon and said, 'children, where are you going?' I told him that we were going to my grandfather. He said, 'I know the town. I will take you there.' I didn't know if this man was a goy or a yid. Until today I don't know how he appeared. There were just fields as far as the eye could see. There was no road and we had a long way to go. It would have taken us twenty-four hours to walk there. He just appeared. We could hear the planes, which were not above us now, throwing their bombs. Poland was attacked from only one side.

We came to the town of Grudek where we saw many Yidden. We left the wagon in the middle of the town and some of the townspeople came over to us. 'Kinder,' they asked, 'where are you coming from?' I told them that I was the granddaughter of the Rav.

My grandfather was the Rav of the town, but we didn't know him because his village was a long way from Krakow. Although we had never met, since we wrote letters to him, we knew that he was Rabbi Yosef Klieger, a great posek and Talmud Chocham in Poland.

The townspeople were surprised and asked 'where do you come from?' We told them which son of the Rav was our father; he was the eldest son, Meshulam. They were great admirers of my father who was well known in Poland for his community activities.

As we arrived at my grandfather's door the whole town followed us to see the children of the eldest son, Meshulam. When my grandfather opened the door you couldn't imagine more surprised people. After settling us inside he asked about the rest of the family. We told him where everyone was and he said 'we will try to get in touch with them.'

There were telephones in Poland at this time, but my grandfather did not have one. When we lived in Krakow we did not have a telephone, however, our neighbours, who were business people, did. On Fridays, my grandparents from Gorlice would call, and our neighbours would fetch us to take the telephone call. It was a ritual that marked the beginning of Shabbos.

Now the wires were cut. I would never see my parents or sister again. I am the only survivor of my family. I was

The cattle truck at Yad Vashem

now on the German side of Poland. We were invited to register to return to the Russian side of Poland, in order to return to Krakow, which was now under Russian control. I stood in line the whole night to register, but it was a trick. A week after I had registered the Polish Police came to the house, in the middle of the night, and asked who was not a citizen of the town. They were cooperating fully with the Russian Authorities. My brothers were hiding, but they took my Aunt and me. One of the possessions we took with us was a down quilt, without which we could not have survived.

We were taken by cattle trucks to the train station and loaded into more cattle trucks. There was standing room only. I think that the Germans learnt from the Russians. We were two or three months travelling by train in the cattle trucks. We sat on each other's knee. My Aunt and I were together. There were occasional stops to take care of our physical needs. Sometimes we got hot water, a little soup or a piece of bread. The train rolled over the frozen tundra until we reached the edge of Siberia.

We were taken thousands of kilometres in the cattle wagons, deep into the heart of Siberia, where nothing grows because there is very little sun and it is mostly winter. I wrapped newspapers around my feet, which were so frozen that the bone showed through. Although it was freezing, whenever we stopped by a river, we would wash our clothes. I know that some women were mesiras nefesh to go to the mikveh by digging a hole in the ice and going in the ice cold water, holding on to some one else for dear life.

When we arrived at our destination we lit fires and slept in shacks. We were given meagre rations in exchange for the work that we did, a little bread, margarine and barley. If you didn't work you got no food. My Aunt couldn't work so I shared my food with her. If you had jewellery you swapped it for food. I had a ring, which I gave to a Russian family in exchange for potatoes, which was a lifesaver. We got acquainted with the people who looked after the horses and they gave us the husks of the oats that they fed to the horses, in exchange for our possessions such as pillowcases. We mixed these husks with water and cooked them on the fire.

I was a good knitter although I lacked the materials. Occasionally the Russians gave us an old sweater, which we unravelled for the wool. Although they were goyim, the doctor and his wife were very fond of us. They gave us knitting needles. She brought me old sweaters and I made gloves, earmuffs and hats for her children. I knew the patterns from siyata dishamaya, heavenly assistance. One of my jobs was being put to work knitting and sewing. We had to walk a few kilometres to work. In the low temperatures I had nothing to wear on my feet. My feet froze. You had to cover your mouth and your eyelids had ice on them.

For my first job I was sent to the woods to cut down trees. It was difficult and dangerous work. A lot of people perished when a cut tree fell on them. I was sixteen years of age and I went to the head of our group to complain that I was too young to do the work. I told him that 'it's too difficult. I am going to die here.' He asked a Polish doctor, who had been sent to Siberia with his family, to examine me. 'She is complaining that she cannot do the work,' he said. The doctor checked me and agreed. 'She is right,' he said, 'she can't do the work.'

In the winter no food came in and we were cut off from the rest of the world because the whole area was frozen. They allowed us to grow vegetables, otherwise we would have starved. You could only get through by sled.

It was our goral, bitter fortune, but we saw nissim, miracles, every day. They wanted us to work in the gold mines the other side of the river. There were no boats, and we had to cross on a few planks tied together like a raft. It was very dangerous. My three friends drowned, but I didn't have to go across. That was a nes, a miracle. I was assigned work in the cafeteria of the workers in the mines. Everything was measured. We served perfectly measured squares of food. Only two jugs of milk were provided. I was responsible for giving out the portions of milk. If I was short I was the one who did without. And they always gave me short measure. Other people got together and shared their milk with me because I was swollen with hunger.

Our plight was very hard, and every day was a struggle because we were put to work in such terrible circum-stances. We slept in a shack that was so cold that the walls had ice on the inside. I slept next to the wall so that my Aunt didn't need to.

When I came out of Siberia I couldn't move my hand because I had slept next to the frozen wall. I didn't think that I would survive the hunger, the cold and the diseases.

After the war Russia and Poland made a pact and the first thing the Poles did was to free the people in Siberia. I returned to Poland the way I had come; in cattle wagons, on a two-month journey, over the frozen tundra.

Tzipora Morgenstern Gilbert
born in 1923

'Deutschland uber alles Juden kaput'

On the same day that Hitler invaded Warsaw, I graduated from a Polish elementary school. I remember the German boots crossing the bridge between Praga and Warsaw. We watched as the boots kept coming over the bridge, across the road and finally they were there. After the invasion we had no water, no light and life itself started fading away day by day. As refugees trudged along the roads with bundles on their backs, towards the Eastern border, my father, an orthodox Rabbi said 'we will not go to the East, to the communists.'

Tzipora Morgenstern Gilbert

One day I went with my girl friend to dig radishes in the field near where the German army was stationed. A young German soldier, no more than a teenager, engaged us in conversation. I still vividly remember him telling us, 'Deutschland uber alles, Juden kaput,' Germany above all and the Jews are finished. I believed him completely. His words left me cold with fear. From then on I dreamed of leaving German occupied Poland. My father, however, sensing our unease, made sure that his daughters would not leave by putting a lock on the outside door.

My brother David and his best friend Abraham Zilberstein left Poland for Russia, as the German bombs were falling. They reached the other side, but Abraham couldn't accept his family's fate and dreamed of saving his parents and sisters and brothers. He trekked back into Poland to the small town where his family lived. Meanwhile the Germans, the Angels of Death, had brought devastation and annihilation to the Jewish population of that small town. People said that the earth at the edge of town trembled for many days because so many people were thrown into pits and buried alive.

Abraham Zilberstein helped us escape from Poland. We formulated a plan. One day when we were supposed, as usual, to go to the Vistula for some water, my sister and I took the pail and left it at my girl friend's house. We told her to go to our mother and tell her that we were leaving and we would write to her. The three of us made our way from Warsaw to the Eastern border of Poland on foot. We were able to eat because the peasants along the way would sell us some food.

We finally arrived at the River Bug on the border between Poland and Russia. The river was in front of us and we stood on the Polish side along with the German soldiers. On the other side of the river stood the Russian soldiers. The Germans allowed us go, and we crossed the bombed out bridge, pieces of which were missing. Abraham told us to look up to the sky, because if we looked down we might fall into the water and be swallowed by the current. When we made it to the other side the Russian soldiers greeted us.

The first Russian soldier who spoke to me asked me about my ambitions in life. I told him that to be a secretary in a nice cosy office would be just great. He laughed and said 'oh, you could become that and anything else that you want to be.' The conversation was in contrast to the one with the young German soldier who only a short time earlier had promised me death. This young soldier spoke about life and a future to look forward to. Then we found ourselves in the city of Bialystok, engulfed in a group of refugees on the way to Brest Litovak. This was the city where Trotsky had, some years earlier, signed a peace treaty with the Germans.

My father's sister lived in Brest Litovak and my sister Mina and I thought that now we could relax after our long journey. My Aunt, whom we had never met before, told us that she had no room for us. Mina and I had to search for a place to sleep. A good family, who were complete strangers, offered us their floor. Eventually another good family offered us a bed. As we had to eat, we quickly learned hand knitting and worked for a while in a knitting factory.

The Russian letters looked so strange and so different from the Polish language, which is based on Latin. The Russian language is based on a modification of the Greek alphabet called Cyrillic. I was young and learning came easily to me. I overcame the difficulties with the language and the new alphabet and soon spoke Russian like a native.

As soon as I felt adjusted to our new life, everything changed. Before I knew it, 1941 came. At 4.00 on the 22nd June, Kiev was bombed and the war started for us all over again. Before we left the city I invited my Aunt to come with us. She refused and said, 'oh no, I will not leave our brick factory and home to go somewhere deep into Russia.' Meanwhile my sister got married and she and her husband, with a group of other people, decided that life in

Russia offered them too many deprivations. They registered to return to German occupied Warsaw. At this time the Germans were still fooling the world and no one believed the reality of Mein Kampf. I didn't want any part of it and after much discussion my sister and I parted.

In the end the Germans refused to let them in and the Russians considered them enemies and sent them all to Siberia.

I joined a group of people travelling on freight trains in order to go deeper into Russia. I remember sitting on top of some sort of grain. As a child I was always hungry and cold. I dreamed of sunshine and warm lands. I chose, therefore, to go to the Caucasus, the Russian South, also known as the Russian Florida. I soon disembarked in a city called Gueorgievsk, a warm and pretty city.

I travelled with Ada Josefovna, who had been a schoolteacher in Poland. With only the clothes on our backs, a small suitcase in our hand and with no money, we entered the Police Station. We gave them all the information they required. I vividly remember an NKVD agent called Mr Bondar. He told me that he would find a place for me to sleep in his house and for Ada, in the house of a neighbour. At Mr Bondar's home, I met his sweet, friendly, undernourished wife and his little girl with freckles. I slept in a cot in the kitchen. They were as nice to me as a good brother and sister.

At that time my command of the Russian language was good enough for me to apply for an office job where I was hired as a clerk. I remember two wonderful women in the office, the accountant Zenaida Pavlovna and a bookkeeper Tatyana Ivanova. The husband of Zenaida was an officer at the front in Rostov.

The Germans were knocking at the door of the Caucasus. They wanted Rostov and they wanted Baku, the oil centre of Russia. The Germans wanted the oil, the land and they wanted to annihilate the population. They wanted the roads of Europe free for the master race to roam at will. Most of the population of Europe were to be annihilated, with just enough people left to do the slave work for the master race.

Zenaida made a trip from Gueorgievsk to Rostov to visit her husband. She lived in a clean little house. She was good and kind and often took me into her house and gave me food. In Russia, people who offered food to others were giving them life itself. Zenaida had two beautiful greyhounds, and she was as proud and considerate of them as any Fifth Avenue lady is of hers.

Tatyana was married to a man who occupied a position in the communist hierarchy and who was away most of the time. She had several children, some his, some theirs. She kept wondering why she ever married him, resentful of having to feed so many mouths.

At the end of 1941 and the beginning of 1942, the Angels of Death, the Germans, knocked more and more vigorously at the gates of the Caucasus. During this period I became acquainted with some girls aged twelve to eighteen, who belonged to a girls' school that had been evacuated from Leningrad. These children lost their parents in the siege of Leningrad, mostly dying of starvation. As the Germans came nearer, I carried in my mind the promise of death the young German soldier had offered me in Warsaw. I immediately joined the group and was evacuated with them to a city on the Volga called Kuibyshev. In Czarist times it was called Samara. I remember passing Stalingrad, which still had its old architecture.

There were thirty to forty girls in the group. My best friend was Sima Romanova, a kind, sweet girl, whose mother had hanged herself in Leningrad when Sima was three years old. Sima never forgot it. An Aunt who was a nurse in a hospital brought her up. In 1942 we arrived with our teachers and supervisors to a town a few miles from Kuibyshev, called Bezymianka, which in Russian means no name. Bezymianka was in the process of being built. The Russians were evacuating their factories from Moscow and with the factories came the workers, their families and teachers. Schools were also being built.

Our group of girls was taken to work in an airplane factory called Frunze and we were given our jobs to do. The good man who selected us for different kinds of jobs, G-d bless him, did not put me in the assembly line where the girls were making different screws and parts, I suppose roller bearings. They had their hands in oil most of the time, which resulted in the developing of rashes on their hands and face. The good man put me at the end of the assembly line to check and measure the finished product.

We were given places to sleep in the nearby barracks that were still under construction. In the barracks we were given double-deckers and each girl was given a mattress and a blanket. The summers were tolerable and even nice, but the winters had sub-zero weather. We were always freezing and always hungry. We were half starved and lived in perpetual cold. We washed under an outside cold water pump in cold weather and the toilets were holes in the ground surrounded by frozen faeces and urine, which we stepped on. We were lucky not to break our legs, and not to fall in. Once a week we were taken to the public baths.

Sima and I shared the food we had. When our salary came on paydays, we used to go to the black market and look for something to buy. We ended up buying cucumbers, because they were cheap but they gave us stomachache.

After I had a job and a place to sleep, I started investigating the possibility of enrolling in the nearest High school. In the factory we worked shifts, two weeks on days, two weeks on nights, these were twelve-hour shifts from nine to nine. In order to go to school I applied to my factory director to work only nights. The factory director said, 'little girl, how can you do it?' I answered, 'Sir, I will try.'

From then on, for many years I worked in the factory from nine in the evening to nine in the morning. In the morning I returned to the barracks to sleep on my cot for several hours. Since the High school operated on several shifts I enrolled in the late afternoon shift. I was the only one who came to the school from the factory. The roads were not paved and the soles of my shoes had the habit of falling off in the mud. I never had a cold or a headache during that period and didn't know the existence of emotional problems.

My major dreams of those days were that a bakery truck would pass by, drop a loaf of bread and I would be the only one to grab it.

Gerry Benson
born in 1935

Grey days
and penny chocolate bars

T he war started in 1939. They say that a child's memory storing process usually starts around the age of four, so naturally all I can recall of my very early years is ...WAR! Now war seemed a perfectly normal event, as it was the only one I knew. A child is equipped with an incredible built-in ability to adapt to his surroundings, whatever they may be so WAR was, well, almost fun!

I call them the 'Grey Days', because when the footage of the war years from the BBC archives are broadcast, they are always depicted in black and white. But it seemed, through my eyes as a child, that not only the film but also real life unfolded in colours of grey. Women wore turbans and trousers. The advent of trousers for women was heralded in, and remains a permanent fixture right up until today. The reason for this was highly practical. The fine work they did in the garment factories making uniforms, and working in factories which produced armaments, necessitated, with all the dangerous machinery around, the wearing of turbans and trousers for obvious safety reasons.

Since all of the industrial installations were commandeered for the purpose of producing all the many and varied items needed to fuel a conflict of such enormity, the clothing and material mills were turning out uniforms and all their necessary accoutrements. Items that were considered luxury goods were not produced. One of these speciality items was women's stockings. At that time a stocking was manufactured with a back seam. As stockings were hard to come by, women used to circumvent the dilemma by painting a black line on the back of their leg to give the impression that they were wearing stockings.

They were grey days because there was rationing and items, which are now casually dropped into the supermarket trolley in passing, were at the time, a most coveted luxury. Eggs! Cox's apples! Sweets and chocolate! I can recall my father castigating my mother for having purchased a pound of Cox's apples on the black market for the princely sum of half a crown [twelve and a half pence.] This was true extravagance. Today's equivalent buying power is around three pounds sterling. Those apples tasted like nectar.

I vividly recall standing on a railway station platform with my mother and discovering a rusty metal contraption, about eight inches wide and two feet deep, mounted on the wall. Printed on the front were the words 'Nestlé's Chocolate − One penny per bar'. There was a slot in the top to place your penny and assumedly the bar of chocolate would fall into the aperture for collection by the lucky recipient. I gazed, at the age of seven, literally transfixed at this beautiful, magnificent rusty contraption, which before the war and rationing, used to actually dispense chocolate for a penny. I remember imagining how wonderful that, in another world, in another dimension, on another planet, one could actually approach this now empty, magnificent contraption and for the sum of one penny receive ... chocolate.

The world where such a coveted, hedonistic experience could occur sat only in the deeper enigmatic realm of my imagination. Sometimes, when I travel on the London underground, where there is a marked predominance of chocolate machines even more magnificent and beautiful because of their colours and the enhanced lighting, my head turns to look at them and I smile as my mind rushes back down the corridors of time to that rusty, obsolete, but truly beautiful contraption on the wall of that dingy railway station.

During the war we had occurrences known as 'Air Raids'. This was when the aeroplanes of the 'glorious brave Fuehrer' flew over London and other major cities of Britain, with the sole purpose of dropping as many bombs on as many civilians, homes and installations as possible. Their missions were highly successful. Thousands of civilians, men, women and children, were killed or maimed where they stood or slept. This, too, became normal and commonplace and for me there were no memories to recall to the contrary.

I remember rising to go to school, crossing the road one block away and seeing a complete row of about twenty houses almost completely flattened by bombs. Timbers were still smouldering. Once again a child's mind functions in strange ways, rearranging the order of the priorities of events. One of these was remembering among the wreckage photographs of people not known to me. Photos of babies, weddings, family groups soldiers, children, strewn across the pavement and fluttering away in the wind. These were items that had no earthly value to a passing onlooker, but having treasured intrinsic value for their original owners who were now either dead or maimed.

I recall the memory of a house cleaved in two by a bomb, with a candlestick and a vase on the mantelpiece of the upstairs fireplace, which remained in its original position having avoided the blast.

Every night when the air raids began they would be heralded in by the most stomach-curdling sound of a siren. This siren was located in buildings such as police and fire stations. I was duly awoken by my mother, often at two or three in the morning, and told to hurriedly get dressed and go down to the nearby shelter or cellar, and sit awaiting the 'all clear.' When I see an old film, the sounding of the siren still has the effect of a hand entering my abdomen and inverting the contents of my solar plexus.

Although I was only six or seven years of age, I took note of the terrible events that were unfolding on the continent of Europe. There was a horrendous loss of civilian life with tens of thousands of men dying or wounded in combat against Hitler's massive and highly mechanised war machine. The results of the Holocaust were not fully publicised until the latter years of the war, as the Third Reich used many cunning devices to try to conceal the fact that many civilian men, women and children were sent to their death. The enormity and horror of the Shoah wasn't discovered fully until after the dust of war had fully settled.

During the war, when the German bombing was at its height, there was an evacuation scheme, which was brought into operation for the purpose of getting the bulk of the civilian population out of the large cities to avoid fatalities. This meant that thousands of families were boarded with families who lived in the country and smaller less vulnerable towns away from the bombing. Our fate was to be that my mother, sister and I, my father now being in the army, were billeted in Bridgewater in Somerset, together with three other London families. This was to be, for me, a most pleasant interlude, despite it being imposed upon us. I attended a school where there were only two classrooms! It was something out of a Dickens' novel! It was 'rustic' to put it mildly!

The estate on which I dwelled had an orchard at the rear of the building. With permission of the owner I was allowed to fill my pockets with apples, whenever I saw fit, when they were in season. I remember that there were Russets, Cox's and small green apples called 'Golden Knobs'. I also had to cross a field full of horse chestnut trees, so everyone in the class was armed with conkers and apples at specified times of the year.

Half a century later I visited Bridgewater again. All the green pastureland and the paddock for the horses had disappeared and modern housing had sprung up in its place. The entire area had been developed on every available spot. I walked around, spellbound, trying to relive my childhood memories.

Michel Nager
born in 1937

'Do you think we ate every day?'

In 1936 Hitler took away German nationality from all the Jews. I was born in Berlin in 1937 and at that time because of the Nazi restrictions Jewish boys were compelled to have a German first name. The second name of all Jewish boys was Israel, in order to identify them as Jews.

In 1939 my parents thought that it would be safer in Holland. Since we now had no nationality and no passports we had to enter into Holland illegally and we did not exist in any official capacity.

People believe that in Holland there were only good people. This was not so. There were only a few special people who were not indifferent to the plight of Jewish children. Even fewer individuals were prepared to risk their lives to rescue a Jewish child during those times when the Germans were taking Jewish families to the camps in Germany.

One such person was a Jew who had converted and now regarded himself as a gentile. When the Germans took the families to the place from where they would be sent to Germany, he tried to smuggle out as many as he could. He had to find a place for every Jewish child he tried to save. There were so few people prepared to hide a child, even for a few days. The neighbours would go to the Gestapo, who would pay seven and a half guilders or around three dollars to the informer for such information. Many non-Jews could not withstand the temptation. I went, with my brother, from one address to another,

*Mrs. Van Drakestein and my brother.
I am on the left*

staying only a week at each place. The family was split up and neither our parents nor we knew the whereabouts of each other.

At one point they could not find a place for me. They knew a lady in a small village near Amsterdam. She was a young widow, with no children, well known in the village since her husband had been the Mayor. Her name was Mrs Johanna Bosch Van Drakestein. The Dutch resistance contacted the lady and told her that they wanted to leave my older brother and myself with her for a week. She said 'okay, let them come.' During that week HaKadosh Boruch Hu sent me a middle ear infection, which was very painful. In the war you couldn't trust anyone and the lady could not take me to the doctor. When the girl from the Dutch resistance came back a week later, the lady told her 'I can't let him go, he's too ill. Leave him with me another two or three weeks.'

When the Dutch resistance came back the lady said 'you don't have to find anyone else. I have become attached to them.' The doctor had told her she couldn't have children. The Dutch resistance said 'it's dangerous for you.' The lady was a staunch Roman Catholic. She replied 'G-d will watch over me. I am not afraid of the Germans. Nothing will happen.'

After the war she married again, to a nobleman, and gave birth to two boys. She was convinced that it was a gift from G-d because she had looked after my brother and I.

During the war, even if you had money, you could not buy bread without ration coupons. Since my brother and I did not officially exist, we had no coupons. A very old woman lived in the house along with Mrs Van Drakestein. She had lost her house in Rotterdam when a bomb fell on it. She had coupons for bread. However, she had no teeth and could not eat the crust of the bread. My brother and I were given the crusts to eat. This was our only food. The neighbours had a goat in the garden and the lady asked if they would let us have a little milk each day.

The Germans came with dogs to search for us many times. We were hidden in the cellar under flower bulbs. Flower bulbs were eaten during the war as food. Mrs Van Drakestein had several sisters. One of the sisters would say to the Germans when they came to search for us, 'my sister is a young widow. We appreciate that you have to do your job, but do it in a gentle way.' Since they liked to talk to the sisters they did not take their task seriously and they never found us.

There were times when there was no bread, and since there was nothing else ... it's too difficult to speak about. We were very privileged to have crusts of bread to eat. The last winter of the war in Holland was called the 'hunger winter' because there was absolutely nothing to eat. The Germans told the farmers that all their produce was for the Germans. The farmers kept some produce back, but that was for themselves. We were so happy to be alive, having no bread was not important.

During that winter, towards the end of the war, the Swedish Red Cross parachuted white loaves of bread and butter into Holland because of the shortage of food. Mrs Van Drakestein made shirts for me out of the parachute silk, so that I would have clothes to wear. During the war, people were preoccupied with staying alive. We thought that liberation would come soon and the main thing was staying alive.

Life in Holland, after the war, was hard for families who did not officially exist. My family survived the war although my father died shortly afterwards. My mother had no money and no means to support us and she could not get an apartment. Although we had nowhere to live, we did have our lives. There was a Jewish hospital, which before the war, used to be an old age home. It was turned into a home for displaced Jewish people who had nowhere else to go. The residents were Jews without Dutch nationality.

In those days the baker came round with the bread, pedalling on his bicycle. Sometimes my mother told the baker 'I don't want bread today.' The baker would say 'why? Is my bread not good?' My mother would tell him that she had no money to give him. The baker would reply 'I know you have small children. I will leave bread for you and you will pay me when you can.' My mother would reply 'I learnt from my mother that one only buys things if one has the money to pay for it. If one doesn't have the money, one doesn't buy.'

We didn't eat if she had no money. In the war do you think we ate every day? Sometimes she would receive money from a family she knew in Germany. All the residents in the home were Jewish and they helped each other.

After the war I was thin and pale and it was suggested that I go to a farm in Belgium, where I could work on the farm, and have home made farm bread. The farmer was a non-Jew and grew his own grain and was able to make his own bread. Bread is the most precious thing there is. We make a special brocha on bread because it is the most important material thing a person has.

Since I did not officially exist it was illegal for me to cross the border into Belgium. I hid on the floor of the car of the couple with whom I was travelling, covered with coats. We worked on the farm very hard all day. We took the horses to the woods where the trees had been cut down, and brought the wood home for the farmer.

At the end of the day we would go back to the farm. The farmer's wife would be standing there, holding a huge loaf of bread against her stomach, slicing it and giving each of us a slice. If there was any bread left over we would have it for lunch the next day. The farmer's wife would bring lunch to the farmer with a huge pot of coffee, which he allowed us to share.

After the war my mother went again and again to the Dutch authorities to try to get Dutch nationality for us. The Authorities did not want to give nationality to the Jews and made it very difficult. They said to my mother 'what favours did you do for the Germans, that you survived the war?' 'Perhaps you are a communist because you come from the East of Holland?' They always told her that they would look into her case, but nothing ever happened. From time to time my mother would try again. They told her that in order to have Dutch nationality she had to speak Dutch. 'But I do speak Dutch,' she would reply. 'Ah, yes, but with a German accent!' they would tell her. Eventually they didn't have any more excuses and after many years we were granted Dutch nationality.

Emmanuel Boruch
born in 1916

'Jerusalem is not on the moon'

I came to Palestine in 1938 from Germany when I was twenty-two years of age. It was very different from what I had imagined. It was not a desert with a lot of palm trees; it was a modern developing country.

I came from Berlin straight to Jerusalem because I had to leave Germany. The Gestapo had said 'you must be out by the end of August'. I had a transit visa to travel through Switzerland to Italy. At that time travel was mainly by ship and, to my surprise, the Swiss behaved in a very bad fashion. They did not want to let me pass. They said 'we have to think about it'. In the end they permitted me to pass on the condition that I would leave the country the same day. I shook my head in disbelief. I couldn't understand why they wouldn't let Jewish refugees pass and I never found out the reason.

I left at twelve that night for Venice. My ship, the Galileo, was to go to Palestine a week later. I had to stay in Venice for a week. I stayed in a very cheap and good tourist hotel that I could just afford with the very small amount of money, 10 marks, the Germans had let me take out of Germany. It was enough to pay for the hotel for a week, but not enough for proper food. I went to the market and bought enough fruit and bread to live on for a week.

At that time I was not yet certain that my wife would join me because she had to have permission from the Gestapo to leave the country. She was working in a small chemical lab and her office was employed on secret projects, which involved military secrets. My wife never told me what they were. I notified my wife immediately I arrived in Venice, and waited for the Gestapo to allow my wife to join me. Two days before the ship left I received a letter that she was on her way. The delivery of mail in Europe was very quick.

Two days before the ship was to sail my wife arrived. She also had ten marks in her pocket. We used that money to make a gondola tour in Venice. 'No matter what will happen we have to celebrate.' We were so happy to be together again.

There was a last minute hitch. I lost my ticket. We went to the harbour and talked to the captain of the ship. He said 'I am sorry I can't do anything about it. If you have no ticket you can't go.' Then a miracle happened. When I went to the harbour to check once again, I discovered that the ticket had been handed in. I was allowed on board and the ship sailed as planned. We were three or four days on board.

Even though immigration had stopped we had acquired a visa for Palestine. Visas were issued in special cases where there was danger to life. An Aunt of mine, who had been in the country since 1925, intervened with the Jewish Agency on the grounds of danger to life since I had been in a concentration camp for six weeks. My wife had not been in the camps.

When we arrived in Haifa we disembarked and went to the hostel in Haifa, where all new immigrants could stay. I asked the Jewish Agency representative at the harbour why it was called the German colony. He told me that it was so called because Christian priests had built a quarter of the town for Christian Germans coming to Palestine. We stayed there only a few days. I had friends in Haifa who took us in for a few days until we could go to

Jerusalem and stay with my Aunt. I tried to find work in Haifa. I had a recommendation from a non Jewish German who had befriended me in Germany. When he heard I was going to Palestine he told me that he had a good friend in the electric company in Haifa. He wrote a letter to the manager. However when I applied for a job he told me they had none.

After a few days we went to Jerusalem to live with my Aunt. They had rooms to let but we were never asked 'can you pay?' It was furnished with everything we needed, however my wife was pregnant and work was difficult to find. My Aunt was the chief nurse in a baby home and she arranged for my wife to work at the home, taking her baby with her to work.

I did occasional jobs repairing household appliances, shutters and locks. It didn't bring in very much money since I am not a good businessman. The financial situation was not good. I remember one incident where we did not have enough money to buy food. We had bread, margarine and one egg and had an argument as to who should eat it. I told my wife 'you eat it,' but she answered 'you eat it you have to work.' In the end we split it in half. Food was available if you had money to pay but it was my Aunt who fed us.

Time went on. I became known for good work at reasonable prices, so somehow we managed, and then the war broke out.

In the beginning the Germans met with a lot of success, they even invaded North Africa. At that time there was quite a strong movement of Jewish inhabitants of Palestine to volunteer for the British army in order to help with the war effort, so I also volunteered.

I joined the British army as a dispatch rider. After training for three or four months I was sent to Egypt to a signals unit that was stationed in Cairo under General Montgomery. I was a dispatch rider for two years. This involved going by motorcycle from unit to unit and picking up letters from commanding officers communicating with commanding officers of other units. I had to go direct, not through the post office, for reasons of security and time.

After two years, I fell ill with tuberculosis of the lungs; I was discharged from the army and returned home.

Jerusalem is not on the moon. There was no shortage of food in the shops at that time. Cheap food was always available from the Arabs, such as cheese made from goats' milk. My Aunt warned us not to eat it. 'It comes from milk from Arab farms that has not been checked. The milk is contaminated and there is a rumour that the milk can lead to illness.'

War was still raging but Palestine was not directly involved. There was no action by the Germans or the Italians in that area. The Germans tried to conquer Africa but were beaten back. For a while they were in North Africa but the Allied forces under Monty [Lord Montgomery] threw them out at El Alamein.

There was a shortage of labour during the war and it was easy to find work as soon as I was fit. At that time I was a practical mechanical engineer, doing only civil work. My company had a small workshop in Jerusalem, but this work did not continue for very long. Afterwards I became a regimental paymaster in an army camp, which used to be an orphanage, which had originally been built by the Germans.

While I worked there I had plenty of time. I studied engineering by post under the auspices of the British Institute. I took examinations in mechanical engineering. The exams were in English. I had learnt English in

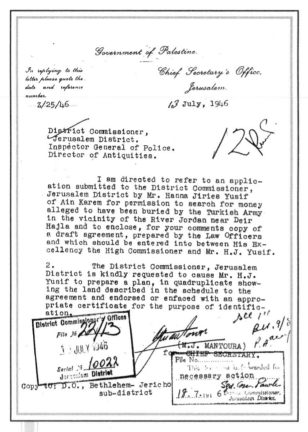

Government of Palestine.

Chief Secretary's Office,
Jerusalem.

In replying to this letter please quote the date and reference number.
2/25/46

13 July, 1946

District Commissioner,
Jerusalem District.
Inspector General of Police.
Director of Antiquities.

I am directed to refer to an application submitted to the District Commissioner, Jerusalem District by Mr. Hanna Jiries Yusif of Ain Karem for permission to search for money alleged to have been buried by the Turkish Army in the vicinity of the River Jordan near Deir Hajla and to enclose, for your comments copy of a draft agreement, prepared by the Law Officers and which should be entered into between His Excellency the High Commissioner and Mr. H.J. Yusif.

2. The District Commissioner, Jerusalem District is kindly requested to cause Mr. H.J. Yusif to prepare a plan, in quadruplicate showing the land described in the schedule to the agreement and endorsed or enfaced with an appropriate certificate for the purpose of identification.

(M.J. MANTOURA)
for CHIEF SECRETARY.

Copy to: D.O., Bethlehem- Jericho sub-district

Germany because of my ambition to emigrate to America.

At that time there were two Jewish underground movements in an active struggle against the British mandate. The British had closed the gates of Palestine to Jewish immigration. Although it states in the Balfour declaration that Palestine is to be the home for the Jewish people, the British Mandate did not take it seriously. The British did not help or further the Jewish national movement. They were not comfortable contending with independent movements, not from the Arabs or from the Jews.

There were frequent curfews. The Jewish underground movements were involved in attacks and they planted bombs, one in the King David Hotel. They succeeded in planting bombs in the centre of Mandate activity. I myself was not involved in the underground and I was surprised by it. I was sure the British Secret Service was kept informed of all underground activity. I was opposed to this kind of struggle.

The siege of Jerusalem in 1948 affected daily life in two respects. It made supplies difficult resulting in shortages, and there was bombardment. I was living on the outskirts of Jerusalem, in the area which is now Gan Sacher.

We had a very small apartment built on an existing house. It had originally been a donkey stable. The landlord was very old and after he stopped riding his donkey he converted the stable into a two-roomed apartment, each room two metres by three metres. There was a kitchenette but no bathroom, and the loo [toilet] was outside. It was difficult to use if the curfew was on and I made a curtain so that we could go outside without being seen from the street. We also had no shower. In the part I had curtained off I put up a shower that operated only with cold water, since there was no possibility of heating it.

We were very lucky. We heard explosions but bombs did not fall in our vicinity. The siege and the curfews continued for what seemed quite a long time, but it was less than a year. This made it very difficult and sometimes impossible, to walk about. The house was a big building. On the ground floor lived the landlord and another family. There was also a public mikveh for the whole surrounding area, and a shelter. On the roof there was a shack that was lived in by a German Jew and his wife. She was a Yemenite and such a marriage was very unusual in those days. When the alarm went off we went into the shelter in the cellar and talked and waited for the all clear to come.

While I was in hospital with tuberculosis I had befriended a young Arab, who was there as a patient. He was a teacher by profession and very friendly. We kept up the connection after both of us left the hospital. He worked as a teacher in an orphanage 10 kilometres west of Jerusalem. When Jerusalem was under siege he sent me a letter since he had heard about the difficulties. If there was any problem with getting food he was prepared to send me a food parcel. I thanked him and said the food problem was not serious and we would manage.

The water supply was limited and a truck with water made the rounds of various quarters. During the siege water was rationed and delivered by truck and food was also rationed. You couldn't go and have whatever you liked, only what there was. In one of my walks I encountered a stray dog that attached itself to me and I brought it home. When the siege finished we were living in Givat Shaul. There were still shortages of certain foods. The dog loved to sit under the bed. Our landlord, who was very religious, lived upstairs. He kept a cockerel for Kaporah in an enclosure. One day the dog got hold of the cockerel and my wife had to go to the market to buy another cockerel. It was not so simple and she spent nearly the whole day trying to find one. That day the dog ate better than any of us!

We were grateful when the siege was finally over and slowly tried to rebuild what had been lost.

William Sopher
born in 1923

'The poor lived and died on the streets'

I was born in Bombay in 1923, at the time of the British Colonial rule in India. My father was a share broker and we were regarded as an aristocratic family. We had two servants, a cook and a butler, who lived in the house with us and slept on straw mats.

We settled easily into British Colonial life with its many aristocratic indulgences such as drivers and servants, possible only because of the availability of cheap labour.

We admired the British and children were given English names. We learnt English at the English school and spoke English at home. Everything was orientated around Britain because they were the ruling Colonial power in India until after the war. Jewish life under these conditions was very peaceful. Anti-Semitism did not exist and there was religious tolerance between the Jews and the non-Jews. The main religious battles were between the Muslims and the Hindus.

After school I usually went to the sports field to play field hockey. The social life centred on the clubs. There were clubs for swimming, tennis, badminton and gymkhana. There was also a Jewish club where the adults would play Bridge or rummy, or other card games, and the children would play table tennis or sing. Refreshments were served and it was a very pleasant way of life.

In Bombay the poor lived and died on the streets. They erected makeshift tents on the pavements, which were basically just a roof. When you walked by you could see the family cooking or eating. Women gave birth on the pavements. It hasn't changed, even now.

The local Indians sometimes made their living as snake charmers. They trapped the snakes, usually cobras, removed the venom and put them in baskets. The cobra's neck swelled up and spread out when it was about to attack. This attracted the passers by who watched while the snake charmer played music on a crude flute consisting of two pipes and a round ball. The passers by would throw coins into his basket.

Other locals performed with monkeys, who danced to music that was played on a crude drum. Durbishers entertained with a drum consisting of a barrel that was narrow at both ends. They attached a thin strip of animal skin to a bow, which they rubbed against the drum to make an eerie noise. The durbisher then took a long rope with which he whipped himself and passers by paid money for this performance.

Some of the locals were idol worshippers and we were subjected to bizarre and ridiculous displays during their festivals. There was a pagan festival called Gunpati. The worshippers made a statue with a human face, the nose in the form of an elephant's trunk, and fifteen pairs of hands. On the day of the festival the worshipers walked along the street with the statue to the ocean and threw the statue into the sea. During another festival, passers by paid money for milk to be fed to snakes. In India the Hindus regard cows as holy and the cows walk freely in the streets.

The Parsees had a strange ritual. When someone died they took the body to the 'tower of silence' and left the body there so that the vultures could eat the flesh. There was another festival that took place in March. People sprayed their body and clothes with different colour dyes as a display of holiness. When I passed by them I would hide my face with my hands because it was petrifying to look at them.

Among the poorer classes there were sometimes three generations of family members all living together in the same house. The children slept on straw mats under the beds of the parents.

There was a small market not far from the house where I went to buy fish and vegetables. For a bigger shop there was another market about five miles away. A porter brought back the food, in a very large basket, which he carried on his head. He walked the five miles with me, and would then have to turn around and walk the five miles back. Payment for this service was minimal. The alternative was to take a rickshaw, which was a small carriage on wheels, pulled by the rickshaw driver. Eventually the rickshaw became mechanised. When I was a child I also travelled by horse and cart. We had no car but there were buses and trams.

World War Two did not affect us, apart from the fact that there was a shortage of flour and rice since imports were restricted. The children still went to school every day. We did not know that atrocities were being committed in Germany because it wasn't reported. When the newspapers and the BBC radio reported the war, we heard that the Germans had overrun France and that they had sunk British submarines. We heard nothing about the camps. There were Indian troops and American troops based in Calcutta, and friends of ours would entertain the Jewish troops on Shabbos.

This was the war experience from the Far East — a vague and distant dream behind the curtain of the Raj.

✦ ✦ ✦

Editors' Note

After this interview a family member told us the following. One of the Gedolim said, in the name of the Gerrer Rebbe, that the Sephardic Jews were hardly affected by the war. The Sephardim are very particular about the honour of the Shul and do not talk in Shul. The Tosafos YomTov said it was revealed to him by Shamayim that the reason the Jews suffered pogroms by the Cossacks, etc, was because they talked in Shul. This is the reason that Rommel did not succeed in North Africa and Tunisia. The family member continued that it was the Gadol's chiddush that we have a Kabbalah that in times of trouble we fast and Hashem answers our prayers. So why did it not help in the Holocaust? Middah keneged middah. You are not listening to me, so you lose the power of prayer.

Matil Miryam bat Shmuel Meir
born in 1911
Told by her daughter

'I am alive
andI am coming home'

M y mother was born in Hungary. When she was five years old her mother passed away during the influenza epidemic that was rampant at that time, leaving my mother, her brother and three other sisters. After a very short time her father remarried a single girl with no children. Together they had five children and she also brought up the other five children. All the children were close to each other and like one family, even now.

My mother's eldest sister married my father and together they had two children. She passed away when the children were three and four years of age. In 1937 my father married my mother. She became ill with an infection on the covering of the heart. Although her condition was very serious, she had a strong bitachon and an iron will to live. This saved her and kept her alive. Although she was not allowed to have children, she thought, 'I must have one.' I was born after the war in 1946.

My father was called up at the beginning of the war to serve in the Hungarian army. My mother brought up my father's children from his first marriage from1937 until 1944. My mother and the two children, her stepmother and sisters were all together for the duration of the war.

The Germans entered Hungary in 1944 and the family was put into the ghetto in Debrecen, Hungary, for a few weeks. The Germans then took them to a factory to make white stones for building, after which they were loaded on a train to Austria. Once they were there, the Germans made my grandfather the head of the group. Since they had food, work and accommodation in wooden houses, it was not considered a bad situation.

My family did not know what was going on in the rest of Europe. The few who heard did not want to believe it.

One day the Germans came and told every one to go outside. They had come to stamp everyone's papers with one of two seals. One seal was inscribed with the letter 'A', the other seal with the letter 'GD'. As the Germans were sorting the people, the big families and the children to one side, the others to the other side, a man approached my mother. This man was a stranger; she had never met him and did not even know if he was a fellow prisoner. He told my mother that she should attempt to be classified with the seal GD and not with the seal A. My mother did not know what the seals represented or what the letters stood for. However she did what he told her to do.

My mother approached the soldiers and cried that she didn't want the seal A; she only wanted the seal GD. This was the way that the whole family went to Gemund, a transit camp; instead of the fate of all the other families who were stamped with the letter A, for Auschwitz.

My mother and the family were taken to the army camp in the town of Teresianstadt. It was in this place that my sister saw, for the first time, Jewish people who looked like skeletons, dressed in striped prison clothing. Some people had come from Auschwitz. They were amazed to see my grandparents and the young children, because all the young and old people in Auschwitz were killed. It was the first time my family heard about Auschwitz. It was only a few weeks until the end of the war.

In this transit camp they were not asked to work and they received food, consisting of bread, jam, margarine and maybe a little soup. The morale of the people in the camp was so low they didn't think about where the food was coming from, or if it was kosher or not. Then my sister got typhoid. Anyone who had typhoid was taken to the crematoria to be burned. This was the first time people heard about crematoria. Because typhoid is infectious, the other prisoners informed the Germans that my sister was sick. However my mother outsmarted them. She hid my sister, moving her from place to place within the camp, covered with blankets, so that no one would see her. Miraculously, without medicine, she stayed alive. Without my mother's constant care, concern and love the Germans would have burnt her.

When the war ended, the prisoners watched the Germans and Hungarians running away. The Russian soldiers came into the camp shooting, gave the prisoners food and told them that they were free. The first thing the people in the camp did was to go into the town to obtain food. They ate it quickly and their bodies puffed up because they were not accustomed to food, and they died. When the American soldiers arrived they gave them meat, which they ate and died. My Aunts went into the town and obtained bread, jam and margarine. On the way back to the camp the Russian soldiers, who were also hungry, saw the food and took everything away from them. This turned out to be a blessing because they didn't die from overeating, as the others did.

My family wanted to go back to their town in Hungary, because they didn't know the whereabouts of my father. Travel was arduous and long because everyone was going home at the same time. The Jewish groups, like the Joint, made camps for the refugees, and gave them food, clothes and sometimes tickets to travel. In spite of this, the situation in the camps was not under control, nor were they able to give out money.

When the family returned to Debrecen, they found goyim occupying their apartment. They looked for and found an empty apartment and tried to find out about my father, to no avail. Then one day they received a telegram, addressed to the last known address. Since they were a well-known family the postman delivered it to their current address.

The telegram read, 'I am alive and I am coming home.' My sister often told me that this was the happiest day of her life.

The next day they went to the railway station and waited there all day looking for him amongst the arriving passengers. They didn't see my father. Towards the end of the day one of my Aunts came running to the station. 'He is home!'

My father had a much worse time than my mother, during the war. We know this from people whom he saved. Many of these people didn't want to continue their lives. In the camps my father, who was no longer a soldier, forced the Jewish people to stand up and clean themselves. He scraped together food for them. If not for my father they would have died. He had connections with a few Germans who supplied him with a few more potatoes, which he cooked, or a little more bread, both of which he was able to give to the sick people.

He knew it was important to keep clean. Even though many of the prisoners in the camps no longer had the will to live, he told them 'don't lie down, stand up, wash yourself.' He carried them through and kept them alive.

After we returned, the communists began to rule in Hungary, which was bad for the Jews. Although I was born in Debrecen, when I was two years old my father paid a goy to show us the way to the border, one dark winter night. My first childhood memory was of wearing a heavy winter coat and being told not to cry or say anything and to be very quiet. My family say it was a miracle that I made no sound as we passed the border and reached Czechoslovakia, the home of my mother's cousin. From there we went to Vienna.

The Joint ran a camp at the Rothschild Hospital, for Jewish refugees, from which the Jewish people could emigrate. My father had a brother who had gone to the United States before the war, and that is where my father and sister wanted to go.

Although I was just under three years of age, my sister recalls that as my father was going to the American consulate, I ran after him crying, 'I don't want to go to the States; I only want to go to Israel. In September 1949, we arrived in Israel.

My father died over thirty years ago. He was sick for four years with leukaemia. However he said 'Hakodesh Boruch Hu has given me a present of twenty-five years and a daughter' and he accepted the verdict in peace.

My mother lived almost ninety-two years and most of the time she was healthy. Every time a doctor examined her heart, he would say 'you have something wrong with your heart.

At the end of the war, my grandmother went to the Rabbi of Debrecen and asked him the reason that the whole family had merited to stay alive through the war. He said 'because you were orphans.' Hakodesh Boruch Hu gave my parents the zechut to save many people from certain death.

Rabbi **Michoel Boruch**
born in 1939

'Come, sit by me'

D uring the British Mandate, my family lived in a one-room apartment, which was half underground, on Ben Yehudah Street. It flooded in the winter. There was no privacy for anyone. I slept in my parent's room with a curtain drawn around my bed.

I remember on my way home from school that I would walk passed the military court of the British army, which was opposite Beit HaNasi. British soldiers would laugh at the children passing by and call them 'ginger fox.'

I was nine years old during the war of Independence in 1948. Most of the teachers were recruited into the army and I stayed at home and did not go to school for around six months. At night children wouldn't walk on the streets as a result of a rumour that British soldiers assaulted children.

We moved to Jabotinsky Street in the western part of the City. At that time Jerusalem was not built up and there were no houses between the Old City and us. From our window we had a clear view of the ancient walls and ramparts. The Arab Jordanian soldiers used to sit on these walls and snipe at any passing Jew. It was dangerous to go outside because of the shelling and shooting. In order to enable the people to walk on the streets, a wall was built on Jabotinsky Street consisting of two layers of tin, between which was sandwiched earth and stones. Only if you walked next to it were you protected from flying bullets.

The shelling had a pattern. After breakfast they would shell for a time, then stop for lunch, and rest. Then they would resume their attacks. Because people knew when it would start and stop, they ran around doing their most urgent errands in between.

I recall one incident that had a profound effect on me. Mother used to work in a lending library in the backroom of a bookstore She took me to work with her every day that there was no school and I would read books, mainly in English, German and Hebrew. The bookstore had a display case on the street. I would sit and read close to the display case. One day mother called from inside, 'come, sit by me.' As soon as I reached her, a shell hit the display case and destroyed it. I might have been killed.

Dodging bullets and snipers wasn't the only hardship. During the war food and water were rationed. Food was distributed by coupons, issued by the Ministry, according to the number of people in the family. Water was distributed by portion, again with coupons, and limited to one litre per person for twenty-four hours, which was scarcely enough for drinking.

Every Jewish neighbourhood had a cistern under the houses and in the courtyards, which filled with water during the winter. During the siege the public water supply was cut off. Mother opened the pipe under the sink to collect water used for washing hands in order to wash the floors and then flush the toilet. Every drop of water, apart from drinking water, was used three times. This water rationing lasted between six to nine months.

Although food and water were limited because of the siege, I was never hungry as a child. Before the siege began we stored away a large quantity of Quaker oats. This was our main staple food, along with eggs that we had once every few days.

In the early 50's people tried to smuggle chickens and eggs from moshavim. Inspectors on the buses would

Beth Mahmoud, Arnona.
P.O.B. 1122,
Jerusalem.
June 24, 1947

The Chief Secretary,
Palestine Government,
Jerusalem.

Sir,

This is our thirteenth day without water – except on two occasions of less than a day's supply and about one pail full supplied last night!

I am bringing this to your notice only after making a great many inquiries among my friends in other parts of the city who apparently never, or very rarely, suffer from our chronic deprivation. I am also doing so after I have ascertained that a great many people in Arnona and Talpiot have complained about the matter and after I have written two notes within the past few days, out of sheer desperation, asking for some alleviation.

I have been advised to put in another tank. That would be quite useless since the tank we now have is rarely filled. For days and days now, it has been as dry as the desert's dusty face. In fact, I am sorely tempted to take my flock of babes down to the Negev for a drink, and discourage the Beduin now trekking North from heading towards Jerusalem. Those photographs of waterfalls at Revivim in the heart of the wastes are better than my mirages. Frankly, I envy our cat who can lick herself clean.

I am aware of the sorry state of water supply in Jerusalem generally, and I have always done my utmost to use the same water twice, e.g. bath(shower water kept in the tub) for washing floors and thence on to the flower beds (which otherwise get only water from the cesspit); dishwater flushes the toilet, etc. etc. but I see no reason why other districts of the city should get an ample supply and our tank should remain completely dry. Of late we have been reduced to eating out of tins and drinking out of bottles, and I have had to take the children to friends in the city for a decent wash. Were it not for the kindness of our Arab neighbours some distance away (from whose well we get water via bucket brigade) we should, I fear, have to leave our house altogether. There is another well nearby kept under lock and key by its Arab owner, but since this water stinks to heaven, we have so far refrained from breaking the lock.

This ventilation of my rage is also a plea to have something done for us. I believe that our house, situated somewhat alone from the rest of the quarter, suffers more than the rest of Arnona. Nineteen people live in this house, however, and I should be grateful if some way could be found of supplying us with our minimum needs. The whole quarter, however, is usually in sore need of water; a need quite out of relation with the rest of the town.

Yours faithfully,

Molly Lyons Bar-David.

Copy to: District Commissioner
Mayor of Jerusalem.

P.S.

"Hi, there, Bath-Sheva! Not so much water in your bath!" -- hmm, shall I send her husband to battle --"Less water, there my girl!"

KING DAVID

requisition the supplies. Convoys would bring in supplies from the more remote areas. When a friend of the family came with a convoy, I remember as a child, being very impressed with his pistol.

As a child I never went to the Kottel, even though before the war of Independence in 1948 it was permitted. In 1967 I went for the first time. The moment I stepped through the walls every turn and twist was familiar. It was as if I had been there before, in a previous life, in another time, long ago.

The Satmar Rebbe,
Rabbi **Yoel Teitelbaum**
born in 1887
Told by the daughter of the household in the story

'Yosef, someone is trying to take a picture of me, but nothing will come out'

In 1945, after the war, the Satmar Rebbe came to Chicago and stayed with us in our home. I was fifteen at the time. My brother, who was very anxious to take a photograph of him, waited for the right opportunity.

One morning as the Rebbe was going to the mikveh accompanied by Yosef, his gabbai, my brother decided that this was his chance. I decided to watch.

Our family had a first floor flat and when the Rebbe walked out I watched him from the front window, until he was out of sight. Our house was on a corner, and when the Rebbe turned the corner I ran into the next room to see him from that window. I heard him say to the gabbai 'Yosef, someone is trying to take a picture of me, but nothing will come out.'

My brother followed him down the block hiding behind the bushes so that The Rebbe would not see him. When I heard the Rebbe's words I was very upset for my brother. I knew that my brother was overjoyed to have the opportunity to photograph the Rebbe, but at the same time I realised that the Rebbe didn't want his photo taken.

When the Rebbe went into the mikveh my brother waited outside to take more photos when he came out.

When the Rebbe returned to the house, my brother came in too. I went into our parent's bedroom because I didn't want the Rebbe to hear what I had to say to my brother. I knew that he would be surprised and in shock. I told my brother what the Rebbe had said to Yosef.

My brother didn't want to believe it. 'But Brocha,' he said, 'he didn't even see me.' 'So wait' I replied, 'develop the pictures and go see.' My brother went right away to have the photos developed and returned very distraught. 'Not one picture came out,' he said. I thought he would start crying he was so upset. I said to him, 'don't worry, but don't try and take any more pictures because they won't come out.'

✦ ✦ ✦

Editors' Note

Pirkei Avos 2:4: 'Treat His will as if it were your own will so that He will treat your will as if it were His will. Nullify your will before His will, so that He will nullify the will of others before your will.'

Ezra Yakhin
born in 1928

'The Foreign Minister was asked to reinstate the name of King George'

M y father married my mother in Egypt, but I was born in Jaffa. My mother's uncle, Nachman Betito was an Egyptian who was appointed the Chief Rabbi of Jerusalem around 1920. My parents moved to the Montifiore quarter, now called Yemin Moshe, to a house inherited from my grandfather. Our house was in the outermost row of houses that bordered the Sultan's pool, opposite the walls of the Old City.

I was six months old when the Arabs rioted in 1929. My father heard that Jews in Sefat and Hebron were being massacred and quickly began to fortify the house, using stones to barricade the frail plywood door. Hundreds of Arabs, screaming 'death to the Jews, let's slaughter the Jews,' made their way to the houses in the quarter, and were close enough to our house to throw rocks at the door. At that moment one of the Arabs was hit on the head by a rock that had ricocheted off the wall, and he was killed, and they had to stop their assault to take him away.

Within a few hours they returned, again bombarding our house with stones. Just as the door was about to give way, one of the Arab women shouted to the mob,' I know a better neighbourhood, let's go to Rehavia where the rich ones live, they have nothing here, you won't get any loot.' They left, but my father's small textile store had been looted, and nothing was left.

The family moved to a safer place, and our house in Yemin Moshe was demolished in the War of Independence. The government gave the family compensation, cleared the land and made a park.

Looking back, I see that we lived in misery, but we did not feel poor, even though the eight members of the family shared three rooms. My brother had a job as a messenger boy.

We had no electricity until I was twelve. Until then we used oil lamps for light and a primus stove for cooking and heating water. There was no running water and when the well ran dry, we used the tap in the yard. It was kept locked and opened once a day when we were able to purchase water from the neighbourhood water supply.

We had so many diseases; I don't know where they came from. Hygiene was very bad, the toilet was a hole in the ground in a cabin and many families used the same place. From time to time someone would throw water down to clear it. We were lucky that there was a sewage system in our neighbourhood because not every place had one. There was almost no garbage because people used everything. You never threw away a newspaper; this was used as toilet paper, or for packing.

We did not have a refrigerator, this came later on, but like everyone else we had an icebox. We cooked fresh food every day. Once in a while, the Arabs would bring their goats to our neighbourhood for us to milk. There were fruit and vegetables, but you had to open fruit like apples and apricots to remove the worms first. There were a lot of worms at that time and there was no way to prevent it.

Everyone knew everyone else. Buildings were identified by the name of the landlord, so although there were few street names and even fewer street numbers, families were located by the name of the building, the Mizrachi building, or the Levi building, and so forth. The streets were narrow and the children of the neighbourhood played together.

We had no toys; but we created our toys from all kinds of things. Balls were made with torn clothing and with a bit of rope fashioned into a kind of a ball. We played with apricot stones, used matches and small pieces of wood sharpened both sides. You hit the small piece of stick with another stick to move it. We played a game with stones where you had to hit a stone that was already on the ground. If you won any of these games, the winner mounted the back of the loser, who was the donkey and he had to carry you on his back.

I remember that we did have glass marbles and fives, now called jacks. Birthday celebrations were not part of our childhood.

In 1944 I read a notice put up by an underground movement called Etzel, warning the British not to interfere with the blowing of the shofar at the end of Yom Kippur at the Kottel. I decided to daven there for Neilah. When I arrived, with my brother, the space in front of the Kottel was crowded with worshippers, but as Neilah drew near, most of then slipped away. Only around thirty young people were left, surrounded by British police. The police were carrying truncheons to use in dispersing demonstrators. Sunset was approaching and the Neilah service was completed. Out of the corner of my eye I saw a boy drawing the shofar from his shirt and passing it to his friend. His friend blew the shofar and the police burst into the crowd trying to reach him. The blowing stopped; the shofar disappeared only to be heard again in a different direction. This happened several times with the police striking left and right with their truncheons. The crowd continued to pray oblivious of the police rampaging all around them.

At the age of fifteen I obtained a job at the Post Office as a messenger boy delivering telegrams. I preferred to deliver in the city, rather than in the outlying districts. There were just three Jewish lads because the Postal Service preferred Arabs since they would deliver any day including the Sabbath and Holy Days, and agree to take their day off any day of the week. A telegram meant news, either good or bad, the Arabs would murmur, 'good news, G-d willing.' When I delivered telegrams in the Jewish Quarter it was like stepping into a different world. After the odour of the exotic spices used in Arab cooking in the Moslem Quarter, I would now be met with the fresh, clean smell of soapy water used for cleaning the floors inside and the courtyards outside. A telegram to a Jewish family was rewarded with a cool drink and a cookie.

I decided early on that I wanted to join the underground movement. I was a member of a club called Brith Hashmonaim. In order to attract the attention of those responsible for enlisting new recruits for the underground, I would freely express my opinions about the underground within the confines of the club. My persistence paid off and late in 1944, when I was just sixteen I was invited to join Lechi, Fighters for the Freedom of Israel. My contact warned me, 'punctuality is compulsory in the underground. The man you are meeting may be under surveillance. The longer you hang around the surer you are to arouse suspicion. You must never be late, nor must you be early. If you feel you are being followed, change your route.'

My contact knew that I was working at the Central Post Office, and he explained that it would be a great advantage for the underground to have the contents of all the telegrams sent to British staff. I told him that I could supply him with copies of all the telegrams sent from the British Foreign Office in London to the High Commissioner, however they were all in code, meaningless rows of numbers or letters. 'Don't worry,' said my contact, 'we have someone who can take care of it.'

One of my jobs was to deliver booklets to sympathizers who were also socially influential. 'Familiarize yourself with the addresses. Learn the exact location of the houses and the letter boxes in the entrances so that they can be distributed quickly,' I was told. I said that reconnaissance wasn't necessary as there wasn't a house I didn't know in Jerusalem.

My work in the Post Office made me a real find for Lechi, and I was assigned to the Lechi information service — section 6. In

A. A. Abdul Hadi,
Former Assistant Palestine
Government Agent in Egypt.
c/o Amin Abdul Hadi Bey,
Supreme Moslem Council,
Mamilla Road,
Jerusalem.

18 October, 1947.

JERUSALEM HEAD ... ATION
R...
Date :
Filo No. _____ A

Dear Mr. Graves,

This will confirm my conversation with you of the 16th instant regarding the necessity of giving names to streets and numbering buildings in the City of Jerusalem.

It is a well known fact that in all civilized communities and, I hope Palestine falls under this category, every street, and every square has a name; and all houses, shops, and other premises carry numbers. Jerusalem, to my knowledge, is perhaps the only civilized Capital in the world where this fundamental rule of town planning is so seriously neglected. It would not be fair of me to deny that only a very few streets in the heart of the town have names; but the buildings on those streets, indeed the fortunate streets, carry no numbers. It is perhaps much easier to solve a Chinese cross-word puzzle for a man who knows nothing of that ancient Oriental language, than to try to locate a house in the residential quarters of Jerusalem. The Jewish part of the Holy City is far better off than the Arab quarters in this respect.

It is needless to point out the numerous unnecessary inconvenience people experience in trying to locate or describe a building which has no number in a nameless street. Sometimes the results may turn to be most serious ending in the loss of human lives. And here is a concrete case.

The other night, to be exact it was Wednesday of this week, at about 11:50 p.m. the Government Hospital telephoned and asked for my brother, Dr. Murid Abdul Hadi, an ear, nose, and throat specialist, to attend to an urgent case at the hospital. I answered the 'phone and said that my brother was at his flat and gave them his telephone the course of my work at the Post Office I often saw letters marked 'Opened by the Censor.' I now inaugurated a new censorship, that of the underground. It wasn't everyone who could supply the organisation with confidential telegrams sent by the Government of His Majesty King George the Sixth to its administration in Palestine.

Eventually I became too old to serve as a messenger boy, so at the age of eighteen I was promoted and became a regular postman. I clas-

(2)

number. Half an hour later, the telephone rang again; it was the hospital. The Sister told me that she could not get my brother on the 'phone as there was no reply from his house. And as I was sure that my brother was home and, that his telephone must have been out of order, I asked the Sister to send an ambulance and fetch him from home. I very carefully described the location of the flat of my brother: at Qatamun, just opposite the residence of Mr. Joseph Albina, the second floor.

But, no sooner I went to bed when the telephone started ringing for the third time. It was the hospital all right. This time an English Sister was on the 'phone. She said that the driver failed despite repeated trials to locate the flat of my brother as he did not know where the Albina house was; and she added that the patient was still suffering and bleeding. I really felt very sorry for the poor fellow. So I requested the Sister to send the ambulance to my house and I would accompany the driver myself to the house of my brother. Of course it took the driver some time to get to my place at the Greek Colony. I, too, live in nameless street, and the house has no number. It was almost two-thirty in the morning when we finally got to the flat of my brother; and as I have anticipated his telephone was dead. By the time my brother reached the hospital it was just before three o'clock. Most fortunately the patient was still alive. These are the true facts of this case.

One could easily cover the whole City of Jerusalem in much less than that wasted time.

Despite that avoidable inconvéence caused to us at that beastly hour of the night, the poor suffering patient may well have passed away.

I am sure that other people have suffered from similar tragic experiences at one time or another; and they will continue to suffer unless a proper system of naming streets and numbering buildings is adopted in this town.

Will it then be asking too much all those concerned to give this vital question some serious thought with a view of arriving at a satisfactory solution to this dilemma. If, however, for some reason or another it is thought undesirable to give streets names, well let them be numbered as it is the case with New York City and Maadi, the beautiful suburb of Cairo.

(3)

I am sorry to have taken so much of your valuable time; but as a citizen of this town I felt it was my duty to draw your kind attention to this question.

I avail myself of this opportunity to convey to you the assurance of my high consideration.

Yours very sincerely,

A A Abdul Hadi

The stone slab bearing King George's name

sified all the mail belonging to Jerusalem into district pigeonholes and whenever I found an official envelope I would put it into the pigeonhole of my own district. I would also filch registered government letters out of other niches and put them into mine. My task was often made easier when the authorities stamped the envelope 'Confidential'; section 6 was particularly interested in those.

Fighting wasn't always done with guns. Proclamations had to be put up, information collected, and people followed in summer and in winter, hail or snow or a hamsin wind. No one would ever know about it, and after many sleepless nights the operation you had worked so hard on might be delayed or even cancelled.

On November 29th 1947 the General Assembly of the United Nations decided to form two states in the Western part of Palestine, between Jordan and the sea. The Jews were celebrating in the streets while the Arabs were preparing for an all out attack throughout the country. The whole city quickly turned into a shooting range, as there were hardly any streets in Jerusalem not within shooting distance of the Arab guns. The British were still in the country and though impotent to rule, they saw to it that the Jews would not be able to protect themselves. Jews were not allowed to carry guns in the streets, although the Arabs had made the streets into death traps.

The underground decided to remove the name of the British King from one of Jerusalem's main streets, and pasted a new sign, 'King David St' over the stone slab bearing King George's name. The public liked the change but after Israel was declared a State at the end of a vicious and bloody war the Foreign Minister at the time was asked by the British Ambassador to reinstate the name of King George. The Mayor of Jerusalem agreed to make this gesture to 'friends in the past.'

During this time I met a boy who had a pad over his eye and I thought he must have been fighting with the underground so I asked him what had happened. He hesitated before he told me the story. In 1929, during the riots, the Arabs attacked a Jewish neighbourhood near the Damascus Gate. It was a Friday and they murdered about twenty of the most vulnerable people, the women and the children. When the men came home from work, it was too late to bury the dead. They took the bodies to the mortuary at the hospital, but there was no refrigeration at the time. On motzei Shabbos they returned to bury the dead, and heard the screaming of a baby. One of the men saw that his wife had been stabbed, clutching her baby, who had been stabbed in the eye. 'This baby was me', he said.

Shirley Granovetter
born in 1927

'We were learning to live without money'

W e came to Israel in March 1948 and lived in a little cesspool near Ra'anana. We were learning to live co-operatively by working the land in order to form a kibbutz. Before forming the kibbutz you learnt to work co-operatively.

Everyone worked, but nobody received any money. We were learning to live without money. I was twenty-one and had a young baby. My job was washing clothes, and my husband's job was working in the garden. It was not a nice place, but at least they put up barracks for the married couples. Single people had to live in tents. The government helped us to come to Eretz Yisroel on aliyah to work the land. When we arrived the government decided where we were most needed.

We came by boat from New York, which carried members of the same Jewish social group. We were not affiliated to any religious organisation. The women were connected to Hadassah and the men to a general Zionist organisation. There were less than eight people from our group on this boat. When we docked at the port in Haifa, they took us to a giant, empty building with wooden cots, but no mattresses, where we slept overnight. The building was reserved for our group and had just ten beds. We were amazed at the conditions of the lavatory. We thought that the construction was not yet finished. However, it was as it was supposed to be, a hole in the ground.

We slept here only one night and then travelled on to Ra'anana. Someone from the settlement drove us there in an old truck. They knew which boat we were coming on but there were no telephones to confirm arrivals or to relay messages. What an experience!

The settlement was so new it did not have a name. It was outside Ra'anana, which, at that time, had two stores and five houses. There were no street names. I know that we received letters because we used them as toilet tissue. There was nothing else to use. There were no real bathrooms, only similar ones to the one we used in Haifa — an outhouse with a hole in the ground.

There were thirty people on the settlement. It was a learning place, to learn how to co-operate with each other and work together. I remember the shower room had no individual rooms. Men and women did not shower together. I don't think we had a problem with water. At the settlement we slept on wooden cots with hand made mattresses stuffed with straw.

The food problem was horrible, just unbelievable. There were no chickens in Israel at that time so consequently all eggs were imported. There were plenty of flies, which

---

FC/7/30/1

DISTRICT FOOD CONTROLLER
JERUSALEM DISTRICT
P.O.B. 587
JERUSALEM.

16th February, 1945.

Your Worship,

    I have the honour to inform you that a large consignment of Scotch herrings will shortly be made available for distribution to the public.

2.   With a view to securing a method of distribution equitable to all interests concerned, I am directed by the Food Controller to request your kind cooperation and to invite you to nominate a member of the Municipality to attend a meeting, at such time or place as may hereafter be agreed on, to discuss the question with myself and representatives of the two local Chambers of Commerce.

    I have the honour to be,
     Your Worship's
     Obedient servant.

JERUSALEM MUNICIPAL CORPORATION
REGISTRY.
Date: 19 FEB. 1945
File No. 7/30/33

A/DISTRICT FOOD CONTROLLER
JERUSALEM DISTRICT

The Mayor,
Municipality of Jerusalem.

cc:- District Commissioner,
  Jerusalem District.
  ref. Food Controller's letter
  FCL/87/45 of 13.2.45.

EJH/CP

carried terrible sicknesses. We cooked on a kerosene stove, which cooked poorly and the smell and taste of kerosene lingered in the food. The group had one refrigerator but it was full of flies. Every time we opened the fridge the flies would fly in and out.

The first privilege the settlement gave us was to take two weeks and see the land of Israel. I went with another girl and my husband looked after baby Zachariah.

On our trip my friend and I felt that Arabs, hiding behind the rocks as we walked down lonely roads, were watching us. Once when we visited the Kinneret, a Christian monk stood by the edge of the water watching us swimming and called other monks over to take a look. We hitch hiked over parts of Israel. I remember one kibbutz in the North that was muddy and unattractive.

Despite everything, nothing discouraged us. We loved every minute of it because we were going to build the land. We came with friends from New York who also had a young baby. We lived by our ideals, until we became sick. My husband was the first to get diarrhoea. I was the second one to get sick. At the time I was pregnant again, but I didn't know. When I miscarried, I walked a mile or so to the hospital in Ra'anana. Then baby Zachariah became ill.

We couldn't take him to the hospital; they said the hospitals were so full the beds were in the hall. We tracked down a doctor who came on a bicycle and wrapped the baby in cold wet towels. The baby survived even though there was no penicillin in the country. The doctor came just on that one occasion.

In June we decided to return to New York since the baby was now well enough to travel. When we arrived at the port of Haifa we were informed that our boat was expected two days later. We only had enough money to get us onto the boat and not to last us for two extra days. There was a travel agent at the port and we asked him to help us get in touch with our parents through the American Consulate.

The agent wanted to know what we needed from our parents and we told him we needed money to buy food and accommodation for the extra two days. The man pulled a roll of bills out of his pocket. 'Take whatever you want,' he said, 'when you get back to New York please send me food packages in return'. We sent him food through the mail when we got back to New York — cans of fish, salmon, and other food that wouldn't spoil. In Israel the situation was very bad. Even with money you couldn't buy food.

*Rabbi **Yehudah Davis***
Told by a Talmid

'That was the Shalom Aleichem that saved America'

F ifty years ago I had the zechus to learn with Rabbi Yehudah Davis, in Brighton Beach, New York. He was not content with running a Yeshiva and instead preferred to teach a chaburah, group, of older boys. As one of these boys I received, along with everyone else, a tremendous amount of understanding and clarity of thought from this Gaon, genius. He presented everything in a crystal clear manner, not only in English, but also in all Semitic languages. He was not only proficient in languages but also adept in mathematics.

Rabbi Yehuda Davis

Together with Rabbi Nosson Wachtfogel, Rabbi Yehudah Davis created a revolution in the Yeshiva world in America, whose total impact is still reverberating today. Rabbi Nosson Wachtfogel was learning in the only Yeshiva that existed at that time in New York. Other bocherim were Rabbi Mordechai Gifter, Rabbi Aaron Paperman, Rabbi Chaim Pinchas Scheinberg, Rabbi Mordechai Yaffe and Rabbi Avigdor Miller.

Reb Nosson, a young boy at the time, recognised that the Yeshiva was going off the derech of the general Yeshiva system. He went to the Rosh Yeshiva and told him that he was taking the Yeshiva off the derech of Yeshivas and steering a foreign course. The Rosh Yeshiva said 'if you don't like it you can leave.'

Reb Nosson was disturbed by this meeting and went to the Beis Hamidrash and started speaking to the bocherim, without success. Finally one of the bocherim saw that Reb Nosson was very despondent and asked him why. Reb Nosson told him that the Yeshiva was going off the derech and he was at a loss about what to do. The bocher said 'at the other end of the Beis Hamidrash is Yehudah Davis. Give him a Shalom Aleichem and explain to him what is going on. If he agrees to help your problems are over.'

Reb Nosson went over to the other end of the Beis Hamidrash and gave a Shalom Aleichem to Yehudah Davis. That was the Shalom Aleichem that saved America.

Yehudah Davis spoke to Avigdor Miller and Mordechai Jaffe, and together they travelled to various Yeshivas in Europe. Avigdor Miller went to Slabodka; the others initially went to Mir.

After one year in Mir, Rabbi Davis transferred to Slabodka where he met the Chofetz Chaim and other Gedolim of the time. After two years in Slobodka he returned to America for a shidduch, but after his marriage he returned to Slobodka. During that period in the States he learned karate. One day, he and Avigdor Miller were walking in the streets of Slobodka when they saw some local ruffians beating up some bocherim from the Yeshiva. Yehudah Davis said to Avigdor Miller 'let's go and teach them a lesson.' Avigdor Miller said 'me? Do you think I want to get killed?' Yehudah Davis said 'then I will do it myself.' He single-handedly smashed them to bits. After that, when the goyim saw Yehudah Davis walking in the street, they would whisper to each other 'be careful, there goes the American gibor, hero.'

People think that the Baal teshuvah movement is a new phenomenon that started just a few years ago. This is not the case at all. Rabbi Davis had a chain of Talmud Torahs in Baltimore teaching Chumash, Neviim, Mishnayos and Gemorrah in depth. In the summertime Rabbi Davis took the boys to a farm in the country, where they milked the cows themselves, so that they could have Cholav Yisroel, kosher milk.

Rabbi Davis was a Gaon in everything. And this expertise in a wide range of disciplines held special appeal for his young talmidim. He could wrestle with three people at the same time. When he played baseball, he hit the ball so far it disappeared and you couldn't find it. He was also a terrific swimmer.

The Telshe Yeshiva started in America only because of his intervention. When Rabbi Elya Meir Bloch went to America, he had only four Talmidim from Telshe in Europe. The Yeshiva had been so decimated that they went to New York. At that time there were already three Yeshivas in New York and no help was forthcoming to rebuild Telshe in America. Finally, someone suggested to Rabbi Bloch that he approach Rabbi Davis, who was then a Rav in a shul in Baltimore. Since Rabbi Davis had a chain of Talmud Torahs, maybe he could help. Rabbi Davis listened and responded by sending ten, raw American Talmidim to Telshe.

The Telshe Yeshiva started in America with those ten American talmidim from Baltimore.

Rabbi Davis was indeed multifaceted and his numerous talents were just cause for admiration. For a number of years I taught Malbim's commentary on Chumash to a wealthy man on Shabbos and I never took a prutah, coin, from him in payment. One day I said to him 'I have learned with you for quite a while and have never asked you for anything for myself. However I have a Rebbe who has a Yeshiva, and the Yeshiva needs money. You are in a position to give.' 'Who is your Rebbe?' he asked. I said 'Rabbi Yehudah Davis.'

'Rav Benjamin,' he said, you don't have to tell me. I was going to give to his yeshiva anyway.' I said to him 'you were going to give anyway? How is it possible? He is a nistar, hidden person. You can't find his Yeshiva if you wanted to. There are no signs and if you don't know how to get there and don't have a compass you will never find it. So how do you know who Rav Yehudah Davis is, that you want to give money to him?'

'I was very close to Rabbi Aaron Kotler,' the wealthy man explained, 'I helped his Yeshiva financially. When Reb Aaron felt he was going to leave this world he called me to his bedside and said 'you should know that there is a tzaddik who lives in Brighton Beach and his name is Rabbi Yehudah Davis and you should help him.' That's why I was going to give the money anyway.'

Rabbi Shalom Rotenberg once asked me if I would be willing to interview any bocherim that want to leave Israel to go to the States, to ascertain if they are the right people for the Yeshiva. I responded 'you are learning in the Yeshiva a long time. There are no stipends in the Yeshiva, no bein hazemanim, vacation time. You have a family. If you were in a different kollel you would receive payment. Why do you stay there? Go to Mir or Lakewood.'

He answered 'if I would be in a different Yeshiva I wouldn't see what I see in that one. When I see Rabbi Davis, I see the Chofetz Chaim; I see the Tanaim and the

Amoraim, sages from the past. I see how they talk and how they walk and how they thought. That's what I see over there, I can't see that in any place else.'

I remember when I first went to Rabbi Davis' home in Brighton Beach; it was like going into the Chofetz Chaim's house. Apart from the table and chairs, there were beds, and that was it. That was the house. Later on Rabbi Davis became Rosh Yeshiva in Mir in Brooklyn. They needed him very badly because there were a number of bocherim who only spoke Loshen Hakodesh, Hebrew, and Arabic. He taught there for a number of years where he attracted quite a number of talmidim.

Eventually a number of talmidim asked him to start a Yeshiva. This was a big nisayon, test. In the Mir, Rabbi Davis had a nice parnossa, he had salary on which he could live. To leave the Yeshiva to start his own meant that he would have no parnossa. However he listened to them and started his own Yeshiva, Yeshivat Zichron Meir. In order to fund the Yeshiva he had to take out a mortgage on his house. His talmidim, his feeling for Torah and his mesiras nefesh for what he knew must be accomplished for the glory of the Torah was a Kiddush Hashem for the entire Jewish people.

Rivka Leah Silver born in 1875
Told by her grand daughter

Charred mealies, pootu and Zulus

B obba Rivka Leah came to live with us in 1948 when she was seventy-three years old. We lived in Orange Grove, Johannesburg and the family had decided that she shouldn't be living on her own in Berea. After much heated discussion she agreed to come. My Bobba's mother tongue was Yiddish since she came from Eastern Europe. Fortunately, as a child of ten, I had no difficulty communicating with Bobba because I had absorbed the Yiddish my parents spoke in our house when they didn't want me to know what they were saying.

Bobba was a lady of great dignity and warmth and was regarded in her birthplace of Rezeta, Latvia, as a learned person because she could read and write and was committed to a Torah life. She was very refined and never raised her voice, but this did not preclude her possessing a strong will and a fierce independence.

When she was in her twenties, Bobba arrived from Lithuania by boat. Her betrothed was already in South Africa where he plied his trade as a hawker. He took goods round the suburbs of Johannesburg on a horse and cart. When he gathered enough money he traded in second-hand clothes and then eventually opened a general dealers' store.

By the time my mother was born, the youngest of seven children, he had become very wealthy. My grandmother was regarded as an aristocrat because she could read and write, whereas most people then were illiterate. It was at this time that grandmother built a shul and maintained a minyan in it for many years. When a drought came it wiped out grandfather's business and he lost his fortune. The community then assumed the responsibility of maintaining the shul.

I remember when Bobba came to live with us. She taught me all the morning prayers in Hebrew and as I watched her I tried to understand that her constant davening was an intrinsic part of her love of Torah.

Bobba had zerisus for kashrus and insisted on maintaining her own cooking facilities that she alone used. On the Thursday before Bobba's first Shabbos with us, she asked me, when I returned home from school, to help her with the preparations for Shabbos, which eventually became a weekly event. On my arrival I noticed a large, live chicken in a wicker basket squawking loudly, feathers flying, as it tried to escape. Bobba rushed around cleaning and cooking in a haze of Shabbos preparations not seeming to notice.

I cautiously approached the basket and saw that the chicken's feet were tied together so it couldn't get out and fly away. Bobba noticed me and smiled as she beckoned me to come to her. 'I've managed to buy a live chicken which has to be shechted [killed], she explained. 'Take the chicken to the shul and the shochet will help you, here is half a crown.' She folded the money in a hanky so that I would not lose it.

When Bobba handed me the basket with the anxious chicken inside, I realised that in the adult world there is no place for squeamishness. I held onto it with both hands trying to balance the fluttering bird and made my way to the shul.

The route to the shul took me up our street, past Paterson Park along a lane between the park and the workers' compound, which I passed with a mixture of fascination and fear. African gardeners worked in the park and stored their tools in a series of sheds. As well as containing their tools, the sheds also housed their families who used these sheds as their living and sleeping accommodation. There was water and outside toilets but all the cooking was done outside on a primus stove, where women, dressed in brightly coloured clothes and head-scarves, cooked traditional 'pootu', maize meal porridge, spoke Zulu and talked very loudly while small naked children played in the dirt. The mothers would often be singing or eating with their children and occasionally one might see a couple of old men smoking pipes, repairing things and discussing serious matters in their deep base voices.

Although I had been warned by my mother not to linger at the compound, I was drawn by the unusual sights and familiar smell of charred mealies [burnt corn on the cob.] The staple diet of the Africans was corn, and there was a patch of growing corn. Although I was only a child I realised that this was subsistence living.

The shul was nearby on a busy road, which I needed to cross with skill, clutching the squawking, restless chicken in the basket. As I approached the Shul the gate opened and a bearded man, wearing a white shirt, dark trousers, a black cotton jacket and a kippah on his head said 'are you Mrs Silver's grand daughter, I've been expecting you. Take the chicken inside, I won't be long.'

He came back wearing a black and white striped apron and carrying a large, sharp knife. He deftly lifted the squawking bird out of the basket with his back turned towards me and then everything went quiet. I saw a splash of blood on the floor and then the chicken, which had escaped the shochet's grasp, running around the yard without a head!

The shochet picked up the chicken, which had collapsed, and casually wrapped it in large sheets of newspaper, before putting it back into my basket. I paid the shochet, picked up the lifeless basket and returned home to Bobba in a daze. She plucked out the feathers and then singed the ends over her primus stove,

This early experience has stayed with me all my life.

Rabbi Dr. Joseph Kaminetsky
born in 1911
Told by his granddaughter

'Suppers consisted of only a piece of bread and an onion'

R abbi Dr. Joseph Kaminetsky was born in New York, the third of nine children, to a Russian Jewish couple living in East New York, Brooklyn. The community had many Jewish youth groups and synagogues, and its residents ranged from Modern Orthodox to Chasidic Jews.

The learning of the Torah and adhering to its teachings was the most important thing for Mr. and Mrs. Kaminetsky to pass on to their children. It was so important to them, in fact, that they sold their beautiful home in East New York so that their son could learn in a yeshiva rather than the public school he attended. They bought a new home in another large Jewish community in Brownsville, Brooklyn, at that time also known as "the Jerusalem of America", because of the vast numbers of Jews who resided there.

In 1918 when my grandfather was seven years old, World War One began. All he remembers of that terrible time was being told one day in school that New York would soon be bombed. He slept with his head under the covers that night to protect himself from the fictitious bombs hovering in his mind.

Grandfather graduated from a yeshiva high school and began Yeshiva College [the forebear of today's Yeshiva University] in 1928, at the age of seventeen. He decided to go into education, even though earlier he had been considering the Rabbinate. Everything seemed to be falling into place when the depression struck in 1929. It was a terrible time for many Americans, including the Kaminetskys. Mr. Kaminetsky lost his carpentry business and developed Parkinson's disease and Mrs. Kaminetsky had cancer. Money was scarce and grandfather remembers suppers consisting only of a piece of bread and an onion. Mr. Kaminetsky had brought over a niece and a nephew from Europe so that there were thirteen people living in five rooms with very little food.

Grandfather remembers that the worst thing about this time was watching his parents suffer as they did with their illnesses and their poverty. Very little was known about Parkinson's disease and cancer at that early period and large sums of money, which could have been used for much needed food, went to "quack" doctors with "quack" machines in the hopes of recovery. When I asked him what his life was like when he was nineteen, grandfather responded, "I must say that I was a very unhappy young fellow".

Despite these hard times, he continued his education in Columbia's Teacher's College where he enjoyed school and did well, graduating in 1944 with many honours. Now was the time to enter the career world. As a result of everything he had gained from his education, both secular and religious, grandfather realised what kind of education was needed for Orthodox Jews in America. Most Jews in America didn't have Hebrew day schools in their communities linking religious and secular studies. The fear was that because of this problem, Orthodox Jewry in America would soon come to an end. This fear was greatly magnified by the massacre that was occurring in Europe at that time. Grandfather made up his mind to put all his efforts towards preventing such a tragedy from occurring.

His first professional position had been working as principal in the after-school learning program of the Jewish Center in New York City. He thoroughly enjoyed his work there as well as the fringe benefits that came along with his position. He had a lovely young secretary, Selma Lefkowitz, whom he promptly began to court. He and my grandmother were married on June 23, 1940, and began to raise a family, which has now grown to three generations.

His experience working for the Jewish Center together with his doctoral degree in education, catapulted grandfather to his next position where in 1946, he began working under the leadership of Rabbi Shraga Feivel Mendelowitz to create Torah Umesorah, a foundation built to organize Hebrew day schools across America to educate Jewish children. The beginning of this undertaking was slow and difficult. People are naturally hesitant to accept change, and there was also the financial question of a private school when education was free in public schools. Then things began to pick up slowly with the idea of Hebrew day schools appealing to many Jews in America who felt the spiritual void of public education.

In 1948, grandfather found himself in what he describes as one of the most critical moments of his life. Rabbi Mendelowitz suddenly passed away leaving him as the head of the great and growing Torah Umesorah. He suddenly found himself burdened with a tremendous amount of responsibility and a very difficult task he had not expected, which became even more difficult with the death of his mother, of whom he was very fond. But he was determined to pull through for himself, his family, and the thousands of Jews across America who needed him.

Another event of 1948, which had a great impact on his life, was the formation of the State of Israel. Grandfather got involved in helping the newborn state by volunteering in an organization called Hapoel Hamizrachi [literally worker for the east, meaning Israel). Its purpose was to encourage American Jewish youth to settle in Israel and to help the new State in any way possible.

In 1942 he was elected national vice president and later on ran for president, losing by four votes. Grandfather, as well as many other Jews, kept a close watch on the current events, politics and happenings in Israel. This connection was strengthened when, together with my grandmother, they visited Israel for their first time in 1958, which he recalled as the most moving experience of his life. Meanwhile, as his success in building Hebrew day schools through Torah Umesorah continued and he was becoming well known and respected in various Jewish communities, he enjoyed some of the benefits that came along with this recognition including meeting many of the most respected and revered Rabbis of America and the rest of the world. He thought it a great honour to meet such people and considered himself fortunate to become personal friends with a number of them.

Grandfather also met with many United States politicians and in 1962 President Kennedy invited him, along with many other prominent Rabbis and educators, to the White House to discuss the civil rights legislation he sought to have enacted by congress. He became involved in United States politics only when the passing of certain education laws that affected his work were being discussed. Apart from President Kennedy, grandfather met with many senators, mayors, and a number of other presidents.

After he took over as national director of Torah Umesorah in 1948, the number of Orthodox day schools in America jumped to five hundred, with nearly one hundred thousand students. After thirty-four years with the organization, building a strong foundation to expand upon, at the age of sixty nine he decided to retire. In 1980, grandfather and grandmother decided to pursue their dream and they bought an apartment in Jerusalem, where their youngest daughter had been living for three years. They split each year between the United States and Israel.

For many years, he had a hobby of collecting, smoking and cleaning different kinds of pipes. He had a beautiful collection in his study. However in 1983, at age seventy two, his doctor informed him that he had a heart condition, which would require a triple bypass surgery that was caused by his smoking. Grandfather then stopped smoking and immediately gave all his pipes away. After his surgery, when I asked him how he felt about growing older, he said 'I am grateful to the Almighty that I am growing older gracefully.'

Herman Greenstein
born in 1949

'I believe you have to be Jewish first, everything else is second'

I lived in Mumkach, which before World War One was in Austro Hungary. Between World War One and World War Two it was in Czechoslovakia, and after World War Two it was part of the Ukraine in the Soviet Union. Now it is in the Ukraine. Between the wars seventy per cent of the inhabitants of Mumkach were Jewish.

Every place has its history and culture. When it comes to Mumkach the Jews had their own culture. Their mentality was that of ultra orthodox Jews, similar to that of orthodox Jews in Israel today. Not only did the Carpathian Mountains separate us from Russia there was a separation between the Russian Jews and us. We kept Shabbos. No one mixed or associated with the goyim, that was the unwritten rule. Gentiles did not exist in my life.

After World War Two there was no one left of the Jewish population in Mumkach but Jews came into the village from the surrounding areas.

My grandfather was the wealthiest person in his village of Kopinoutzi. Although he was an orphan, he created his wealth. He owned land, grapevines, a factory making alcohol and a mill for flour.

My grandfather was killed in the concentration camps. He had had twelve children; but only six of his children came back from the camps alive. When the Soviet Union occupied the village they tried the left over members of the family for exploitation of the general population. In 1945 the boys were jailed for being kulaks. The Russians did not use the word capitalism, the word kulak means fist. With a fist mentality you abuse someone else in order to become rich.

My father spent two years in jail. After he came out of jail he was not allowed to work for five or six years, therefore he worked at home as a tailor. When Stalin died he was allowed to go back to work, and he was employed by a government organisation as a tailor. My parents had four children and I was born after my father came out of jail.

When you cannot work, you don't live. You survive. If you have bread, water and salt your stomach could be full. I have no idea, even now, how people survived. We owned a piece of land next to our house and in the summer we grew vegetables and raised a few chickens. That helped a bit. We ate kosher and never broke the rules of kashrus. When we didn't have our own chicken to eat, we bought one. A chicken lasted our family of six a whole week.

My Dad had a house in Mumkach in a nice location. It was a big house and until 1961 we did not have running water. There was a pump outside in the yard and we brought water into the house in a bucket. My mother boiled water on the stove and emptied it into a zinc tub in the kitchen when we needed to wash ourselves or do the laundry. In order to water the vegetables in the garden I would have to schlep twenty buckets of water. We had electricity for four or five hours a day, the rest of the time we used a kerosene lamp.

Our clothes were second hand. My Dad obtained used clothes, took them apart and turned the material around. We rarely wore suits made from new material, but our clothing was respectable.

It didn't seem terrible to us at all. We did not regard ourselves as poor. At my age now, I give credit to my mother who never told us that we were poor. She used to say 'we are rich people but we are cash short.' The interesting thing was that in our village Jewish life was paramount. The synagogue was not in a building; people opened their houses for minyanim. On Rosh Hashanah we had a minyan in our house since we had a sefer Torah.

In the 1950's I went to a Russian school six days a week, which was three or four miles away from home. Since we were now in the Soviet Union my mother wanted me to go to a Russian school. In town there were Russian, Ukrainian and Hungarian schools. I spoke Russian, Hungarian, Ukrainian and Yiddish. Our class in school was fifty percent Jewish. Although our teacher was a Russian Jewish lady who was not anti-Semitic, we were not allowed to wear yarmulkes in school. The singing teacher said to me, when I was a soloist in the chorus, 'take off your hat, this is not a synagogue.' If he could make fun of me he did.

Up until the age of fifteen I wore a hat all the time. However, there was an occasion when some punks took my hat off in the street and stamped on it to show their superiority. My father defended me and the punks beat him up so badly that his face was bloody. After that I never wore a hat in order to protect my father. Russian law did not allow anti-Semitism and the police went after the punks. I don't know what happened to them.

In those days you had to belong to the youth communist party in school. This entailed wearing a red handkerchief around your neck. They said it was voluntary but in fact it was enforced.

The Russian government forced the Jews to work on Shabbos. My father was forced to go to work on Shabbos, but when he came home it was Shabbos, no question. When we came home from school it was Shabbos. We were not allowed to turn on the light and a Shabbos goy came in to put wood on the stove. My mother baked challah for Shabbos.

On Rosh Hashanah we did not go to school or work. On Easter, which sometimes coincided with Passover, the Russian government forced us to volunteer to sweep the streets, or to beautify the City, or clean the factory — for free. Not only the Jewish people, but also the goyim were forced to take part, in order that people should not celebrate religious holidays. This was to make sure that no one had a religious life. The doctrine of the communist party was to dominate the mind of the human being, and suppress religious views.

We studied scientific communism. This was a form of organised religion. The goyim were hated for being religious; we were hated for being Jewish and religious.

The KGB had religious seminaries. First the goyim would become members of the KGB; then they would go and train in the Seminaries to be priests in the Russian Orthodox Church. They became priests in order to spy on the population. If you were Catholic and went to the priest and made a confession, the priest reported everything to the authorities.

My father had a Jewish friend who became a Catholic priest for the KGB because it was a job. As a priest he had a good job, which paid three or four times the normal salary for government officials. He had a limousine and a driver, a place to live, servants, a good name and a beautiful lifestyle. However, at home he and his family remained Jewish. Jewish government officials would come to our house in the middle of the night to have a religious wedding ceremony after the civil ceremony.

There is a Russian joke. The big synagogue in Moscow was looking for a Rabbi. The first candidate Chaim was a good Jew, very knowledgeable but not a member of the communist party. He was turned down for the post. Yanky was Jewish but not knowledgeable so he didn't get the post either. Boris was well educated in Judaism although not Jewish, but he was a member of the communist party and he got the job as Rabbi in the synagogue.

In Russia my nationality on my passport stated that I was Jewish, not Russian. I believe that you have to be Jewish first, everything else is second.

Simon Braun
born in 1918

'There are no open miracles, but there are many ways of hashgacha'

I t is forbidden to rely on miracles, say our sages. Even in times of desperation, a man should try and undertake some action to save himself. Miracles do happen, but at that moment of time people do not realize that what is happening to them is miraculous. Only later when they reconstruct the events, can they recognize the hand of Hashem.

My story begins on a December night in 1956 in the midst of the Hungarian revolution. My wife, my nine-year-old daughter and I were escaping from Hungary and crossing the border into Austria. I paid four thousand Hungarian Forints in advance to smugglers to hire a truck. In exchange they promised to drop us at the nearest point in Hungary to Austria, from where we would find our own way across the border.

The truck left us on a dark field full of mud and puddles, with short instructions, "carry on to your left, until you find a road which will take you the nearby Austrian village called Deutschkreuz." The truck then disappeared leaving seven people, alone, in total darkness. The family who joined us had a baby with them who cried and screamed continuously. We walked and walked and the thick mud stuck to our shoes. I had to clean the shoes of my wife and daughter with my hands, because it was impossible to continue walking. The weight of the mud was too heavy.

There was some discussion between the two families, over which direction to go. I clearly remembered that the man said left, the same side I put on my Tefillin. I had no doubt that we should go left. We had to cross difficult trails on a little hill, which was no easy job. We climbed up the hill in total darkness with nothing to hold on to and nothing marking the way. All we had was in one suitcase and a knapsack. At one point the suitcase rolled all the way down to the field below. I had to go on my hand and knees all the way down to find it. This was all we had on earth — a few clothes stuffed into an old suitcase.

The Hungarian border guards, who heard the baby's cries, shot rockets in the sky to light up the area. They failed to locate us and at last, after we crossed the train tracks, we suddenly saw a road, and a tree. To our horror we discovered that somebody was standing behind the tree. As we got nearer, he stepped out from behind the tree, and we realized, to our relief, that he was an Austrian border guard. He escorted us to the Austrian village, where there was a temporary shelter, lined with straw, where refugees could sleep.

We were happy to be safe, but I couldn't sleep. We had no money, no gold and no jewellery; all we had were the clothes we wore with a few more in the suitcase. While I was lying there full of worries, I heard two people talking. The first said that he had three thousand Forints, which he would like to change to three hundred Schillings. (At this time currency change was totally forbidden!) In my heart I thought how nice it would be if I had some Forints with me, but I had given all I had to the smugglers. I got up and went for a walk.

At a bus stop I heard two peasant women talking and discovered that they were on their way back to Hungary. One of the women said: 'I have three hundred Schillings, and would like to change them to three thousand Forint.' I immediately remembered the man who had the same sum in Schillings. The two peasant women were waiting for a bus that would take them back to Hungary. I ran back to the shelter as fast as I could and found the man I heard speaking about exchanging his forints for schillings. 'Listen,' I said to him, 'if you want to have two hundred Schillings for your Forints, then give me the three thousand Forints and I will return with two hundred Schilling. Maybe you don't believe me but look, here are my wife and my daughter, so you can be sure that I will come back with your money.' The man, wonder of wonders, gave me, a total stranger, his three thousand Forints. I ran again as fast as I could to catch the two women before the bus came. What luck! Baruch Hashem, the two peasant women were still waiting at the bus stop. I started to talk with them asking, 'where are you travelling to?' One of them said, 'I am going back to Hungary, and I only have Austrian Schillings.' 'What would you do in Hungary with Austrian Schillings?' I asked. 'You know it is against the law to have foreign currency! Here,' I offered, 'I can give you three thousand Forints for your schillings!' She immediately agreed, we exchanged money and I ran back to man in the shelter and gave him two hundred Schillings, as I had promised. In this way I earned one hundred Schillings, a big sum in those days, with absolutely no investment from my side.

Only later, when I reconstructed the events I understood how incredible it all was. Why should someone trust a stranger with his money? Why did he agree to accept one hundred Schillings less than the going rate? Why did the two peasant women trust a total stranger in the darkness? Maybe the notes were false? How did I suddenly have hundred Schillings, when I left Hungary without a penny? There are no open miracles, but there are many ways of Hashgacha [Divine Providence]!

Katya Brajtman
born in 1976

A fabulously wealthy gift – of two onions

As a child, life in the Soviet Union meant that at one year old you went to kindergarten. From about eight months old a child is toilet trained. In the kindergarten you were forced to eat the meals and if you didn't eat them you were punished. You had to sleep during the day and if you didn't sleep you were punished.

At seven years old I went to school close to my home in the workers district of the city of Kostroma, which was situated on the river. The old city was on one side of the river, and on the other side were the factories and the sleeping district. We lived in the workers district.

Our apartment was in a huge building of two hundred families, where each family was given one room. Our room was twelve metres square. There were two or three communal toilets in the communal area on each of the six floors. Forty families shared two kitchens in the communal area. On the bottom floor was a showering place, which was a big room with cabins, each with three walls, the fourth side was open. There was one area for the ladies and one for the men. On the first floor there was a huge room with giant bathtubs for hand washing laundry. There were two washing machines in the building, but they were not reliable and we mostly washed by hand.

I remember a huge slogan on the wall outside saying that the People and the Party are one. The children loved living there because they had lots of friends and the doors to the apartments were never closed.

This building was the hostel for my father's factory. He was a white-collar metal engineer researching different alloys. In the Soviet Union the industrial system worked in this way. The factories would specialise in making only one part, and a hostel housed all the workers in the factory. If you worked for many years you were eligible for a better apartment.

The school was enormous with two thousand boys and girls from age seven to seventeen. The uniform for girls was a brown dress with a black apron for regular days, and a white apron worn only for holidays. You sewed a piece of lace to the cuffs and collar. You took it off to wash it and then sewed it back again. You wore brown or black ribbons in your hair on regular days and white ribbons on holidays. No colours were permitted. A girl I knew was thrown out of the school for wearing a red ribbon in her hair. This was at the height of the Soviet Empire. After the Second World War no one could afford a uniform.

In school you sat with your arms folded on the desk. If you wanted to ask a question or leave the room, you raised your forearm off the desk. When teachers went in or out of the room you stood up as a show of respect.

Our history book was called a reading book about the history of the Union of the Soviet Socialist Republic. There it described the happy union of two nations, the Ukraine and Russia, which decided to be one. Currently, under the present regime, Ukraine says that it was annexed. Describing the Second World War, the book explained that at four o'clock in the morning of the 22nd June 1941 a cloud of planes approached the border and a treacherous war broke out, which was started by Nazi fascist Germany. It conveniently left out the Molotov/

Ribentrov pact completely. It left out the fact that in 1939 Russia annexed the Baltic countries, much of Poland and Galicia. It left out Stalin's repressions. In fact it didn't mention Stalin's name at all because it was already Khrushchev's time and Stalin's government was finished.

The history book romanticized and revised the history of Russia. It didn't mention famines. Whenever Russia fought a war it won. Russia was never the aggressor and it always fought a noble war to protect itself, which ensured her victory. It was not because G-d granted anything. When the people are fighting a noble cause, they prevail.

Every day on the television there was a movie about the Second World War. There were books about the war. Because Russia was under occupation twenty million people perished. The Nazis wiped out whole villages. After the war Russian historians pointed out that the war was a tragedy for all the people and one ethnic nation should not be singled out. So the tragedy of the holocaust was not singled out as a crime against the Jewish people. The Soviet people and the people of the world perished from Nazi fascist oppression. There should not be a distinction in death. It was shared pain.

When I was eight years old, I was in second grade. At that age we were called 'Children of October.' We received a red star, with a picture of Lenin at the age of eight, to wear on our uniform. At the age of ten we were Young Pioneers, and the Communist Party structure was introduced into the class. We had a national newspaper, called the Pioneer Pravda. It introduced the cult of Pioneer heroes, who fitted nicely into our revisionist history book.

One example, which was considered an heroic act, occurred in the 1930's. Armed groups of soldiers would go into the villages and confiscate food from the peasants who would then starve. The father of the first Pioneer hero hid some bread. The hero told one of the armed groups and the father was executed. The peasants killed the son who then became a Russian hero.

My grandmother was fourteen years of age when the Second World War broke out. She lived in the Jewish city of Smolesk. The day before the city was entered and occupied by the Nazis, the huge Jewish population decided to get away. The people could not decide whether to go on the train or go to the outlying villages, because the trains were often bombed and people died in the bombed trains. My grandmother was with her mother and they were still undecided at the train station about what to do. An Officer forced them onto a train.

They reached the Northern Urals city of Asbest, a city that made asbestos and they went to work in a factory. The whole factory made shells for the war. When my grandmother was sixteen a group of friends gave her a fabulously wealthy gift of – two onions.

My grandfather was sixteen when the war broke out. He was starving, so he lied about his age to go into the army. He was conscripted early and went to a military academy. This saved his life. When he got to the front he could shoot and he had boots to wear. During the war he got a safe job to do. He crawled in the fields where the battle was in progress in order to deliver fifty kilo boxes of shells to light tanks in his division. He was awarded many decorations, but the commander sent them back because he was Jewish. After the war he was shown a stack of the official orders for his decorations.

My great grandfather was a shoemaker. In order to survive he would raid the garbage dumps looking for scraps with which he made shoes and sold them to buy bread

My grandmother was a faithful pioneer at the age of ten. On one occasion she was wearing her pioneer uniform and red scarf and held in her hand some black bread and schmaltz. She walked into her house and saw the whole family gathered round the table. She was hurried out of the room. Many decades later she realised that the family was having a Pesach Seder and they didn't want her to know. They wanted to protect her and themselves from the Young Pioneer ethic. In addition she was holding bread.

Her father was in charge of a secret minyan, which he never told anyone about. There were mailboxes on every building into which you could drop a written report about someone. You did not have to sign your name. In 1936 someone reported that my great grandfather was a spy. In the middle of the night the KGB, the committee for State Security, came in and frisked the apartment. My grandfather was a youth communist league member and told the KGB that he could attest to his father's innocence and that it was a mistake. The KGB responded 'step aside youth league member'. During the search a gold watch disappeared.

Two years later the head of the KGB was accused of something and executed and then replaced by a new head. There was an amnesty for the victims of his policies and great grandfather came back without his teeth. He was illiterate and could not sign any papers that he was a spy. This saved him.

Things have changed in Russia, but I thank G-d for allowing me to view the changes from the outside, here in Eretz Yisroel.

Jack Krantz
born in 1912

'The Queen,' he replied,
'likes to keep everything'

O ne of my earliest memories occurred around 1917 or 1918, during the First World War, when I was six years old and living in my father's house in Chelsea. Our neighbourhood, known as Edith Grove, had old-fashioned houses all along the road. One morning I noticed a policeman on a bicycle blowing a whistle. This was the official signal for an air raid. Father hurried us down into the basement. In those days some of the houses had basements, which were also used as bomb shelters. Even today, some of those old houses are still standing, basements intact. When nobody was looking, I climbed out of the basement to have a look. Everybody was gazing up at the sky, so I also looked up and saw that just above us was a German Zeppelin. Zeppelins were filled with hydrogen so of course the easiest way to bring it down was to use incendiary bullets. I believe that it might have been the first one they'd shot down because before that, they'd never used incendiary bullets.

Another early memory is of 1924. I was fourteen years old and going to school near my home in a neighbourhood of Chelsea called Park Walk. My father had recently bought a car, and at that time we were one of the few families who had one. Of course it wasn't really new, it was an old French one called a Mathis, I believe. It was a curious looking box-like model and my brother, who was four years older than I was, and my father, used to drive it.

On my way home from school I would pass a famous place called 'World's End.' It was famous, I was told, because Charles the Second used to visit his friend Nell Gwen, who lived around there. The King was so amazed that she lived so far from the Palace that he called it 'The World's End.'

One day, as I walked past 'The World's End' I heard a commotion behind me. I looked around to see a whole crowd of people gathered together in the first of what is now known as a general strike. The people were very militant and had already overturned two cars. I quickly ran home to warn my father to put the Mathis in the garage. My brother ran out and drove away in the car just as the mob came around the corner, a hundred yards from our house.

Sometime between 1923 and 1926, I recall attending an inventions fair. My father spoke broken English throughout his entire life, but nevertheless made himself understood. He was an inventor, and invented many things relating to clothes. He invented 'plastic wardrobes', an entirely new concept in those days. They were plastic protective coverings for clothes that kept out dirt and moths. He exhibited this invention at the fair, which was held somewhere in the West End of London.

I remember going to visit him at his stand, one day, and next to his stand was a man with a peculiar looking machine. I didn't really know what it was, nor did any one else. His name was Baird and he was the man who perfected television. He was exhibiting a very ancient type of television, which worked by rotating a turntable rapidly in order to 'catch' the voice and image of the person. At this stage there was still a lot of static, nevertheless, people were interested in watching his demonstrations.

My father told me afterwards that Baird would often talk to him about how he struggled to perfect this machine because, like all inventions, the ideas improved as he went along. The television that we have today bears no resemblance to the early primitive machine invented by Baird.

In the early 1930's my mother and father took a trip to Germany to treat my mother's asthma, from which she suffered all her life. The doctor recommended a certain German spa, famous in those days for it's curative properties. The four children, my siblings and I, the youngest, were left at home in London.

From Germany, after the treatments, my parents travelled to Poland to visit their many cousins. Hitler was just starting his campaign against the Jews and Poland's large Jewish population was feeling the incitement. Some towns were almost entirely composed of Jews. The Jewish people were religious. They didn't call themselves ' Ultra Orthodox', because everyone lived that way in Poland. There was no question of Reform Judaism, everyone was Orthodox. They all did the same thing, living in the same way. That alienated the local Polish population, inciting envy and later hatred.

When my parents visited Poland, my father's many cousins begged him to take them out. He couldn't get them visas and he had to leave them behind. Those with insight knew what was coming.

In 1937 my father had a stand at the Ideal Home Exhibition and he wanted to hire a girl, as he did not speak very good English. He went to an agency to ask for someone who could do this kind of job. They enumerated all the various qualities he would need in such an employee. When they finished he was so exasperated he told them he didn't need such a professional person. The clerk jumped up exclaiming 'for crying out loud!' to which my father replied 'vell, I don't want somebody wot cries out loud'.

Unfortunately, father died during the war in 1942 and I was called up to serve in the army. One day, during a training exercise we saw German prisoners at the end of the field hundred and fifty yards away. My sergeant, a sadistic man, ordered us to fix our bayonets and charge at them, 'until I tell you to stop', he added. I will never forget the looks on their faces, although it pales into insignificance compared to the horror on the faces of the holocaust victims when they were led into the gas chambers.

After the war, material for manufacturing plastic wardrobes was still rationed. However, the giant Plastics Company, ICI had just started to manufacture their products and since we made the wardrobes out of their plastic we were able to resume production.

In the early 1960's, we were fortunate to sell a lot our goods to the Royal household and I applied for a royal warrant, which was granted to our company by the Duke of Edinburgh whom we were supplying.

Occasionally, my brother went to the Palace to take measurements for the various royal garments at the behest of the Duke. However on one occasion, in 1962, my brother was indisposed and I went to do the measuring in his place. In those days I drove an old car and I remember driving up to the gates of Buckingham Palace just before the changing of the guard. I presented my card to the guard at the Palace gates, he opened them for me and I felt most embarrassed as the crowd outside the gates, hoping to catch the glimpse of a Royal personage, stared at me as I passed though in my old car. I drove up to the side entrance where the tradesmen were and waited in the waiting room until a servant of the household beckoned for me to follow him.

We went to a very old-fashioned lift, which looked as if it dated from Queen Victoria. Just as he opened the gates of the lift, out jumped another of the palace servants with a couple of Corgi dogs who rushed passed me. It was a most extraordinary scene but that was nothing compared with what was to come. I got into the lift, which shuddered as we entered it and we went up to the private apartments, on the first or second floor.

The servant took me around the outside of the gallery and as we rounded the corner I saw a whole load of broken toys, including rocking horses and dolls with broken limbs and missing heads. They looked a sorry mess, so I turned to the servant and asked 'what are all these old toys?' 'Oh, he said 'they belonged to Queen Victoria'. I asked him what they were doing there, to which he replied 'the Queen likes to keep everything'.

From there, he took me to the Duke of Edinburgh's private quarters, where we entered a room which was almost as long as a football field. If I recall clearly on the side of the room there were about two hundred huge glass mahogany cases, beautifully crafted, each displaying some sort of uniform in them. Every type of uniform you could possibly imagine was there, all belonging to the Duke of Edinburgh. My job was to supply the covers for these.

I continued to walk through that room and entered his private quarters where his personal servants were working. There, I had the surprise of my life. We passed a room where a man was sitting cross-legged, like an old fashioned tailor and he appeared to be knitting something. The servant said to me 'that's one of the Dukes tailors darning a pair of the Duke's socks'. 'You must be joking!' I said. 'We don't waste anything here. Everything is used.' He replied.

I was really astonished.

Etta bat Shlomo HaLevi
born in 1912
Told by her daughter,
the Librarian of the Telshestone English Library

'Mille et mille fois'

My mother in the middle
with her mother and sister

My mother was the youngest of eight children. Her mother Elizabeth was a first generation immigrant from Lithuania and she could barely speak English (she referred to her shiny pine floors as "my Polish floor"). Elizabeth signed her name with an "x" but ran two successful dress shops, describing her eight children as her stock, and 'better than money in the bank.'

My mother had three children. As she walked the third child, aged two, around the park she thought 'what a waste of a brain' and resolved to qualify as a barrister. It was difficult studying with three young children. She began her law studies only after she put them to bed. My father would often find that she had fallen asleep over her law books.

She qualified as a barrister in 1944, at a time when the younger members of her chambers, the rooms of the barristers, were still on army service. She was one of the first women to join the bar. However, before that she had to overcome considerable male hostility. On her first day at law school all the other students were men. The lecturer turned to her and said, "wouldn't you be better at home making the dinner?"

In her pupillage (apprenticeship as a barrister) her barrister principal said, "You can sit in my room and you can read my papers, but I don't need your views". My mother read each bundle of briefs, solicitors' requests for her principal's opinion. Ignoring his remarks, she wrote out her own opinion of each case and placed it

My mother

with the papers. One day, when he was very pressed for time, the barrister principal read my mother's opinion. It was so good he sent it out as his own work, and from then on her place in the barristers' chambers was assured

As a barrister she never gave up in Court. If a judge was against her she carried on, as she always said "mille et mille fois" (thousands of times) until she got over her point. Her motto was, 'unless I tell the judge what to do, how will he know the right decision?' On one occasion she argued a case in the County Court. As persuasive as ever she said to the County Court judge 'I argued this point only yesterday in the Court of Appeal.' The judge countered with 'but Mrs Frazer, did you win?' Pulling herself to her full height she replied, with her usual charming smile, 'Your Honour, I regard that question as an insult.'

On another occasion she appeared in the County Court for the defendant. The plaintiff gave his evidence, was cross-examined and then his barrister called the plaintiff's witnesses. After cross-examining them, my mother stood in her place in the well of the court, waiting to open the case for the defendant. As she stood there waiting for the nod from the judge to begin, he turned to her and said 'well I think it's clear, judgement for the plaintiff?' How I longed to be in court on that day to hear how my mother handled such a very delicate situation. We only know that she won her case!

As the child of immigrants, who had fled from the country of their birth, my mother understood what was needed to persuade people to her way of thinking. When she addressed a jury she would say the same thing six times. She explained to me that the first time the members of the jury were aware only that someone was speaking in the Court. The second time they realised she was speaking to them. At the third repetition she would gain their attention. The fourth time they would listen to what she was saying. The fifth time they would assess the value of her remarks, and then finally they would be persuaded to give a verdict in the favour of her client.

She was a champion of the underprivileged. She gave her best efforts to the many complicated legal issues involved with marriage, divorce and custody cases. In a succession of cases before the Court of Appeal, my mother managed by expertise, determination and charm, to obtain a fair outcome for many disadvantaged families.

She was persuasive. She always smiled when she spoke. She never scolded her children. She allowed them to make their own mistakes. When one of her daughters was nine and needed new school shoes, she was too busy and sent her daughter to the shoe shop by herself. The child came back with silver grey strapless shoes. Mother just smiled and said that that was part of learning for life.

She always saw difficulties as challenges to be overcome. In her early seventies, ten years before she was niftar, she had one leg amputated. Her attitude was that although she only had one leg she felt sorry for people who had no legs.

Her determination never left her. She practised full time as a barrister until she was eighty-three. After her leg was amputated she was determined to continue. She would arrive at Court every day by 8.30 am to get the parking place nearest the Courthouse. She sat in her car, which she had had adapted so she could drive with her remaining leg, working on her papers until 10.00 am when the Court usher came out. He carried her barrister's blue bag and papers and helped her up the Court steps. In those days the Court would sit till 6.00 p.m. to finish a case. Sometimes the hearing was extended because of her refusal to give in until the judge saw it her way.

Once towards the end of her career, when the ravages of time had taken their toll and she struggled to walk with the aid of two sticks, she was accompanying her client into Court. The other barrister enquired of my mother's client "have you brought your grandma?" At the end of the case which my mother won convincingly, the other barrister muttered under his breath "sly old witch". On another occasion, while disrobing in the robing room, after another hard fought victory, she heard her adversary being asked by another barrister how he had fared in the case. He said 'I was Yettaed.'

Most barristers take a pile of law books into Court and quote from previous cases to try to persuade the judge to follow a previous similar case. My mother knew the cases thoroughly. She never took law books into Court, and when the other barrister quoted a certain case, she would lean over and borrow the other barrister's law book. She quoted other parts of the same case to the judge to persuade him that her view of the case was correct, and she usually won.

I worked at the Citizen's Advice bureau, representing bureau clients in unfair dismissal cases. On one occasion when I had had a spectacular success in the Industrial Tribunal, the Chairman of the Tribunal was uncharacteristically complimentary about the way I had presented the case. I went home and telephoned my mother, to share this moment with her. She listened in complete silence while I spared no words in describing to her exactly what the Chairman had said. I had even taken notes so that I would not forget one syllable. Eventually my monologue petered out and I waited for her response. I have never forgotten what she said, and have used her comment many times in giving advice myself. She said 'what you have told me tells me more about the Chairman, than it does about you.'

Her work was her life and she rarely took a holiday or a day off. Once when her granddaughter Rebecca, aged five, drew a bird with three legs, my mother told Rebecca that she had never seen such a bird. Rebecca replied, "that's because you have never been anywhere Grandma". My mother never wanted anything, and was generous to her children and to her grandchildren. Her philosophy, which she passed on to her children, was 'if you can't get what you want, want what you can get.'

When she was eighty-three, and I was living in Israel, she telephoned to tell me she was thinking of retiring. I knew that if she retired she would lose her reason for living and I told her that she should not retire. 'Can you think of anyone who is still working at the age of eighty-three' she asked. It was the time of the elections for Mayor of Jerusalem. At the age of eighty-three the incumbent was not intending to hand over the reins voluntarily. When I reminded my mother of this there was silence at the other end of the phone. 'No-one,' she said, 'has been able to answer the question except you.' I could not persuade her to continue working and, sadly, she was niftar barely six months later. Judges, solicitors, colleagues and her clients, mourned her as a person who had been a character and a fixture on the legal Midland circuit for half a century. She refused to be elevated to the Bench to serve as a judge, preferring instead to fight for justice for her clients.

My mother once told me that she would like to be remembered as eccentric. However I hope that her values, her fight for justice, her determination and her honesty, will be the legacy that she has passed on to her children and many grandchildren and great grandchildren.

My mother's father, **Shlomo HaLevi ben Yehoshua HaLevi** was born in 1870 and died in 1923. On his matzevah [gravestone] inscribed in Hebrew are the words 'A dusty pearl known to many but honoured by few, a spark covered with embers and ashes, floundering between the waves of the present and the past.'

Upon reading the stories that are told in this book, one sees how difficult it was for our parents and grandparents when they were plucked from the womb of orthodoxy in Europe and thrown into the abyss of secularism of the goldene medina and beyond.

My grandfather was the sacrifice that enabled his family to escape from pogroms and the fires of the holocaust. Even though he was crushed by the embers of his own life, his Torah is now blossoming through many of his descendants and his sacrifice was not in vain.

The compilers of this book hope that the sacrifices of our storytellers, their parents and grandparents will also not have been in vain and that the Torah of our ancestors will be the beacon that lights up our life.

Noach Haltrecht
born at the end of the age of elegance

Fifty Years is Half a Century

"I t's got a *haskomah* from Rabbi Akiva Eiger" shouted Reb Leib excitedly bringing amazed gasps from the studious readers in the silence of the reference library at The Hebrew University in Jerusalem that memorable morning.

He was looking at a copy of "Toldos Noach" published in Warsaw in 1830 by a son of Reb Noach miLissa, the first named Haltrecht. It had been a long search to find the Sefer which came to light in the pursuit of family genealogy. "Halt recht — keep the Derech" was the name chosen by Reb Noach, who lived in Lissa, (now Leszno). In Germany most people had adopted surnames by the 1500's, but patronymics continued in some areas until various different states adopted decrees requiring permanent surnames between 1771 and 1820. In 1808 Napoleon made Jews in France take a fixed surname.

His name was bequeathed to subsequent generations who travelled and settled in different parts of the world remembering and naming their sons after Noach miLissa, even now. From Poland the family, in common with many of the families whose histories are included within this book, settled in England, America, Canada, Argentina, France and Israel. My grandfather reached London around 1904 and my father became Bar Mitzvah in *Machzikei Hadass* in the East End of London in 1910.

Subsequent *Hashgochah Protis* revealed further treasures in writings by the sons of Reb Noach miLissa, one with a *haskomah* from The Malbim and a *perush* on the Pesach Haggadah hidden in the Library of Jerusalem University together with some *kisvei yad* originals on *T'nach* and *Gemorrah*, yet to be translated. Family history is not merely the tracing of ancestry; it is what we inherit from our forebears and perhaps today, even more, is how we deal with this legacy.

Parshas Lech Lecha begins with G-d's commandment to Abraham, "Go out of your country, from your birthplace, and from your father's house unto the land that I will show you. And I will make of you a great nation and I will bless you and make your name great..."

Haskomahs to Sefer Toldos Noach

Haskomah from Rabbi Akiva Eiger

Thus, at the age of seventy five, Abraham became the first wandering Jew.

He and Sarah left their families and birthplace and went to an unknown destination – the land of Canaan. When they finally arrived there, G-d brought a famine upon the land and again they were forced to move. This time they journeyed to Egypt where they experienced many trials and tribulations.

The Midrash uses the following analogy to explain why G-d made Abraham and Sarah move from place to place. This is compared to a bottle of perfume which is located in the corner of a shelf. As long as it remains there, no one realises its value nor do they have any benefit from it. Only when the perfume is moved from place to place does everyone benefit from its wonderful fragrance. The same occurred with Abraham and Sarah. G-d wanted them to move from place to place so that people could get to know them, learn and benefit from them. Rashi says that Hashem wanted his arrival at the final destination to be precious in Avrohom's eyes, as well as to reward him for every word of Hashem that he obeyed.

Yet, Abraham's travel was not only for the benefit of others. The Torah uses the expression "Lech Lecha" which can be translated as, "go for your benefit."

Fifty years is half a century and seventy per cent of the normal allotted lifespan of a human being. "L'd what is man that You should care about him, mortal man that You should think of him? Man is like a breath; his days are like a passing shadow." (Psalm 144: 3-4; Yizkor Prayer).

The truth is that fifty years is half a century of moments strung together. Each moment at its birth is a step towards the future, unknown, next moment. In this way, life at seventy years of age is only different from those years of half a century ago by the view from "under the passing shadow." The memories which spring to mind of incidents which are etched both into the mind and the personality are mostly ones which can never happen again and thus this collection reveals treasures that have to be preserved within the "cedar chests of time."

If pressed to recollect moments from these years, how does one arrange them into tangible events and into words with meaning? This indelible memory was never meant for sharing. Recapturing them now in a different setting only reveals the arena wherein they were part of the panorama. They revive emotions, joy, tears and sighs, blushes and shivers up the spine. "Man tracht un Gott lacht!" "Man thinks and G'd laughs!"

The Hashgochah Protis in the pieces of the jig-saw of life become more evident with the aid of hindsight. "Teach us to count our days rightly, that we may obtain a wise heart" (Psalm 90:12. Yizkor). A glimpse of decades of a life — indeed but a passing shadow — can never be recaptured by future generations, not with photographs or with words. The emotions and the "breath" which is a man are in the past now and within the covers of this book the portraits give evidence of an age consigned to the description of being "old-fashioned" Of course it is and thus it has been since creation.

My father with Queen Mary in 1931

Each new age brings with it its own *mores*, fashions, technology and lifestyles. However, it is the values of the past generation that this book has set out to portray. The strengths, the ideals and the principles by which our parents, grand parents and great grandparents lived, in the way of their upbringing, connect us to them. It is these values which have been collected into these "passing shadows", for it is from their history and their "breath" that we can inherit their legacy and live the message of "counting our days wisely to acquire a heart of wisdom."

The days of Noach spanned three ages, he saw three worlds. Noach saw the world before the *mabul* – the flood –in its settled state, and in its destruction of the flood and in its resettlement after the flood.

My life span before the destruction was indeed short, but I can bring to mind the thrill of a three year old child waving to the engine drivers as the steam trains puffed their way past the end of our garden, and the pure joy when one of them returned the wave. None of my descendants will appreciate such a moment because progress has long retired these named and puffing smoke-belching monsters for the impersonal diesels of today. *Chazal* teach us to be the first to greet one's fellow man and to do so with a *"ponem yofes"* a pleasant demeanour. Maybe this was an early introduction to a character trait implanted for life.

In "Strive for Truth" part one of Michtav Me-Eliyahu rendered into English by Rabbi Aryeh Carmell, (Published by Feldheim 1978) Rabbi Carmell notes on page 208 that the article 'The ego, the inclinations, the spirit and the soul' is from a letter to his students, written in the train between Bournemouth and London on Thursday 4 Adar II/16th March 1940. Rabbi Dessler had been to Bournemouth, a seaside town two and a half hours from London, to visit another pupil who was living there because of the war.

As an evacuee, I recall the aftermath of "Dunkirk" in Bournemouth in 1940.

On 12th May, 1940, Adolf Hitler ordered the invasion of France. The German Army employed 136 divisions and 2,500 tanks in its invasion of France. The French, supported by Belgian and British troops, had a total of 125 divisions and 3,600 tanks. The Germans were dominant in the air with 3,000 aircraft against the allies 1,400.

By 14th May, 1940, the German tanks had crossed the Meuse and had opened up a fifty-mile gap in the Allied front. Six days later they reached the Channel. When he heard the news, Winston Churchill ordered the implementation of Operation Dynamo, a plan to evacuate of troops and equipment from the French port of Dunkirk.

On the 14th day of May, 1940, the BBC made the following announcement: "The Admiralty have made an Order requesting all owners of self-propelled pleasure craft between 30' and 100' in length to send all particulars to the Admiralty within 14 days from today if they have not already been offered or requisitioned". These ships were required for harbour services and national defense and thus the idea of using private yachts as naval auxiliaries was quite well established by the time the emergency of Dunkirk broke upon the Nation.

On the 27th of May, the Small Craft section of the Ministry of Shipping was telephoning various boat builders and agents around the coast requesting them to collect all small craft suitable for work in taking troops off the beaches where the larger ships could not penetrate. What was needed were boats with shallow draught, in particular pleasure boats, private yachts and launches on the Thames and also in muddy estuaries and creeks in deserted moorings along the South and East coasts which would be suitable for such an Operation.

As a result of the Operation of the Little Ships and the considerable fleet of Naval and Merchant Marine vessels, which operated off the Dunkirk beaches and the harbour between the 28th May and the 4th June 1940, no less than 338,000 British and French troops were evacuated. Approximately one third of these were taken off the beaches and, within this number, approximately 100,000 Frenchmen returned from England to fight again.

I can still smell the seaside and the immaculate beach from the cliff top road and a walk down the "zig-zag", which stirs strong emotions even at the time of life of being a "frail human being." Fifty years on, introduced for the first time to Michtav Me'Eliyahu, I wonder whether I am, perhaps, entitled to say that I was in the same town as Rabbi Dessler in that momentous year?

It is impossible to argue with one's "aleph beis" teacher because what he imparts is complete *emes*, the absolute Truth. Mr Schneider was a refugee from Germany who used "Reishis Chochmah," a slender brown covered primer, to introduce my sister and me into the wisdom of the Hebrew alphabet. By then we had been evacuated to Bedford, leaving an ailing father to be nursed in London by our mother. I doubt that I rendered Mr Schneider the due respect or gave the *hakoras hatov* that was richly deserved. I have a vivid and stark memory of being in a school playground when the teachers suddenly started to yell at us to move inside to the bomb shelter, but being mesmerised by the sight of black "things" falling out of an aeroplane, which was being hotly pursued by two Spitfires.

In the course of our wanderings we sojourned in Cambridge and in Ayr and thus we had travelled north, south, east and west. — "Hashem said to Abram after Lot had parted from him 'Raise now your eyes and look out from where you are, northward, southward, eastward and westward.'" (Parshas Lech Lecho, Bereishis 13:14)

We endured the blitz in the heart of London. Air raids were almost an adventure, sitting in the dark eating the burnt toffee used by my mother to pacify us as we heard the thumps of the bombs and the doodlebugs. The "morning after the night before" took on a new meaning for us as we walked to Hyde Park to watch the soldiers cleaning their "Ack Ack" — anti aircraft — guns after the battles of the night against the German bombers. We gleefully collected the rolls of silver strip thrown from the German aeroplanes in an endeavour to distort the radar from tracking their flight path

There were many American service personnel in the streets of London on leave from the war theatres and taking advantage of everything that London could offer them. We saw chewing gum for the first time and the "Got any gum, chum" request to an American soldier was a password to a treat from Heaven! We endured a long period of rationing and ration books. Gas masks were carried in their square boxes and from time to time we had a drill to learn how to use them. Blackout curtains drawn at the windows every night and the merest chink of light becoming visible was enough to attract the wrath of the local A.R.P. warden patrolling the streets wearing his regulation armband and tin helmet.

It is impossible to forget the drama of 6th February 1952 when the entire school was summoned to the Assembly Hall. The Head Master entered, complete with cap and gown, mounted the platform and solemnly announced "The King is dead. Long Live The Queen." The rest of the day was a holiday as was the day of the

Aircraftsman 2ⁿᵈ class 2729146

coronation in 1953. We enjoyed a spectacular view of the procession which passed in the road beneath our third floor flat.

In the mid fifties, the days of compulsory National Service in the UK, before the Air Officer Commanding-in-Chief arrived for an inspection of the camp, the grass was cut by recruits with a pair of scissors! Does that still happen? Upon reporting to the cook house with the letter requesting that "every facility be given to this man to observe his Jewish religious laws and dietary laws" I was amazed at the care with which the RAF cooks produced new mess tins and cutlery and saucepans for me, as required by RAF Queen's Regulations. Then they kindly gave me some eggs. "There you are," they said, "Now you can cook them" and gave me the bacon fat in which to do so.

This story and the true life travels and events recorded in this collection of memories would not have been available without the Hashgochah Protis that guided us on our journeys, journeys in which many were forced to ""Go out of your country, from your birthplace, and from your father's house unto the land that I will show you. And I will make of you a great nation and I will bless you and make your name great..." (Parshas Lech Lecho, Bereishis 12:1).

"Rescue me, save me from the hands of foreigners, whose mouths speak lies and whose oaths are false.

Happy are the people who have it so, happy the people whose G'd is the L'd." (Psalm 144 v 11 and v 15).

More than fifty years after Rabbi Dessler was in Bournemouth, I had the zechus to be the ba'al hago-

In Bournemouth with the Manchester Rosh Yeshiva zt'l

leh (driver) to The Manchester Rosh Yeshivah during his lengthy visits to Bournemouth. It is impossible to be in the presence of a Gadol and not to be influenced by their actions and speech and to internalise the lessons derived from being with them. One can equally be affected by reading the life stories both of the Gedolim and of the ordinary person surrounding us. The Manchester Rosh Yeshivah claimed that he was only able to give b'rochos because he was "an hediyot" – an ordinary person. The stories in this book can teach us how our forebears overcame their hardships and endured their difficulties and thus they become a great "chizuk" in our own lifestyles.

Rabbi Ya'akov Kamenetsky zt"l was once hospitalised with an IV inserted into his right hand which caused him pain and discomfort. However, when Rabbi Kamenetsky came to have a drink, despite the pain, he held his cup in his right hand to make his b'rocha. His fundamental being could not allow him to do otherwise, it is Halacha. This story affected me when I read it and strengthened my resolve to try to follow the Halacha more carefully.

The following story of Rabbi Kamenetsky was told by a Rabbi in the course of an interview for this book.

"When our son was three and a half years of age he became cross-eyed. His pupils would not stay in one place. We went to a succession of eye specialists who told us to wait until the child was older. When he was older we made enquiries of parents with a similar problem with their children and were recommended to a Doctor who promised a seventy per cent success rate. While in the waiting room of this Doctor, waiting for our turn to go in, I spent the time with my Gemorrah. Reb Yaakov was also in the waiting room and asked to be advised as to the problem. Upon hearing the problem Reb Yaakov gave my son a *brocha* that 'Hashem should enlighten his eyes in Torah.' We had not asked for a *brocha*. We then went in to see the Doctor. He told us that he could only promise us seventy per cent success. We went ahead with the operation. The Doctor was amazed that not only was the operation a hundred per cent successful, but my son no longer needed to wear glasses. At school my son moved from the bottom of the totem pole and shot up like a meteor in the sky. Today he is a *maggid shiur* and renowned in the Yeshiva world."

From the examples of our Gedolim we learn that it is essential to *ma'aser* our time. Rabbi Kamenetsky once remarked that the older you become the more demands are made upon you. This is the excitement of life which presents us with new opportunities and challenges almost daily. Through the Aleph Institute I discovered the plight of some ten thousand Jewish individuals who are imprisoned in America and who are frequently totally neglected and forgotten by family, friends and community. I signed up to become a Pen Pal and using their database the Aleph Institute Pen Pal programme connected me with correspondents with similar interests to mine.

Through the Aleph Institute finding a Pen Pal and corresponding has been a two way exchange bringing light into a prisoner's daily life and hope for a positive future. It is one of the most rewarding activities of my life. The Aleph Institute Pen Pal Programme Internet site can be found at http://www.jewishpenpals.org or e-Mail: penpal@a-leph-institute.org and at The Aleph Institute 9540 Collins Avenue, Surfside, Florida 33154   TEL: (305) 864-5553 Fax: (305) 864-5675

The last word in this book comes from one such prisoner in which the appreciation of having a Pen Pal demonstrates the depth of feelings and the effects it has displayed in this short poem.

✦ ✦ ✦

The Purpose of a Candle

by Chaim ben Ephraim

in a closed cell
        under darkness of shame
                a prisoner felt — no one could care after all no one
knew
        unseen was the spark of Good
        eclipsed by his crime — all were unaware

in a open world
        under brightness of Love
                a candle felt — everyone had light to share after all
                        everyone knew
        the spark of Light is always good
                outshone by the sun — it's light seemed hardly there

the prisoner wonders
        what is the purpose of my repentant fight

no one will see — prison walls block the sight
    the candle wonders
what is the purpose of my small light
no one will see it — I'll mail some into the night

in his darkest hour
    when he can't see the Rainbow through the rain
        a secret prayer is granted — it came none to soon
        Light! blessed Light
    shining from an envelope and the words therein
        connection, love, and hope — lit up an erstwhile unlit
room

just another hour
    when it can't see the Gift through the routine
        a secret prayer is granted — in the mailbox one
afternoon
        Light! its own light
    returning from an envelope and the words therein
        now it seems so bright — shinning back from the
gloom

the pen pal knows
    the purpose of a candle is to join the fight
    to destroy darkness with a warrior's might
    the pen pal knows
    the purpose of candle is to brave dark night
    to find an unlit candle and share the Light.

"Our brothers, the entire family of Israel who are delivered into distress and captivity whether they are on sea or dry land — may the Omnipresent One have mercy on them and remove them from distress to relief, from darkness to light, from subjugation to redemption, now speedily and soon and let us say Amen." (Tachanun).

לזכר ולעילוי נשמת

חיים יהודה בן דוב אריה ז״ל

ואשתו
עטא בת שלמה הלוי ע״ה

יהודה בן נח ז״ל

ואשתו
יענטלא בת יהודה ע״ה
ואת בתם לאה ע״ה

תנצב״ה

לזכרון עולם בהיכל ה׳

ונח מצא חן בעיני ה׳

אלה תולדת נח נח איש צדיק תמים היה בדרתיו

את האלקים התהלך נח.

לע״נ

הר״ר נח בן שמעון ז״ל

HaRav **Noach miLissa Haltrecht** zt"l

Author of *Toldos Noach*, published in Warsaw, 1830

And his descendants from Przedecz, Plock,
Warsaw, Zgierz, Lodz, France, Germany, Spain,
Argentina, America, Canada, England, Israel.

"Keep the *derech*."

לזכר ולעילוי נשמת

חיה בת יעקב מרדכי

לזכר ולעילוי נשמת

רב **אשר ושינא בילע צפתמאן**

לעילוי נשמת

החבר ר' **אברהם** בן החבר ר' **צבי זוטרמן** זצ"יל

תנצב"ה

לעילוי נשמת

אפרים נתן סגל

לעילוי נשמות

אבי מורי **אליהו** בן שמרי'

אמי מורתי **רייזל** בת ירחמיאל מאיר לייב

אבי מורי **זאב יהושע** בן מרדכי

אמי מורתי **פריידא הדסה** בת חנה

לזכר ולעילוי נשמת

גרשון בן שמאל

Dedicated to Zeide ע״ה
Akiva Yosef ben **Fattel Shraga**
whose support and determination
were an inspiration to all who knew him.
May he be a meilitz yashar for clal Yisroel

Dedicated by his children and grandchildren

This is in the merit of my
very special Aunt and Uncles
Mina bat **Eliezer**
Yosef ben **Eliezer**
Shmuel ben **Meir**

In loving memory of my parents,
Freida Hadassah bas **Yitzhak**
and **Ze'ev Yehoshua** ben **Mordechai**
Their love of words and knowledge
brought their children to His words

לזכר ולעילוי נשמת
Miriam bat **Leopold**

מרדכי צבי בן חנה
חנה בילה בת חיה שרה
In gratitude for all they have done

Mazeltov to our beloved grandparents
Grampa Les on his 73nd birthday
Granny Zeida on her 72st birthday
Until 120 may they always see nachas

From their children and grandchildren

Telshestone English Library

יהושע בן פרחיה אומר

[עשה לך רב] וקנה לך חבר : (אבות ו, א)

Rashi: One should acquire books —
they are the best friends and are essential
for acquiring Torah knowledge

The Library acquires the newest books!

The Library lends them without counting!

The Library remembers when we forget to return them!

The Library loves fines!

And we love the Library

In all weathers

With a smile and a welcome

With advice and encouragement

With fervour and competence

Our Own Telshestone English Library

From avid and grateful readers